Women in Prison

Women in Prison

Gender and Social Control

edited by
Barbara H. Zaitzow
Jim Thomas

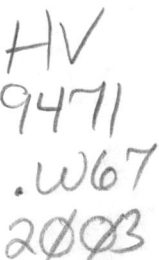

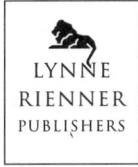

LYNNE
RIENNER
PUBLISHERS

BOULDER
LONDON

Published in the United States of America in 2003 by
Lynne Rienner Publishers, Inc.
1800 30th Street, Boulder, Colorado 80301
www.rienner.com

and in the United Kingdom by
Lynne Rienner Publishers, Inc.
3 Henrietta Street, Covent Garden, London WC2E 8LU

© 2003 by Lynne Rienner Publishers, Inc. All rights reserved

Library of Congress Cataloging-in-Publication Data
Women in prison : gender and social control / Barbara H. Zaitzow and Jim Thomas, editors
    p.   cm.
  Includes bibliographical references and index.
  ISBN 1-58826-228-6 (alk. paper)
  1. Women prisoners—United States.   2. Sex role—United States.   I. Zaitzow, Barbara H.   II. Thomas, Jim, 1941–
HV9471.W67   2003
365'.43—dc21

                                                                                                 2003046720

British Cataloguing in Publication Data
A Cataloguing in Publication record for this book
is available from the British Library.

Printed and bound in the United States of America

The paper used in this publication meets the requirements
of the American National Standard for Permanence of
Paper for Printed Library Materials Z39.48-1992.

5 4 3 2 1

Contents

Preface	vii
Acknowledgments	ix

1 Gendered Control in Prisons:
   The Difference Difference Makes
   Jim Thomas — 1

2 "Doing Gender" in a Women's Prison
   Barbara H. Zaitzow — 21

3 Gendered Perceptions of Dangerous and
   Dependent Women: "Gun Molls" and "Fallen Women"
   Esther Heffernan — 39

4 Women's Stories of Survival and Resistance
   Kathleen J. Ferraro and Angela M. Moe — 65

5 Abused Women and Incarceration
   Lori B. Girshick — 95

6 Imprisoned Mothers and Their Children
   Susan F. Sharp and M. Elaine Eriksen — 119

7 Gender, Race, and Sexuality in Prison
   Mary Bosworth — 137

8   Parallels in the Prison Experiences of Women and Men
    Richard S. Jones and Thomas J. Schmid   155

9   Ultramasculine Stereotypes and Violence in the
    Control of Women Inmates
    Faith E. Lutze   183

10 Conclusion: Moving Forward
    Jim Thomas   205

References   215
The Contributors   239
Index   243
About the Book   251

Preface

The Italian existential dramatist Luigi Pirandello (1867–1936) masterfully displayed the blend of both comedy and agony that characterizes the human condition. His plays juxtaposed the absurdity of everyday life with the blurred boundaries that frame freedom and despair, while also blurring the boundaries between reality and its opposite. He challenges his audience to examine the authorship of the social scripts that constrain our choices, limit our authenticity as actors, and confine us to the roles in which we are complicit in creating. Everyday life thus becomes a type of Pirandellian prison in which we create and maintain the conditions that limit our ability to understand the forces that dominate us and act to change them. One of the most powerful forces that dominates us is gender roles and identity. Where better to examine the Pirandellian prison and the power of gendered constraints than by turning our gaze to the more tangible and dramatically intense stage of prisons that house female offenders in the United States?

In two decades, the number of women being held in the nation's prisons increased fivefold and at the end of 2001, 93,031 women were in state or federal prisons, comprising 6.6 percent of the total prison population. Even though their crime rate is not increasing dramatically, women represent the fastest growing segment of imprisoned populations. The reason for the steep rise in the number of women prisoners is mainly due to the growing numbers of women prosecuted and convicted of drug offenses, the increasingly harsh sentences for drug offenses, and the lack of both treatment and community sanctions for women drug offenders. Hence, the surge in the imprisonment of women has more to do with politics and policy than with an actual increase in the number of crimes women commit. The overreliance on incarceration consumes excessive public resources and exacts enormous social and human costs—for offenders, their families, and communities.

The differing needs and expectations of women, the expectations of society, and the patterns of female crime will continue to influence the directions taken by corrections for women in the twenty-first century. A recognition of these gender differences and their implications for dealing with the crime committed by women will give courts and correctional administrators a basis for making choices about the sentencing and correctional alternatives that best serve society and these women. For example, many women currently serving prison terms could safely and more economically serve their sentences in community-based programs. For those with drug problems, there is a need to expand treatment programs. For many others, the economic crimes they committed resulted from their disadvantaged position and lack of marketable skills. And finally, for many women offenders who are victims of abuse, there is a need to embrace and assist these women with programmatic and community support.

Although the contributions to this volume are not about, or even allude to, Pirandello, each frames the existential dilemma of gender and incarceration in a way that helps illustrate the relationship between gendered power relations and identity on both sides of the wall. The contributors explore women's prison experiences with the broader gendered processes that shape them in order to take the next step of contributing to changes both to the debilitating prison system and the broader patriarchal structures that support it.

Acknowledgments

As with most projects in life, we owe heartfelt thanks to many individuals for their varying roles in this project. Innumerable people in our professional and personal lives deserve recognition; however, space limitations preclude listing everyone. We therefore offer our humble thanks to all the unnamed but important people in our lives.

This book has special significance in that it reflects the intellectual contributions of a gifted group of individuals who are committed to the ongoing struggle to bring voice to the issues and experiences of women prisoners. It has been an honor to work with such a dynamic and respected group of scholars. We thank all the contributors for their willingness to share their expertise in this forum and for their patience throughout the publication process.

We wish to thank Lynne Rienner Publishers for their commitment to this project. In particular, Bridget Julian was initially responsible for encouraging us to write this book and provided invaluable input in the beginning phase of the project.

Our editor, Alan McClare, deserves special credit for his support and guidance, without which the completion of the book would have been far more difficult. We also are indebted to the reviewers of the early manuscripts and thank them for their insightful comments and suggestions.

And to our colleagues, staff, and students in the Department of Political Science and Criminal Justice at Appalachian State University and the Department of Sociology at Northern Illinois University (NIU), we thank you for the various forms of support that have been provided for our prison-related projects over the years. NIU's Eric Behr provided calming influence in so many ways, and Bill Minor and Kay Forest were generous with university resources.

In the big scheme of things, family and friends make possible the pursuit of dreams. Here, BZ would like to extend love and appreciation to Peter V., Jack, Daniel, and "the girls" for being my pillars of strength and my personal safe haven during emotion-packed times. And to Rock and Don—and family members whose spiritual impact continues to influence my work—I offer my thanks and appreciation for their unfailing belief in my abilities and never-ending love and support throughout my life. From the bottom of my heart, I thank all of you for your love and devotion, which make good times better and bad times a little easier to take.

Finally, we wish to thank the women prisoners who have touched our lives and informed our research, and who continue to fuel our commitment to prison reform. We hope that, by the sharing of their stories and experiences with the outside world, the hearts and minds of the uninformed or misguided will blossom into compassionate appreciation for the plight of women prisoners and ultimately into active participation in reformation of the entire correctional system.

—Barbara H. Zaitzow
Jim Thomas

Women in Prison

Gendered Control in Prisons: The Difference Difference Makes

Jim Thomas

> Oh, sir, you know well that life is full of infinite absurdities, which, strangely enough, do not even need to appear plausible, since they are true. (Pirandello, 1922: 7–8)

Surely it cannot be plausible that heterosexual norms and gender roles can be a means of oppressive control in prisons. It may seem implausible also that gender-neutral attempts to treat female prisoners the same as male prisoners by ignoring sex and gender differences add more layers of punishment to the female carceral experience. It's equally implausible that many prison researchers, while challenging the prison conditions that lead to physical violence, nonetheless often produce images that promote an equally harmful form of symbolic violence that reproduces gendered control on both sides of the wall. Yet as the contributors to this volume illustrate, all this is not only plausible, but true.

Social control mechanisms in prisons are not restricted to cells, bars, and security staff. As Foucault (1979) suggested, control includes the culture in which ideology, cultural icons, and other symbolic artifacts become implements of control and domination. Although some of these mechanisms are so basic that we rarely recognize them, they nonetheless contribute to control and punitive processes, especially in women's prisons. One example of such a process is gendered culture.

At first blush, the works of Pirandello have little to do with women's prisons, gender, or social control. So, of course, this volume isn't really about Pirandello. It's about reality. Our reality. Gender reality. And mostly, it's about the existential absurdity of prison culture and the reality of gender-based control in women's prisons. Organizing the experiences of female prisoners around an existential framework provides one way of understanding how the complexity of a gendered social order restricts action and opportunity in tightly controlled environments.

Prison Culture as Absurd

Absurdity, a core existentialist theme, suggests that social life is inherently permeated with oppressive conditions for which there often seem no obvious rational solutions. One absurd aspect of the human condition lies in confronting fundamental cultural constraints, such as those imposed by gender, that promote unnecessary forms of social domination and often make us unwittingly complicit in our own subjugation. Borrowing from Esslin (1961: xix), absurdity refers to a condition of existence out of harmony with reason, a set of circumstances devoid of ostensible purpose that makes behavioral choices difficult. An absurd existence is one in which we are unable to discover the obscurely oppressive meanings and significance of our social world. An examination of this absurdity highlights the tensions between freedom and constraint in the prison social world, composed of ambiguous rules, mysterious forces, and no immediately observable remedies to redress gendered power imbalances. This is the "Pirandellian prison" of everyday life.

If social existence outside prison walls is absurd, then meaning and purpose in the social world of prisons are even more so: inmates are faced with high-stakes dilemmas in their relationships with those in positions of authority over them. Women prisoners especially exist in an atmosphere of subjugation that is at best institutionally paternalistic, at worst systematically repressive and arbitrary. They are expected to develop autonomy and individual responsibility even as conforming to conventional gender roles promotes passivity and dependence within their prison culture.

Prison culture symbolizes oppressive authority, intensifies powerlessness, and constantly reminds prisoners that, even if they are able to manage the physical deprivations, there is no escape from daily confrontations with their dysfunctionally absurd environment. The stripping away of the prisoner's identity through a series of degradations, abasement rituals, humiliations, and profanations (Goffman, 1961: 14–21) dissolves conventional frameworks of normalcy that guide and give meaning to conventional existence. This contributes to "learned helplessness" (Goodstein, MacKenzie, and Shotland, 1984), in which prisoners suffer reduced motivation, "cognitive deficits," and a restriction of choices proportional to the loss of control over their environment and existence. As a consequence, what outsiders often interpret as abnormal behavior in prisons instead may reflect normal attempts of prisoners to adjust to abnormal conditions (Milovanovic and Thomas, 1989). Absurdity emerges from this dilemma of restricted freedom of action and choice on the one hand, and the need to successfully confront debilitating conditions in a regulated environment on the other. The irony that administrative or legislative attempts to promote equality between male and female prisoners has arguably done the opposite provides our entry into the absurdity of prison culture.

The Difference Difference Makes

It's old news that the conditions and policies of women's prisons are different than those of men's prisons. As the contributors here demonstrate, considerable evidence also confirms that incarcerated women experience their incarceration differently than men. However, less evident is how gender differences shape policies and experiences of control, and how gender identity and roles shape women's adaptation and resistance to prison culture and control. Historically, gender-based policies shaped many of the differences between men's and women's prisons, as men's behaviors and needs provided the model for all prisons. This often led to fewer resources, gender-stereotyped programming, and inattention to gender-specific needs such as health care, child care, postrelease preparation, and other issues that affect women more than men. Most significantly, control mechanisms in prisons and the corresponding policies, staff training procedures, and resources tend to be designed to control men, who are more aggressive, violent, and predatory, cope with and experience time differently, and resolve conflicts more competitively.

One challenge facing both policymakers and researchers is whether gender and biological differences between men and women should be recognized more fully and translated into corresponding prison practices. As Barbara Zaitzow and Esther Heffernan argue in their chapters in this volume, the belief that women are innately different than men shaped the patriarchal systems of carceral control in which female offenders were viewed as incorrigible "fallen women" who could be "fixed" by restoring their adherence to and dependence upon traditional images of femininity. Yet women's biological differences undeniably create issues that men do not face, such as pregnancies, hysterectomies, mastectomies, and gender-specific geriatric health and psychological needs.

Biological differences extend beyond medical issues. They also add a level of punishment by increasing powerlessness and uncertainty. For example, drawing from my own prison fieldnotes and Illinois prison monitoring reports (1980–2003), women prisoners in Illinois believed that prison doctors were overprescribing hysterectomies, allegedly to generate revenue for local medical personnel. No evidence supported the belief, but the helplessness and fears that women experienced, when faced not only with surgery, but also with the possibility that overprescription "could happen to me," contributed to distrust of medical personnel, increased health-related stress, and reinforced feelings of helplessness and dependency. When pregnant women enter the Illinois prison system, they normally give birth in local hospitals. The prenatal anxieties of labor and delivery add to the stress of the prison experience. In Illinois until the late 1990s, women were shackled to the delivery table while giving birth (IDOC, 2002). Although no longer practiced, the security procedures required for transporting women to and from the local hospital, combined with close monitoring by security staff while in labor and delivery, increase feelings of powerlessness and anxiety. Mothers with normal delivery are allowed to stay with their infants for twenty-four hours; those with C-sections are allowed forty-eight hours (IDOC, 2002). The subsequent separation from the infant can be traumatic, adding additional layers of loneliness and depression on return to the prison general population.

In addition to biological differences, incarcerated women also bring their gender-based frameworks with them into the institution. As the contributors to this volume illustrate, unlike men, women are more likely to have medical problems exacerbated by substance abuse, be HIV positive, and face child care and other domestic problems needing attention while incarcerated. Coupled with the likelihood that women are more prone to experience abusive relationships with family or male partners, are less educated than their male counterparts, and have fewer vocational skills, they begin their prison experience with less social capital to adjust to, and cope with, incarceration. The prison experience also subverts the mother-child bond, and when reunited with their children most women are unable to maintain stable relationships with their children or to successfully overcome substance abuse problems, which leads to a cycle of repeated incarceration for the women and an intergenerational cycle of incarceration for their children (Dalley, 2002). In addition, Greer (2002) found that women prisoners' emotions and the expression of those emotions influence, and are influenced by, the environment of prison. This differs dramatically from men's emotional coping strategies. For women, previous life experiences shaped by poverty, abuse, drug addiction, and disregard by significant others hindered their emotional management (Greer, 2002: 123). These emotional coping techniques, constructed on the outside, perpetuate gender stereotypes inside the walls in ways that sustain traditional roles of passivity and acquiescence to male power.

Equality or Parity?

Especially since the 1970s, scholars and policymakers recognized that, because women composed barely 5 percent of the nation's prison population, they were the "forgotten offenders." Influenced by feminist scholars, a combination of civil rights activists and prison reformers advocated establishing parity between male and female prisoners by eliminating gender-based prison policies and treating both men and women identically. To some extent, this parity has been achieved, and gender differences have been leveled such that policies are generally created and applied identically. However, parity in policy does not necessarily translate into equality of treatment, especially when policies for women continue to be driven by the control imperatives designed for men.

Parity denotes gender-neutral quantitative sameness or parallel standards of equivalence without consideration for mediating factors. The underlying assumption, quite reasonable on its surface, is grounded in the belief that, by eliminating gender differences and applying policies identically across the board, women would begin receiving resources on a par with men. Equality, by contrast, is a qualitative concept suggesting nonparallel equivalence. Attempts over the past three decades to improve the conditions of women's prisons and provide resources and amenities on a par with men have either stressed parity as a way of subverting gender-based asymmetry and establishing identical standards, or de-emphasized the distinction between parity and equality.

A single example from Illinois prisons illustrates the difference between gender parity and equality. In 1999 the Illinois Department of

Corrections implemented a policy under which prisoners were prohibited from wearing street clothes. They could wear only apparel issued by the prison or purchased from the prison commissary (IDOC-Rules, n.d.). At the same time, a second policy specified that all prisoners' property must fit in two small boxes. The first, a "property box" slightly bigger than a military footlocker, holds clothes, commissary items, and other personal belongings. The second, a "correspondence box" about the size of a small personal computer, is restricted to papers, letters, and pictures. Books may be kept in either box. The only property exempt from property box storage includes authorized electronic items, such as radios, televisions, typewriters, or fans. The policy was initially imposed on male prisoners, but concerns about complaints from men and administrators' concerns for equal protection litigation contributed to identical application of the policy to women. Further, women's additional sex-specific property, such as undergarments, cosmetics, and feminine hygiene needs, exceed those of men, leaving them with more items to store in identical space. Therefore, policy parity trumps equality, because the policy places greater hardship on women, one seemingly minor but nonetheless significant difference.

The contributors to this volume illustrate how women's experiences of prison, and how they cope with confinement, reflect their gender-based experiences in the outside world. Past victimization and abuse, culturally defined ways of coping with problems and interacting with others, cultural ways of encouraging traditional "gender-appropriate" behaviors, and women's strategies for adapting to social control are a few aspects of their previous existence that women bring with them into the prison. As Wheeler and colleagues (1989) have shown, women's legal needs reflect these preprison experiences and differ from the legal needs of men. Women's litigation centers more on such issues as child custody, programs, health care, prison discipline and control, and visitation than does men's, suggesting that establishing parity and rigid gender neutrality is an insufficient criterion for guiding prison policies. Failure to recognize this both in policy and in research adds to what we will call the symbolic violence resulting from distorted images of the relationship between gender, control, and prison culture.

What Is Prison Culture?

Although the dysfunctional nature of prisoner culture was a staple for researchers over the latter half of the twentieth century, few studies focused on the difference gender makes in the cultural experiences for male and female prisoners. The contributors here begin to fill this vacuum by examining the links between gendered culture on the outside and its re-creation inside prisons. To address this, it helps to review the role of culture in social existence.

Culture is the socially established set of public codes, the syntax and lexicon, that guide the conventions of "reality construction" by which we understand and act upon our everyday roles, set our daily priorities and routine, and live our lives (Berger and Luckmann, 1967: 99). As the totality of all learned social behavior of a given group, culture provides not only "systems of standards for perceiving, believing, evaluating, and acting" (Goodenough, 1981: 110), but includes the rules and symbols of interpretation and discourse as well.

Like the broader culture, prison culture reflects meanings that are manufactured, imposed, negotiated, altered, and highly structured yet permeable and amorphous, and provides the behavioral codes for the controllers and those they control. Following Hayner and Ash (1939: 362), many scholars have distinguished between prison culture (which encompasses staff, civilians, correctional officers, and others) and prisoner culture (which reflects norms, language, coping mechanisms, behaviors, artifacts, and other characteristics shared primarily by prisoners themselves). However, in reality the two cultures intertwine, as prisoners and staff reciprocally create, negotiate, and modify rules and norms in a dance of power and control, each providing patterns of mutual expectations, meanings, and interactional strategies for the other (Thomas, 1984). In prisons, the cultural work of staff and prisoners and the formal and informal structure imposed by state and administrative personnel combine to create rules and resources that form prison culture. The rules and social resources are patterned by gender, and as Owen (1998, 1988) describes, the gendered culture of prisons is reproduced in a complex interplay between and among staff and prisoners.

Since the pioneering studies of Sykes (1958), prison scholars have been fascinated with the source of prisoner culture. One view centers on whether prisoners import their culture into the prison with them (the importation model). A second approach addresses whether prisoner culture arises from attempts to adjust to and resist deprivation and control (the deprivation model). Advocates of the importation model see prison culture as resulting from behaviors intended to reduce the pains of imprisonment (Clemmer, 1958; Goffman, 1961; Sykes, 1958; Toch, 1977; Useem and Kimball, 1989; Wheeler, 1961). Advocates of the importation model argue that prisons reflect a microcosm of the broader street subculture, and prisoners build their social world around the predatory norms and socially incompatible values and behaviors that guided them on the streets (Irwin and Cressey, 1962; Schrag, 1954; Thomas and Peterson, 1977). Unlike many studies, the contributors to this volume avoid the importation/exportation dichotomy by reconceptualizing it: How does imported gender-based culture shape how women prisoners create and respond to their prison experience and reproduce mechanisms of control, domination, and even resistance? In varying ways, each chapter illustrates how both sex and gender combine in ways that help women accommodate to prison deprivations while also providing mechanisms of control and resistance. The contributors draw from their research of female prisons and prisoners to explore how gendered characteristics such as roles, scripted behaviors, norms, and identity are re-created behind the walls in ways that reinforce conventional patriarchal images and policies. Each author describes how gender performances reinforce control and add to the punitiveness of women's carceral experience.

How well prisoners "do culture" affects how they experience their time. Not all prisoners master gendered culture equally. Jones and Schmid (2000) demonstrate how poor cultural skills among male prisoners can mark one as weak, resulting in consequences that range from minor humiliation to predatory victimization. When and at whom to smile, the limits of self-revelation, the boundaries of sharing histories of abuse or victimization with staff or peers, the subtexts of verbal jousting matches, or learning with whom one can safely associate are a few examples of the types of gender-based cultural rules that must be learned quickly. The prison gender culture is thus an extension of the larger gender survival game played on the streets. Whether inside or outside the walls of the prison, when recognizing that her gaming skills might be out of the ordinary, a woman is constantly aware of the consequences should she fail to make the right moves. For example, Lori Girshick suggests in this volume that appearing too feminine may put women at risk of staff harassment or worse. But just as appearing too feminine in a men's institution can lead to predatory assaults or intimidation by other prisoners, in women's prisons, failing to appear sufficiently feminine or "ladylike" risks sexually related ridicule by staff or other inmates, and can lead to a staff-imposed label of "not with the program" or "an aggressive troublemaker."

As Barbara Zaitzow, Lori Girshick, Susan Sharp, and Mary Bosworth describe in this volume, women bring their gendered forms of behavior with them into the institution. However, the unique demands of prison control may make many of these behaviors inappropriate, especially when they reflect dysfunctional street backgrounds, such as victimization by intimates or substance abuse. "Doing gender" then becomes complicated by the need to learn new rules, including how to develop a rhetoric of self-expression, construct a new identity and self-concept of independence and self-reliance even while submitting to passivity and control, and learning where the boundaries of appropriate gender expression lie between staff and other prisoners (McCorkel, 1998). Mastering gender in prisons can thus become a manipulative exercise in coping, and doing gender becomes an integral part of control in which the complex relationship between identity, self-expression, and manipulation of others becomes intensified. The chapters in this volume explore aspects of the gender-based ways of creating and reinforcing the existential barriers that serve to subjugate and control women in prison.

Symbolic Violence and Prison Research

Smith (1987: 19) observed that most people do not directly participate in the making of their culture, and our ideas about it may not arise directly from everyday lived relationships: "Rather, they are the product of the work of specialists occupying influential positions in the ideological apparatus (the educational system, communications, etc.). Our culture does not arise spontaneously; it is 'manufactured.'"

Yet, most of us do not perceive this manufacturing process, especially that of the prison research process itself, as a potential act of violence. In subtle ways, uncritical conventional scholarship imposes, distorts, and twists our cognition, and subsequently our actions, forcefully and with often injurious consequences. Too often, conventional prison scholars commit the violence of rupturing the researcher from the people being studied in what Van Maanen (1988: 46) calls "realist tales." In realist tales, the author vanishes from the finished text, making the reader dependent on the author's experiential authority with no opportunity to reflect on the researcher-researched process. The result imposes the meanings of outsiders, including researchers and the audience of the research, on the messages we hear from our data.

Symbolic violence refers to the power of symbols to impose, devastate, attack, suppress, and distort ways of seeing, thinking, talking, and acting. Symbolic violence often can be more destructive than physical assault in that it more deeply imposes and reinforces social harms caused by race, gender, and class in what Collins (1990) calls the "matrix of domination." It strengthens social barriers and reinforces culturally embedded domination games. In describing one way that dominant groups can exert their will over others, Bourdieu (1991: 209–210) observes that symbolic power presupposes a misrecognition of the violence exercised through it and therefore requires some unrecognized complicity by those on whom the effect is exercised. Our images and understandings of prison culture derive from the productions of outsiders, and researchers are a significant outside source of our understandings of prison culture.

The ability to exert symbolic violence exists in the ability to impose meanings as legitimate, thus concealing the underlying power relations on which they are based (Bourdieu and Passeron, 1979: 4). In prisoner culture research of both men and women, images of deviance, marginalization, and stigma can constitute a form of symbolic violence. One way this occurs is through oppressive discourses that reinforce and fail to challenge existing social relations, including those of research. Discourses are sets of symbols that we use to communicate who we are, or who we think we are, the context in which our existence is located, and how we intend ourselves to be understood as well as how we understand our topics. Discourses impose sets of formal or informal rules about what can be said, how it can be said, and who shall say what to whom (Schwalbe et al., 2000: 435).

As an example of how symbolic violence occurs, Heffernan describes in this volume how administrative processes of classifying women prisoners perpetuate gender domination through the image-laden official categories and language of prison bureaucracy. This discourse reinforces stereotypes and imposes behavioral expectations through corresponding policies based on uncritical assumptions of heterosexuality and gender roles. Just as these rhetorical images connoted by official documents create a culture-defining reality that reflects a form of symbolic violence, so too do research discourses shape images in ways that reproduce subtle forms of domination in how we examine prisons and prisoners. By failing to recognize the hidden, yet powerful, ways that gender becomes a mechanism of control, our research reaffirms and re-creates an invisible source of oppression and domination by misconceptualizing and ignoring the crucial element of heterosexually based gendered culture.

As a cultural artifact, conventional discourses often impose metaphors that wrench prisoners out of their shared humanity and create conditions that exacerbate qualities such as animosity, distrust, and predation. In research, the images from these discourses are violent because they arbitrarily impose symbols in ways that may grotesquely distort the "reality" of what is seen and what is signified by what is seen. The distortions reflect oppressive power relations that promote the interests of the more powerful. The conventional discourses of prison research impose images that obscure and distort the deeper structures of the culture and limit the possibility of seeing alternative meanings and connections. Each of the contributors to this volume provides an antidote to the potential symbolic violence of research by critically examining how the gendered foundations of social life are re-created in prison culture and serve as an ironic mechanism in games of control and resistance. All follow the prescription that critical social research should contribute to emancipation by encouraging us to both emotionally and cognitively rethink repressive emotional ideas and identities.

The question remains, however, as to why outside researchers, even those with a critical eye, should be credible in assessing and reinterpreting the meanings of prison life as experienced by insiders. This question poses a challenge that becomes part of our methodological problem, lest we, too, simply impose an alternative, but no less destructive, discourse on those we study.

Standpoint: Outsiders Looking In

There is no lack of methodological or reflective commentaries by prison researchers who ponder over their role as outsiders. Generally, these focus on personal emotional experiences (Bosworth, 1999b), ethical conundrums (Thomas and Marquart, 1988), the difficulties of balancing competing and often hostile inmate and staff groups (Jacobs, 1977), or methodological issues (Jones and Schmid, 2000). Here, the outsider-insider question is reframed in the context of the standpoint perspective to ask: How can well-meaning, white, middle-class, educated, nearly middle-aged, nonincarcerated academics "really know" the experiences of generally economically disadvantaged, uneducated, incarcerated, usually ethnically different, and much younger subjects? This question challenges males writing about the female prison experience, and raises credibility issues when translating the standpoint of research subjects into our own research narratives intended for a wider audience. The question recently has taken on more urgency as "convict criminologists" (Stephens, 2002) have challenged the credibility of outsider nonconvicts to "really know" what occurs in prisons.

In writing about the experiences of female prisoners, we should reflect on the insider/outsider question for several reasons. First, all contributors here write as outsiders looking in. How can we transform our subjects into what Smith (1987: 112) calls "my puppets who speak, see, and think the words, sights and thoughts" that we attribute to them? Second, the prison people with whom we interact are demographically quite dissimilar to us. How do we respond to the extreme essentialist view that only "identity groups" can understand their own culture? Third, most of us teach or work with racially, ethnically, and economically diverse groups of students. What obstacles subvert our credibility when attempting to speak about and to prisoners' culture and experiences from our own dissimilar biographical and experiential standpoint?

Sociological texts characteristically relate us to others and even to ourselves as objects. Criminologists, perhaps more than other social scientists, find themselves on the outside looking in, making objects of our subjects in courts, criminals, gangs, deviant groups, or prisons, among our topics. In reflecting on whether scholars could really fully understand the experiences of their research subjects, sociologist Georg Simmel reputedly asked nearly a century ago: "Must one be Caesar to know Caesar?" Max Weber (1965: 90) provided the answer: One need not be Caesar to understand Caesar, he suggested, but it helps.

Standpoint research, or the "privileged knowledge" thesis, holds that the views and claims of insiders are more credible than those of outsiders. White scholars received heated criticism in the late 1960s and 1970s from those who argued that white experiences and assumptions narrowed and distorted their research lens when focused on people of color. This, the critics argued, obscured the experiences of the subordinate group by producing partial, even erroneous, understandings. Feminist scholars further refined standpoint methodology. Smith (1987: 112) nicely illustrates the insider/outsider problem when describing her experience of watching a "family of Indians" on a rail platform in Canada. The passing of the train, she realizes, provides an image-creating metaphor that distances the observer and observed in ways that silence both. In conceptualizing this "family" of "Indians" and in describing their activity, Smith replaced others' identities and interpretative frameworks with her own, thus making "the other" less visible.

Excluding, distorting, or discrediting the experiences of people we study provides, at best, only partial understandings. At worst, we recreate and maintain systems of privilege and domination through a process of "othering," in which we impute identity and experiential meanings to others that they might not prefer, by labeling them, attributing motives, virtues, and defects, and, implicitly, by saying how we are different from them (Schwalbe et al., 2000). Othering creates imputed selves that stand in a relationship of superiority and inferiority to each other, thus making researchers complicit in preserving the asymmetrical power hierarchies they intend to reduce. Our standpoint matters, because it reflects our ideological, existential, and theoretical lenses, which can distort how we see, interpret, and report our studies. It guides the topics we address, the questions we ask, and how we ask them. It also shapes the uses that we intend for our research. Participatory researchers attempted to resolve the insider/outsider problem by "celebrating the subject" and fully integrating members of the culture being studied as full participants in the research design, data collection, analysis, and writing. Conventional scholars tend to ignore the issue, although some (e.g., Van Maanen, 1988) have suggested reflectively critiquing how the types of narratives we employ can set us apart and often above our subjects. In penology, the "celebration of the subject" emerged in part with conflict theorists and symbolic interactionists who began to give voice to the targets of social control to express their motivations and view of the world. This provided one antidote to the dominant voices of the controllers. More recently, the emergence of "convict criminology" (Stephens, 2002) has mobilized a cadre of ex-offenders and others who have experienced the "dark side of the law" to present what is perceived as an alternative to conventional prison scholarship.

The belief that a culture is best studied by insiders, or that the claims and interpretations of insiders about their culture should be given more credence than the observations of outsiders, however, raises the problem of relativism, in which all standpoints risk being judged equally valid. Mannheim (1936) provides a way out of this potential problem. For him, "standpoint" was not a form of relativism, in which all perspectives are of equal value with no transcendent rules to sift out meritorious claims from those less so. He put forth what he called "relationism," or knowledge seen in the full context of the historically and socially shaped ideologies that shaped it: "Relationism signifies merely that all of the elements of meaning in a given situation have reference to one another and derive their significance from this reciprocal interrelationship in a given frame of thought" (86).

Multiple audiences (or stakeholders) present the challenge of multiple standpoints on both ends of the researcher/audience continuum. The trick is to recognize the dialectical process that elevates the claims of one audience over another, and to activate the process of critical dialogue about competing claims. Although not specifically drawing from Mannheim, Smith, or others who directly address the outsider/insider problem, the contributors here each follow their spirit:

> Locating the standpoint of women in the everyday world outside the text (in which the text is written and read) creates a whole new set of problems to be solved, problems of the relationship between text and reader, problems of how to write texts that will not transcribe the subject's actualities into the relations of ruling, texts that will provide for their readers a way of seeing further into the relations of organizing their lives. (Smith, 1987: 47)

While it may help to "be Caesar" to present his standpoint, individual lenses are no less subject to distortion than other prisms. A constant iterative dialogue between insider and outsider cognition and interpretation, as the contributors here demonstrate, provides an antidote both to relativism and to the dogma of "privileged knowledge." In this volume, we recognize the difference between "speaking as," "speaking for," and "speaking about" women prisoners. In the aggregate, we allow women to speak as themselves in order that we may, as outsiders, speak on their behalf. By integrating their views with our own theoretical insights, we allow our readers to examine the invisible ways in which gender shapes the prison experience in a dialectical game of resistance and control. Our intent is to expand the dialogue by which we understand how gender contributes to the punitive context of prisons for all prisoners.

Core Themes

Seven themes unite these chapters. First, things are rarely what they seem, especially in the absurd world of prison culture. Our social reality is distorted by images that mask the contradictions, tensions, and ironies embedded in gendered social constructs. The contributors, as outsiders, offer alternative ways of looking at and talking about women in prison that reduce the distortion of conventional images by translating prisoners' experiences from one set of cultural symbols (those of our research subjects) to another (those of our audience). This modest exercise in cultural liberation subverts symbolic violence by loosening the unrecognized constraints that distort our perception, interpretation, discourse, and action, and alerts us to alternative meanings that ordinarily might be obscured.

Second, gender images function as an ideological mechanism that sustains male power and privilege, even in women's prisons. Ideology refers to those beliefs, attitudes, and basic assumptions about the world that justify, shape, and organize how we perceive and interpret it, thus providing the conceptual machineries for maintaining social order:

> Gender expectations are essentially ideological constructs that serve the material interests of dominant groups. Hegemonic masculinity reflects and actively cultivates gender inequalities, but it also allows elite males to extend their influence and control within intermale dominance hierarchies. (Sabo, Kupers, and London, 2001: 6)

These gendered ideological constructs support male privilege, in which males on both sides of the walls tend to be exempt from many challenges faced by women. In prisons, this leads to policies framed through the gender lens of male needs, which de-emphasizes or ignores the less visible needs of women, both biologically and culturally. Something as seemingly insignificant as differences in emotional coping or adapting to the aging process are experienced differently by men and women. Yet prison policies are slow to address these and numerous other gender-derived differences in attempting to humanize prisons. This requires that we more fully explore the dynamics of ultramasculine environments such as prisons in order to display how their creation and maintenance also shape women's existence.

Third, gender matters. The idealized practice of identical treatment does not translate into gender-neutral treatment. Recognizing the difference gender makes neither reflects an essentialist position nor need it lead to what Bem (1992) calls "gender polarization." It only requires that we take into account biological and cultural differences and reject the assumption that a system designed for males is also appropriate for females.

Fourth, just as males and females "do time" differently, not all women experience deprivation and control in the same way. The culture of any prison is heavily influenced by variations among prisoners with respect to age, race, educational attainment, nature of the crime committed, and sentence length, as well as institutional location, population, and security level. As Heffernan observes in this volume, women do not share the same social, cultural, or economic capital, such as class position, education, financial resources, networks, race/ethnicity, language skills, or class position (Bourdieu, 1986). Women who possess more capital do easier time than those who do not, because they are more able to draw from their existing assets to "play the prison game" both with staff and with other prisoners.

Fifth, Girshick reminds us in this volume of the irony of considering abuse of and violence against women as a "women's problem" when it is perpetrated by men. Attempting to formulate appropriate prison policies for women while avoiding the broader social context of ultramasculine control mechanisms that sustain abuse is absurdly futile. Prisons, as Sabo, Kupers, and London (2001) cogently argue, reflect in microcosm and in the extreme the culturally embedded practices that promote the ultramasculinity and patriarchy by which men create and preserve power over women, as well as the hierarchical processes in which higher-status males subjugate males of lower status. This suggests that expanding studies of men in prison can supplement feminist theory by including a critical analysis of males and masculinity (Sabo, Kupers, and London, 2001) in order to connect broader issues of gender domination to women prisoners. This requires continual deconstruction of the gendered processes that frame the bases of identity and action.

Sixth, Mary Bosworth, and Richard Jones and Thomas Schmid shift the analytic focus of prisoner culture formation from the importation/deprivation model to one of prisoner identity formation. They demonstrate in this volume that, for prisoners, the production and display of gender involve a style that announces to others who we think we are. But to borrow from Kondo (1990: 48), the relationship between style and identity is not static. It is ongoing, as women create, construct, revise, and enact their identities and sometimes creatively challenge the limits of the cultural constraints. Kondo's accommodation to a Japanese American female identity in patriarchal Japanese society included a "collapse of identity" and a "distancing process" similar to that of women prisoners in accommodating to their own controlling culture (1990: 18). Ignoring the link between identity and culture risks post-release reintegration problems resulting from the need to readapt the prison identities to an often dysfunctional street environment.

Seventh, women are not simply passive recipients or totally powerless victims in the gender game. Femininity can be employed as a power chit both to obtain resources and to resist control. Women may also engage in what Miller (2001: 178–197) describes as "contradictory gender dynamics," in which women's doing of gender reinforces patriarchy, bargains with patriarchy, and reinforces gender status hierarchies. This requires exploring the dialectical relationship in which prisoners are both authors of and subjects in the drama of their own oppression.

Chapter Summary

The contributors here develop these core themes in their own individual theoretical and conceptual styles. But in the aggregate, they display the absurdity of prison life, its existential dilemmas, and how gender is played out in prison as shaped by broader social, historical, and cultural factors.

Barbara Zaitzow provides a framework for examining gendered experiences of women in prison by illustrating how their struggle to accommodate to prison life reflects problems in their outside lives. She argues that relationships (with outside family members, inside friends/family, and staff), programs, rules, and the culture itself combine to reinforce a definition of "womanhood" that may not have relevance or practicality for women, either in prison or on release. Further, the deceptive nature of women's prisons, often seen as "soft," "campus-like," or "easy time," masks repression that, while subtle, is stronger than in men's institutions. Introducing a theme that other contributors build on, she concludes that identical treatment of male and female prisons would not be beneficial to women, and that we cannot eradicate gender differences within prison while they persist in the outside world.

Prisons, of course, have not emerged de novo, separate from the broader culture. Esther Heffernan illustrates how they are embedded in a historical process reflecting gendered ideologies of punishment. Drawing from Bourdieu, she develops the concept of "symbolic violence" to illustrate how the traditional classification of women prisoners arose out of and reinforced gender domination by imposing images of "proper femininity" on female prisoners. This symbolic imposition is violent because it ruptures women from part of their humanity. This forcibly deprives women of their social capital, and only by challenging this outside the walls can we transform prisons as well.

Women in jails, who—like men—can serve up to several years,

tend to be excluded from studies of incarcerated women. Kathleen Ferraro and Angela Moe correct this by illustrating how women are controlled through routinization that subjectifies them and reinforces institutionalized power asymmetries of race, class, and gender. They remind us that women are not simply passive agents or totally powerless victims. They possess means, albeit limited, to resist the imposition of control in ways that partially mediate domination. In challenging the use of incarceration for most women offenders, they argue that activists on the outside, especially feminists, should take a more active role in recognizing the relationship between gender oppression and incarceration.

In coping with imprisonment, prisoners engage in a dialectical dance in which their past experiences combine with the control and deprivations of prison culture to add to the punishment. Lori Girshick details how an overwhelming proportion of women in prisons and jails were physically, sexually, and emotionally abused prior to entry. The sexualized environment of custodial institutions, which includes physical constraint, surveillance, and intrusive searches, retraumatizes women with a history of prior abuse. Existing carceral policies fail to take this into consideration in policies of control. As a consequence, the sexualized nature of control in prison must be reconceptualized as a social problem in order to prevent the revictimization of women when incarcerated.

The androcentrism of the criminal justice system and corresponding research, Susan Sharp and M. Elaine Eriksen argue, would leave the impression that all prisoners are alike. One significant difference between male and female prisoners is that women, far more than men, tend to have dependent children on whom incarceration has devastating consequences. Lacking social capital, these women and children become society's "throwaways." As a consequence, we cannot fully understand women's prison experiences without also understanding the relationship between children and mothers, and how maternal incarceration contributes to punishment. The class and racial underpinnings, which affect both prison and postrelease adjustment, reinforce the need to reassess the so-called impartiality of the criminal justice system. This requires, the authors contend, not only the need to develop creative programs to address the needs of imprisoned mothers, but also the need for researchers and others to examine the broader implications of this gendered layer of punishment and its impact on the families left behind.

Our social identity tells us who we think we are and announces us to others. An identity is not only a status, but a cue-card that prompts others with shorthand summaries of what they can expect and how they might respond. The message of an identity conveys strength, weakness, honorability, accessibility, and other valuable attributes. But identities also can be constructed in ways that challenge or reinforce asymmetrical control. Using data from her study of three women's studies in England, Mary Bosworth illustrates how the intersection of gender, race, and sexuality shapes prisoners' identity. She argues that these identities can be shifted, manipulated, and transcended to challenge the power mechanisms in prisons in an ironic game that uses the gendered and racial forces of domination to renegotiate and restructure prisoners' stigmatized status. In developing their identity as women or as members of an ethnic group, they shift from being passive recipients of power to agents resisting it.

Most studies of prisoner culture focus either on males or on females. Few do both. Richard Jones and Thomas Schmid correct this by illustrating parallel adaptation strategies of females and male prisoners in two midwestern institutions. They introduce the metaphor of "cultural sojourner" to describe the border crossings from the outside world into prison terrain, crossings that require creative identity work. Like Bosworth, they describe how control in women's prisons is partly a dialectical identity struggle in which women can resist some of the dominating forces that constrain them. Focusing on identity assaults, in which prisoners' former identities are replaced with new, more degrading ones, their analysis illustrates how building on identities as mother and other noninstitutional statuses helps women from seeing themselves only as captives. Reversing the traditional approach of applying to females concepts used to study males, Jones and Schmid suggest ways to use our understandings of women to examine the male prison experience.

We cannot fully understand gendered power in women's prisons without also understanding how conceptions and practices of masculinity shape a hierarchical power structure. Faith Lutze moves us beyond the prison arena by arguing that even women's prisons reflect an ultramasculine environment based on traditional sex-role stereotypes and male models of domination. Male power, she explains, defines individual interaction (private and public), the law, and the formation of policy and institutions. This inhibits especially women with histories of prior abuse, for whom the institutionalization of ultramasculine sex-role stereotypes reaffirms their powerlessness. The irony is that even "women-centered" approaches to programs intended to empower women are likely to fail, because the current structure of prisons magnifies the structural inequalities of society that women will confront upon release.

Although the explicit theoretical perspectives underlying individual pieces vary, the central organizing theme that unites these pieces combines critical gender theory with an exploration of the absurdity of gendered experiences that extends beyond the walls. The strength of this eclectic integration lies in pulling together seemingly conventional empirical studies within a broader framework that allows gender domination to be displayed as part of our Pirandellian existential prison on both sides of the walls.

2

"Doing Gender" in a Women's Prison

Barbara H. Zaitzow

The horrors of life in men's prisons are already part of our common currency—prison fights, riots, prison gangs, inmate-on-inmate rape, the threat of contracting HIV. Our lens on women's prison has a softer focus, largely contrived by B movies in which tough, curvy broads with sharp tongues and snake tattoos start catfights in the cafeteria. A few trays are thrown and peas tossed, but in the end, the matronly guards restore order. It's titillating, lurid, harmless. The truth, of course, is much more alarming.

When women enter prisons and jails they essentially become invisible. Statistically, women inmates are much less likely to be visited by their friends and family, in part because their facilities are in remote locations. Women have less money at their disposal than most men when they enter prison, since the crimes that land them in prison in the first place—drug offenses, theft, and welfare fraud—are crimes of poverty. Slave wages for their labors behind bars don't help them achieve any level of self-sufficiency, even to buy basic goods like aspirin or toothpaste. Stripped of their rights, money, and contact with the outside world, they feel powerless, helpless, and that they are easy to manipulate.

As a result, women behind bars are saddled with an added level of punishment, which is, of course, not sanctioned by any prison system, but is so overlooked and so common as to be essentially institutionalized. This chapter explores the gendered experiences of women in prison with special attention to how prisoner culture is maintained and experienced by the women who live there. Moreover, the impact of institutional regimens of daily life on the prison culture that develops in women's prisons will be discussed in the context of how such regimens may (not) be of benefit to the women upon release from the prison setting.

Characteristics of Female Offenders

As in any examination of women prisoners, the first point is to note that they constitute a small percentage of the total number of people incarcerated in the United States, contributing in part to their being labeled the "forgotten offender." And while their relative proportions are small, the growing numbers of women being sent to prison is disproportionate to their involvement in serious crime. Women imprisoned in state and federal correctional institutions throughout the United States totaled 94,336 at midyear 2001, representing 6.6 percent of the total prisoner population (Beck and Harrison, 2001). This represents twice the number of incarcerated women held in jails and prisons one decade earlier. Moreover, the impact on women of color has been disproportionately heavy. For African American women, the incarceration rate is eight times that for white women; for Latinas, it is almost four times greater (Beck, 2000)—circumstances that reflect issues not only of race, but also of poverty.

Female offenders share many characteristics with male offenders and are very similar in terms of age, socioeconomic level, and race/ethnic background. Female inmates are young (about two-thirds are under thirty-four years old), minority-group members (more than 60 percent), unmarried (more than 80 percent), undereducated (about 40 percent are not high school graduates), and underemployed (Beck and Mumola, 1999). Unlike men, large majorities are unmarried, mothers of children under eighteen, and daughters who grew up in homes without both parents present. Moreover, a distinguishing characteristic of incarcerated females is their significantly increased likelihood of having survived sexual and/or physical violence, particularly by a male relative or intimate partner (Greenfeld and Snell, 1999b). Research also shows that women in prison have experienced unusually high rates of extremely abusive "discipline" from parents, involvement in drugs, and prostitution, whether they were imprisoned for these crimes or not (Harlow, 1999).

The increased use of imprisonment for women offenders has been attributed to changes in legislative responses to the "war on drugs," changing patterns of drug use, and judicial decisionmaking (Mauer, Potler, and Wolf, 1999). In other words, the criminal justice system is more willing to incarcerate women. Increasingly, women who are incarcerated in this country for nonviolent, drug-related offenses account for the largest source of the total growth among female inmates (38 percent nationally). The popularity of imprisonment as a sanctioning tool has significant implications for corrections, which traditionally has allocated few resources for institutional or community-based programs for female offenders. Because the overall proportion of women prisoners is still small relative to the total prison population, the special problems of women prisoners—while creating a wide range of recent individual and social concern—continue to be minimized.

The picture that emerges of the female inmate is troubling. Female criminal behavior in society at large appears to be the product of continuing personal and social problems—the impact of physical and emotional abuse and extreme disadvantage, exacerbated by economic problems as well as drug and alcohol abuse. Often overlooked is the fact that these personal and social problems are imported into the prison setting and become a part of the intricate web of the prison culture through which women negotiate their daily existence. At the same time, there is a need to address how institutional rules and programmatic opportunities available to women in prison contribute to the continuation of the disadvantaged status of women prisoners. The gender stereotypes that influenced the first women's reformatories—the idea of "treatment" for women entailed the fostering of sexual morality, the imposition of sobriety, the instilling of obedience, and the prescribing of the sex-role stereotype of mother and homemaker (Chandler, 1973: 7; Freedman, 1981)—continue to affect the treatment, conditions, and opportunities of incarcerated women today.

Deception of the Prison Appearance

On the surface, most women's prisons are more attractive than men's. Some have been converted from country mansions or children's homes and the obvious aspects of security (such as gun towers) are often lacking. Indeed, it has been acknowledged by various departments of correction (personal communications with administrators in California, 1976–1980, Virginia, 1983–1987, Illinois, 1988–1993, and North Carolina, 1994–present) that security considerations for women offenders do not loom so large because there is less public anxiety and fear when women escape from custody. Yet as the inmates point out, there is only the appearance of a campus. Repression is every bit as strong as in men's prisons; it is simply much more subtle. The social control in women's prisons is best described as "pastel facism"; control glossed over and concealed by a superficial facade of false benevolence and concern for the lives of inmates. What few possessions they have are often confiscated or destroyed, and they are subject to arbitrary body searches at any time (Cambanis, 2002; personal communications with women inmates housed in a maximum-security prison in the southeast, 1994–present). When women in prison fail to conform to expectations, physical control is quickly instituted.

In the following sections, the insights of several women who live or have lived the prison experience will be shared. The voices of these women echo the sentiments and realities of many women in prisons throughout the United States.

Upon Entry into Prison

The objectives of the correctional system and the crimes of female offenders notwithstanding, once women enter the institution they often go from being a victim of justice to a victim of injustice. Cruel and unusual punishment is not supposed to exist today; however, one would never know it by observing life in women's penal facilities. After arriving at her assigned correctional home, the new female prisoner must go through a series of orientation or "reception" procedures. She may come in handcuffed and be refingerprinted and rephotographed for institutional records. She soon loses all remaining dignity when she is stripped and searched for contraband, showered, and issued prison attire and bedding. When she is given her prison number, she is officially "property of the state."

> Being processed was like an assembly line. Each person had a job to do. You go in there, you weren't a person anymore, you weren't human anymore, they could care less. About forty-two of us came in together. They threw us all in the same room, and we, four of us, shower together, it was awful. We were in orange jump suits, with no underwear. For some girls, it was that time of the month. One girl had to keep a pad on with a jump suit with no panties on. That's

just the way it is. And they don't care. The phrase is always, "Welcome to the real world." (Vanessa at the Central California Women's Facility, in Owen, 1998: 77)

Over the next two to six weeks the incarcerated woman, who is relegated to a communal segregation living unit during this period, goes through medical and psychiatric examinations for everything from venereal disease to mental illness.

By the time she joins the general prison population, she has been instilled with the extensive rules and regulations of her confinement, including her new status of "institutional dependency." Although women's prisons are usually not the maximum-security fortresses that men's prisons are, some suggest that the rules women must abide by are stricter (Carlen, 1994). These rules and regulations, as well as disciplinary actions for infractions, vary from one institution to another.

Many female inmates view the rules and regulations of prisons as willful efforts to "diminish their maturity" by "treating them like children and fostering dependency" (Mann, 1984: 210). The reality of women's prisons is that they create just as much frustration and pain as men's prisons (Giallombardo, 1966: chap. 7; Freedman, 1981; Rafter, 1990).

> From the day we are "received," we been gradually adapting to the loss of our identity and respect. We become accustom to the chaos and lurking danger because we have to. We are forced to accept absurd rules and cope with insane reasoning. (Christy Marie Camp at Valley State Prison for Women, in Camp, 2000c: 1)

The Prison Experience

Sykes (1958) described the pains of imprisonment for men as the deprivations of liberty, goods and services, heterosexual relationships, autonomy, and security. All these deprivations apply equally to female prisoners, and some may be more severe for women. Separation from one's family is an obvious example of this. Women may also suffer from receiving fewer leisure, work, and educational opportunities and closer surveillance than men.

Many have noted that the corrections experience is significantly different for women than for men, because men and women are treated differently by the courts and corrections systems (Chesney-Lind and Pollock-Byrne, 1995). It has been suggested that this differential treatment has to do with the nature of crimes committed by women and the role of many women as mothers. Unfortunately, our understanding of the role that sex and gender play in shaping prisoner culture and experience has been constrained by a lack of recent research.

Although female offenders became the subjects of extensive research in the 1960s, studies examining their adjustment to imprisonment today have received minimal attention. Research continues to focus primarily on the effects of incarceration on male prisoners, suggesting that the female inmate still remains a "forgotten offender" (MacKenzie, Robinson, and Campbell, 1989, 1995). Those studies that have focused on the female inmate, however, have shown that imprisonment impacts women more severely than men, especially if they have family responsibilities (Durham, 1994). As noted by Elaine Lord (1995), superintendent of New York's Bedford Hills:

> Women "do time" differently from how men do time. Men concentrate on "doing their own time," relying on feelings of inner strength, and their ability to withstand outside pressures to get themselves through their time in prison. Women, on the other hand, remain interwoven in the lives of significant others, primarily their children and their own mothers, who usually take on the care of the children. Yet the inmate continues a significant care-giving role even while incarcerated. (266)

Despite the growing number of long-term offenders in the United States, studies continue to focus primarily on the male long-term offender, with little emphasis being placed on females. Since few studies have examined issues of coping among women within the prison setting, very little is known about the special concerns of female inmates. Those studies that have focused on long-term female offenders, however, have produced inconsistent findings with regard to the effects of long-term sentencing.

In a study of female offenders, Carlen (1985) found that long-term inmates were more likely than short-term inmates to engage in one of four responses to the pains of imprisonment: death, institutionalization, self-mutilation, and madness. Her results indicated further that the primary means of survival for long-term female offenders involved the formation of relationships with other prisoners. In contrast, MacKenzie and colleagues (1995) found no difference in the level of anxiety experienced by women serving both short- and long-term sentences, regardless of their time served in prison. In addition, they found the establishment of relationships with other inmates, or "state families," to be a coping mechanism only for newly entered inmates as opposed to those having served their sentences for a longer period of time. A more recent investigation into women's imprisonment experiences noted that "long-termers" and "lifers" have different challenges in composing a life in prison (Owen, 1998: 71). Women serving sentences of ten years or more eventually reach an accommodation by which they can "do their own time." As one young "lifer" shares:

> Can you imagine what it is like being a lifer and sitting in a room with five other people who have three more months they have to sit through before they go home and they can't handle it? They are hysterical because their baby is out there having a birthday without them? I am disgusted with their complaining over nothing. (Mindy at the Central California Women's Facility, in Owen, 1998: 72)

These studies suggest that coping behavior and prison adjustment may in some cases differ among short- and long-term female inmates, although a specific response to long-term incarceration cannot be generalized to the entire female prison population.

The social worlds found in men's and women's prisons exhibit at least two key differences. First, the social climate of the average women's prison is, in comparison to even a medium-security men's prison, far less tense; the institutions are far less violent (Gray, Mays, and Stohr, 1995). Most female prisoners come to prison because of a drug offense or property crime. Far fewer are violent personal offenders. Therefore, women's prisons have a less predatory inmate population than that found in men's prisons (Welch, 1996: 360). Second, the functions served by the inmate subculture in prisons for men and women are different. For example, the inmate subculture in men's prisons exists largely to protect inmates from each other. The subculture also helps to neutralize the rejection associated with incarceration, and provides a buffer between inmates and staff. In prisons for women, the subculture exists for these reasons plus an additional one: it provides female inmates with emotional support (Pollock-Byrne, 1990: 59–63; Welch, 1996: 360).

Numerous historians and researchers have critiqued the tradition and current practice of treating women prisoners as wayward children, as distinct from men prisoners, who are at least accorded adult status (Burkhart, 1973; Carlen, 1985). As noted by Watterson (1996), the controls of prison that attempt to regulate lives, attitudes, and behavior are synonymous with those used during infancy. The women prisoners, like children, are told when to get up, how to dress, what to eat, where to go, how to spend their time—in short, what to do and what not to do. The prison—represented by officers, staff, and administrators—acts as a punitive "parent" imposing rules and sanctions to control a "child." For instance, women have shared accounts of having angered authorities and, as a consequence, being moved from a choice living unit and/or job but being told that such actions were "for their own good." Some women who were caught in a chaotic cycle of drugs and violence may indeed feel relief from the restraints imposed by imprisonment.

> Where would I be if I hadn't been busted? Probably dead. Everyone I was with out there is either dead of AIDS or in prison. I was in a prison within myself. The drugs controlled my life. If I'd been thinking about my child, I wouldn't be here today. . . . I loved my child. I did. But that's not what controlled me. (Judith Clark at Bedford Hills Correctional Facility, in Clark, 1995: 309)

Prison forces this break and provides a "time-out" from such destructive behaviors and compulsive activity as well as a space away from the pressures and problems women faced outside (Clark, 1995). Although external controls may mask problems, they do not solve them. Moreover, some women become dependent on the controlled prison environment.

Prison rules and interpersonal dynamics within women's prisons perpetuate/promote the dependency of their "clients." Ironically, the closed, punitive prison environment can re-create many of the dysfunctional family and social dynamics many of the women experienced as children and as adults, with the resultant negative self-representations and impulses. This is particularly significant given the large percentage of women in prison who report experiences of physical, sexual, and emotional abuse as children and/or adults (Zaitzow, 1996; Girshick, 1999). Forced dependency can undermine a woman's sense of autonomy and responsibility, traits needed to succeed as an individual on the outside.

Adaptation to Prison Life

The first moments upon arrival at prison can be terrifying, when the offender is uncertain where she fits in. Inmate adaptations to prison vary from facility to facility, depending on such factors as institutional and administrative programs, personal philosophy, and inmate characteristics. These adaptations can be grouped under the concept of "prisonization," which describes the degree to which inmates participate in and adopt the prison subculture.

> Prisons are places of intense pressure and like all war zones, produce intense change; for better or worse, no one will leave the same. A day in the system is an endless effort to cope with crisis. The struggle becomes the focus of every thought and deed. . . . Faced with daily evidence of societal rejection and condemnation, with daily blows to their self-esteem and sense of self, prisoners have no choice but to seek their own sources of dignity and pride; their own ways of investing their lives with meaning. . . . All prisoners confront the same problem: how to maintain their sense of self and prove to themselves and others that they are women of substance and worth in an environment designed to destroy this. (Christy Marie Camp at Valley State Prison for Women, in Camp, 2000b: 1)

Women quickly learn to adopt certain inmate identities and lifestyles as ways of adjusting to life behind bars. Female inmates, like their male counterparts, make adjustments to prison life. For many, faced with years behind walls, life becomes a strategy of survival. Their attempts at survival often mean that, compared to male inmates, women are more likely to be rule-breakers. Correctional officers describe female inmates as more emotional and manipulative. They are perceived by guards to be more difficult to supervise than men because they are seen as less respectful to authority and more willing to argue (Pollock, 1986). They are written up for twice as many infractions as men, but usually the infractions are less serious than those committed in men's prisons (McClellan, 1994). Because of prior emotional problems or those induced by the stresses of incarceration, especially the separation from their children or loved ones, female inmates are more likely to engage in self-aggression, including suicide and self-mutilation (Pollock, 1990).

Like men, women become involved in an inmate subculture that includes codes of conduct established by inmates, roles to be acted out, and special terminology that sets inmates apart from staff and the outside world. The subculture facilitates adjustment and coping to counterbalance the negative aspects of confinement (Hart, 1995). Many women incarcerated for the first time do not see themselves as criminals and are called "squares" by other inmates. Those referred to as "cool" are professional criminals, such as con artists, who see the time spent in prison as merely a temporary setback. They maximize their opportunities to enjoy prison life as much as possible by manipulating others. Habitual offenders, referred to as being "in the life," such as drug addicts and prostitutes, find status and acceptance into a family structure (Heffernan, 1972).

Kinships

Women who face the emotional deprivation and cold environment of imprisonment find ingenious ways of accommodating to the world in which they live. The reality for incarcerated women is that no matter the ambiance, degradation, or lack of heat, prison is "home"—a perfect setting for playing house. To play house, of course, you need all the players, including husbands and children. The architectural model is there, the emphasis is there. The only missing elements are the real relationships with men and children and blood relatives. So a family system has developed naturally, an evolution of the model for rehabilitation that reformers first conceived but failed to understand.

Women are more likely than men to form dyads (two-person groups) and pseudo-families. Surrogate or make-believe families—also referred to as "state families"—form groups in which inmates play the roles of father, mother, brother, and sister. Others may attach themselves to the family as aunts, uncles, and cousins. The mother-daughter relationship is the most common. Sometimes inmates "marry" or "divorce" each other. Most homosexual relationships in women's prisons appear to be voluntary and are not present in all kinship families. The woman playing the role of father or husband is referred to as the "stud," and the wife is the "femme." Women who assume the male role and characteristics, sometimes referred to as "butches" or "dykes," may do so because of the associated power and status. This transformation is created by how they dress, style their hair, adopt nicknames, and display toughness. Yet as noted by Superintendent McLaughlin of the Federal Reformatory for Women at Alderson, Virginia:

> Who knows how much of it is real homosexuality? Or how much of what seems to be homosexuality is actually consummated? . . . [I]n our culture, if you ain't got a man, you ain't got nothing. And that model from the outside carries into this institution. People play roles, but a lot of it is just to fill out the public image the culture says women are supposed to project. And a lot of it just has to do with people needing to be close to another human being.
> (Watterson, 1996: 297)

Whether as lovers and/or as "family" members, these kinship groups provide stability, warmth, security, and social bonding for women seeking primary group relationships (Propper, 1982). Having a prison family means that when a woman is sick, she has someone to mother her. If a woman is being bullied or threatened by someone outside of the family, she has family members who will come to her defense. If she receives bad news from the outside, she has people to confide in. Women rely and depend on their family members to varying degrees. Some of the relationships are healthy, some are abusive, others are matters of convenience. And although it may sound peculiar, this world of prison families is extremely natural, somehow, in the unnatural world of prison. Recent research suggests that these pseudo-families are a logical extension for incarcerated women, who like most women, having "been socialized to concentrate their energies on family relationships, . . . presumably miss these relationships more than men do and therefore create pseudo-families to replace lost familial relationships" (Bowker, 1981: 415).

Special Needs of Female Inmates

Women in prison manifest a number of problems in common with men (e.g., drug dependence, lack of marketable job skills, health problems), but they have certain special needs. Separation from one's family is an obvious example. Not infrequently, women enter prison pregnant and give birth while serving their sentences. In only a handful of states are they allowed to keep their children with them for limited periods; in most situations, the infant is removed soon after birth. Mother-child bonding is thus cut off from the very beginning. Incarcerated women are far more likely than incarcerated men to be the emotional and financial providers for their children. A recent study found 90 percent of men who are incarcerated report that the other parent had custody of their children once they were incarcerated. This same study found that 23 percent of incarcerated women report the children's fathers had custody once they were institutionalized (Schafer and Dellinger, 1999). Some children go to relatives, and the mothers try to stay in touch; but others are sent to foster care, and once there, parental rights can be terminated. "Unlike men sentenced to prison, women seldom have been able to rely on a spouse to care for their children; therefore they have suffered more anxiety about the welfare of their families" (Rafter, 1985: 179). In her study of almost 300 women prisoners, Owen (1998: 101) describes most women's relationships with their children as "sacred," providing "a basis for attachment to the outside world not always found among male prisoners." There is no doubt that "Mom is always Mom," and that doesn't stop just because a mother is in prison (Lord, 1995).

Health Services

The quality and quantity of health care received by all inmates have been questioned and generally found in need of reconsideration. Ross and Lawrence (1998) identified the medical problems of women prisoners as asthma, diabetes, HIV/AIDS, tuberculosis, hypertension, herpes simplex II infection, chronic pelvic inflammatory disease, anxiety, neurosis, and depression. The mental disorders, especially anxiety and depression, are high for both mothers and nonmothers, and one study found that incarcerated women had perceived depression scores more than twice those for general population samples of women. Among the more egregious indignities to which pregnant women are subjected is that they are shackled while being transported to local hospitals to deliver their children or when seriously ill. According to a report by Amnesty International (1999), the delegates found that in one ward, every woman was chained by her leg to a bed. Because women commonly need and avail themselves of more medical services than men, the problem of poor medical services for the female inmate is even greater than it is for the male. The street lifestyle of many female inmates (e.g., drug and alcohol abuse, poor diet, possibly indiscriminate sexual behavior, restricted access to medical services, and the tendency to neglect medical problems) means that women entering prison are likely to require significant medical attention and education to help them take better care of themselves on release to the community (Acoca, 1998; Zaitzow, 2001).

With respect to vocational training and placement, the training available in correctional institutions typically "does not necessarily assist women offenders in obtaining meaningful and financially rewarding work" (Prendergast, Wellisch, and Falkin, 1995: 242). The focus on women as wives and mothers clearly belies the vast and growing number of single women who are heads of households. Although this situation has improved somewhat, there is still a theme in prison programming for women to reflect society's bias that the most acceptable role for women is that of mother and wife (Diaz-Cotto, 1996). The work assignments that are available to women incarcerated in the United States tend to be in cosmetology, office skills (including data processing), sewing, and horticulture, but few prisons train women in skills to help them become legitimately independent on their release. By emphasizing training for traditional women's low-skilled jobs and traditional definitions of gender roles, prisons also tend to increase women's dependency, stress women's domestic rather than employment role, aggravate women's emotional and physical isolation, disrupt family and other relationships, engender a sense of injustice (because they are denied many of the opportunities available to male prisoners), and may thereby indirectly intensify the pains of imprisonment. The irony of this situation is that the majority of women currently housed in institutions throughout the United States will be released from confinement and expected to "fit in" with mainstream society. Without providing these women the necessary social skills with which they may become viable contributors to/for society, their chances for successful assimilation as well as day-to-day survival will be impeded.

Victimization of Women Prisoners

The experiences of women in custody can be far more onerous than those their male counterparts face. Once a woman enters a federal or state facility, she gives up all her rights, not only to freedom and daily tasks, but to her body and to ward off sexual advances. Worse than the deficiency of programs for incarcerated women, some studies have found the medical "care" in women's prisons to be abusive, with the psychiatrists among the worst offenders (Faith, 1993).

Faith (1993) recounts stories of imprisoned women coerced into being guinea pigs to test ineffective medications, psychiatrists who viewed and treated all incarcerated women's problems as "penis envy," and hysterectomies given indiscriminately to large numbers of women by unaccredited medical establishments and retired general practitioners with no gynecology experience. As a Nightline (1999) series on the medical needs of female prisoners illustrated, in some institutions, abuses by medical staff may border on sexual harassment and generate litigation.

In addition, female inmates in all but one state have been victims of sexual misconduct by corrections employees, according to a report by Amnesty International (1999). Whether the proportion of incidents of sexual misconduct is increasing or whether more women are willing to talk about it remains to be seen. We do know that women prisoners are far more likely to be subjected to physical and other forms of sexual-related abuse than their male counterparts, including sexual assaults and other forms of nonconsensual coercion. To compound the trauma of these exploitative and abusive experiences, a Human Rights Watch study (1996) of sexual abuse of women in U.S. prisons found that the women who reported the abuses were frequently retaliated upon by the perpetrator himself, other guards, or the entire system. Although some states have made any form of sexual interaction—whether consensual or nonconsensual—a felony, staff-inmate sexual predation remains. Considering the large number of allegations of sexual misconduct by prison staff, the number of actual prosecutions has not been overwhelming. According to the U.S. Department of Justice's own records, only ten prison employees in the entire federal system were disciplined in 1997 for sexual misconduct, and just seven were criminally prosecuted (Gilliard, 1999). Sexual degradation and humiliation of women by staff is so ingrained in the culture of many women's prisons that it seems to have become an accepted mode of control in the custodial environment.

Complicating the problem, of course, is that many women in prison have just left the streets, where the same thing was expected of them, whether they were prostitutes or addicts who gave up their bodies in return for drugs. At the same time, a huge proportion of women serving time have already been sexually victimized in their lives. According to Human Rights Watch (1996), anywhere from 40 to 88 percent of incarcerated women have been victims of domestic violence and sexual or physical abuse either as children or adults. They have already been "conditioned" to believe that they deserve such treatment, and to remain silent, and the prison system plays on that vulnerability to intimidate them and keep them in line. Of particular relevance to the present discussion is this observation by Diaz-Cotto (2000):

> While the literature on imprisoned women seldom mentions how prisoners have sought to reform prison conditions, my study found that when outside sources of support were available, for example, in the form of prisoners' rights attorneys, prisoners were more than willing to join together to engage in litigation efforts against the facility. (129)

Toward Change

In an ideal world, it would seem that equal treatment should be the goal. Given that women and men have such varied experiences in terms of public, private, and criminal lives, however, it is questionable that achieving parity with men's prisons is the best solution. Attempts to provide women with facilities, programs, privileges, and rights on the same level as men is an undeniably worthwhile goal. But it appears that "equal treatment" may have some detrimental effects for women offenders. For example, sentencing reforms designed to reduce class and race bias in men's sentencing may also negatively affect the sentencing of women by increasing their incarceration rates and the lengths of sentences. Nor would complete equality be entirely beneficial for women. To attempt to eradicate gender differences within prison while they persist in the outside world makes little sense. For example, the fact that women continue to be responsible for child care means that prison programs should be designed to take this into account (see Baunach, 1985, for examples of programs that are geared toward helping female prisoners increase contact with their children). As noted by Daly and Chesney-Lind (1988: 526), "Criminologists, especially those involved in the formation of policy, should be aware that equal treatment is only one of several ways of redressing discrimination and of moving toward a more humane justice system."

If we hope to facilitate the reentry of incarcerated women to "free" society, we must attempt to reform current policies and programs, both in prison and in the community, which tend to reinforce women offenders' dependency upon the system.

> When I was released on parole, I discovered that no matter my outlook or my efforts, the world seemed to be closed. I was denied jobs and housing because of my convicted felon status, and I felt like damaged goods. . . . And I cried because I couldn't do anything about any of it, no matter how hard I tried. I could not change public opinion. . . . I realized that all the honest endeavors in the world would not help me gain entry, and I thought I no longer had a place "out here." . . . We can research and write about how women get to prison and what goes on there. It is fascinating and helps us to develop strategies toward prevention. We can do many things to help inmates prepare for a different and better life on the outside. But if we do not acknowledge and address the "set up to fail" situation that parolees currently face, we are tilting at windmills. (Dearing, 2002: 46)

As Richie (2001: 386) notes, "the nature of the reform centers on both enhanced delivery and systemic change especially in low-income communities of color from which a majority of incarcerated female population in this country come from." Here, (1) the provision of comprehensive programs utilizing a case management approach would enable women to deal with multiple gender-specific and culture-specific needs; (2) community-based programs need to build linkages with other services to prevent incarceration in the first place as well as provide user-friendly networks by which incarcerated women might avail themselves of services; and (3) promoting economic and emotional empowerment interventions that facilitate the attainment of individual self-sufficiency. Because women offenders manifest multiple problems that require the services of many different agencies, corrections "needs to move toward a more system-oriented approach . . . that emphasizes linkages and coordination among programs and agencies, joint planning, shared resource allocation, and continuity for clients" (Prendergast, Wellisch, and Falkin, 1995: 254).

Conclusion

A recognition of the differing needs and expectations of men and women, the expectations of society, and the implications for dealing with the crime committed by women will give courts and correctional administrators a basis for making choices about the sentencing and correctional alternatives that best serve society and these women. For example, many women currently serving prison terms could safely and more economically serve their sentences in community-based programs. For those with drug problems, there is a need to expand treatment programs. For many others, the economic crimes they committed resulted from their disadvantaged position and lack of marketable skills. And finally, for many women offenders who are victims of abuse, there is a need to embrace and assist these women with programmatic and community support. We must remember how women's issues and prison issues are part of the same struggle.

Prison issues are important because individual women are being oppressed by prison and, in a wider context, because the judicial/prison system exists to support the larger power structure that oppresses us all. Women in prison are fighting to maintain a sense of self within a system that isolates and degrades—one that attempts to teach submission through the constant exercising of power, in both serious and petty ways, over prisoners. What is generated is not obedience but anger, and since a prisoner risks punishment such as being sent to segregation if she directs her anger at the system that is hurting her, that anger often gets directed inward or at other prisoners.

Our task is to learn about and support the struggles of prisoners. Women inside fight back and resist all the time. Support from the outside is a crucial factor in the success of prisoners' campaigns. The knowledge that people outside care about what is happening contributes to prisoners' strength and makes prison administrators respond much more quickly to demands.

No one can argue with the necessity of prisons and jails for people who commit crimes. However, although incarceration is not a picnic for anyone (nor, some argue, should it be), clearly on a collective basis female inmates are a great deal worse off than male inmates. For one thing, it is arguable that many of these women should be in prison at all. Often their biggest crime seems to be trying to feed their families or having the misfortune to be pregnant or nonwhite. Control-oriented rules and regulations, poor diet, neglectful health care, degradation, lack of vocational training and recreational facilities, exploitation, abuse, and unsanitary conditions typify the conditions in many prisons and jails that house women. Reform is needed both within the correctional system and in a society that condones inhumane treatment of women prisoners.

For most women, prison is just a chapter in their life, but for some, it's the whole damn book. Freedom is a complex issue. There are no simple answers. The liberty to think and do as we wish is one of the greatest treasures of life. Yet we appreciate it most when we have it least. Too often it is more of an illusion than a fact. In reality, freedom is never total, and it is surely never free. But for the legions of women "under supervision" this hour, freedom is the main goal of daily life. Not just physical liberty, but freedom of mind and spirit as well. . . . No matter how long you must remain in prison, there will be only two things you truly own: the power of your will and the quality of your mind. A woman doing days counts hours, a woman doing months counts days, a woman doing a year counts months, a woman doing life counts breaths. (Christy Marie at Valley State Prison for Women, in Camp, 2000a: 2)

3

Gendered Perceptions of Dangerous and Dependent Women: "Gun Molls" and "Fallen Women"

Esther Heffernan

This chapter explores the ways in which deeply embedded patriarchal and heterosexual beliefs regarding the nature and status of women and slaves have shaped struggles over the application to women of incarceration and classification forms developed for male prisoners and prisons. Drawing from historical examples of the incarceration of women in the federal and state systems, this chapter explores the perceived and legally embodied dependencies and sexualities that defined whether women were sent to a corner of the men's penitentiary, cared for in refuges and workhouses, or were fit candidates for the new women's reformatories. Bourdieu's analysis of the symbolic violence that grounds gender domination provides insight into the fundamental dynamics of our incarceration of women (Bourdieu and Wacquant, 1992: 164–174; Bourdieu, 2001: 1–2, 33–42).

The title of this chapter reflects an instructive clash of wills and words that took place during the 1930s in the reports of the Federal Bureau of Prisons. The battle occurred between the male heads of the bureau and Mary Belle Harris, the superintendent of the widely publicized "model" federal reformatory for women opened in 1928 in Alderson, West Virginia. Their exchange introduces us to a historical examination of complex and conflicting beliefs regarding the relationships of power, gender, and sexuality that have shaped alternative responses to the presence of women under the criminal jurisdiction of the state.

Dangerous Women: Madams and Molls

In the 1935 Federal Bureau of Prisons report, Sanford Bates asserted that

> the conviction of a number of women during the past year for serious and desperate crimes or for aiding gangsters and racketeers has made it necessary to provide a special place for their incarceration in an institution of the maximum security type. The Federal Industrial Institution for Women at Alderson was not designed and is not equipped to handle women who are desperate and incorrigible. (Federal Bureau of Prisons, 1935: 18)

Bates had responded to the presence of these dangerous women by constructing a sealed-off section of a cellblock at the male Milan Federal Detention Farm in Michigan, where they were guarded by armed officers and housed "in the more traditional type of steel cell" (Federal Bureau of Prisons, 1935: 18). His successor, James Bennett, in a later report described these "desperate and incorrigible" women as "unregenerate keepers of houses of prostitution, gangsters' 'molls,' and confirmed drug users" (Federal Bureau of Prisons, 1938: 7).

Bennett makes clear in his report, which called for the construction of a separate maximum-security facility for women, that a more fundamental principle was at stake: "We need to specialize our institutions for women just as has been done for men" (1938: 7). Yet Bennett's apparent gender-free position that women should be treated equally or "just as has been done for men" obscured the gendered nature of the offenses he defined as "dangerous." Only women can be "molls" or "madams." What might be the sources for these perceptions?

Bennett and Bates may have assumed that armed guards and steel cells were required for gangsters' "molls" precisely because of their dependent relationship. Either the women of violent men follow "their men" into violence, or violent men will stop at nothing to rescue "their women." Paradoxically, the danger posed by the "madam" was her symbolic challenge to the very nature of women's apparent domestic dependency. As a capitalist entrepreneur selling the sexual wares of her prostitutes as a commodity, the madam was not only an independent woman engaged in public business, but also, in bringing women's bodies into the market as "white slaves," evoked images of supposedly vanquished black slave markets. Stanley (1998) historically explores the implications of the abolitionists' exalting of the labor contract as a mark of freedom, without comprehending the implications of commodifying human relationships in an era of ideological support both for industrial capitalism and for patriarchal domestic families. Stanley examines the symbolic power of the usage of the term "white slavery":

> After abolition the prostitute became a negative exemplar of the legitimate trafficking in human bodies and souls, taking the ideological place of the chattel slave for a nation that enshrined contract freedom. . . . Not labor but sex represented the human essence whose sale as a market commodity transformed its owners from free persons into slaves. (263)

From Bates's and Bennett's perspective, both madams and molls, as well as confirmed drug users, by their challenge to dominant heterogendered cultural expectations, required the same threats of violence and structures of physical control assumed necessary to subdue dangerous men. Mary Belle Harris denied these assumptions. In response to Bates and Bennett, Harris disputed as a matter of principle the need for a separate facility for "desperate and incorrigible" women:

> I do not believe that a maximum security institution for women is necessary and I feel that it would be a decided letting down of our standard if such an institution were proposed. I am convinced that we have made a demonstration here which had set a standard for the country, and that it would be considered a set-back if we should depart from the policy so far adopted here and in well-conducted state institutions for women. (Federal Bureau of Prisons, 1938: 93)

In her prison memoirs, Harris (1936: 301) questioned the assumption of Congress in its enabling legislation for the "reformatory" at Alderson that some women were not "reclaimable." She was convinced that the reformatory program at Alderson was appropriate for most if not all women and, in her estimation, perhaps for men as well.

Determined, Dependent, and Diseased Women

Harris's challenge to the supposed necessity of steel cells and armed guards to protect the nation from "desperate and incorrigible" women arose, however, within an equally gendered and paradoxical historical context. The existence of Alderson as the federal prison for women was not only closely linked to the organized struggle of the women's suffrage movement and the earlier call by women's "benevolent societies" for separate and autonomous facilities administered by and for women, but also by the critical presence for the first time of federal financial support (Lekkerkerker, 1931: 604–607; Freedman, 1981: 146–147; Rafter, 1985: 23–82; Heffernan, 1994: 38–50; Alexander, 1995: 33–66). Ironically, this support was a result of the first federal legislation passed specifically for the control of women—"diseased women"—whose presence near army camps during World War I was perceived as a threat to national security (Lekkerkerker, 1931: 19–20; Connelly, 1980: 137–145; Freedman, 1981: 147). While historically the movement for women's facilities stressed that the distinctive gendered qualities of vulnerability and domesticity required separate institutions and programs, a key impetus for the actual construction of women's institutions was based precisely on women's "dangerous" uncontrolled sexual activity.

Alderson, with its cottage architecture and rural setting, reflected a deeply held belief that "fallen women" were controlled and reformed more effectively through women's care and compassion in rural, "homelike" communal settings, rather than through the penitentiary's use of "terror," silence, and solitary cells (Freedman, 1981: 22–64; Rafter, 1985: 23–51). With kitchens and living rooms in each cottage, provisions for nurseries and child care, and familial staff-inmate relationships, Harris's Alderson appeared to exemplify and reinforce a belief in women's domestic dependency. However, the dependency occurred within a "women's sphere" where facility, farm, and industry were run by women.

The efforts to construct Alderson's buildings and programs, as well as those of other "well-conducted state institutions," were led by women acutely aware of the limitations of their status and the necessity for organized political power. As a consequence, their programs emphasized both the importance and the ability of women to be self-governing and independent, trained in their equal rights and responsibilities as citizens (Lekkerkerker, 1931: 437–511; Freedman, 1981: 131–137; Heffernan, 1994: 41). Harris argued for inmate self-government. Aware of the paradox of teaching "human beings in captivity to live the life of freemen [sic]," for Harris women's experience in their own government was essential (Lekkerkerker, 1931: 438). In turn, Alderson's garment factory sought to provide women with marketable skills, though only in a low-paid, limited field. In rather defensively describing Alderson's domestic arrangements, Harris commented in the 1930–1931 report that not only women, but "men, too, for that matter," should learn "to keep house well" (Federal Bureau of Prisons, 1932: 89). Caring for the home need not be gendered.

Gender: Seesaws and Symbolic Violence

The independent women who shaped Alderson's symbolic message held the same "doubled vision" that Cott (1987: 19) ascribes to the larger feminist effort. Cott likened the movement to a strategic seesaw that at one end moved "to eliminate sex-specific limitations" while at the other "to recognize rather than quash the qualities and habits called female." Harris's sparring with her male opponents while balancing on the gendered seesaw embodied in Alderson's "demonstration" was a difficult feat.

A critical insight that Bourdieu (2001: 120) brings to Harris's balancing act is his recognition that

> one is inevitably trapped in one of the most tragic antimonies of symbolic domination: how can people revolt against a socially imposed categorization except by organizing themselves as a category constructed according to that categorization, and so implementing the classifications and restrictions that it seeks to resist (rather than, for example, fighting for a new sexual order in which the distinction between the different sexual statuses would be indifferent)?

In her effort to maintain a "women's sphere" while challenging the legitimacy of a sexual division of labor, Harris both accepts and rejects this biologized social construction. Bourdieu (2001) argues that this is precisely the source of symbolic violence: "The case of gender domination shows better than any other that symbolic violence accomplishes itself through an act of cognition and of mis-recognition that lies beyond—or beneath—the controls of consciousness and will, in the obscurities" of our taken-for-granted "realities" that are "at once gendered and gendering" (171–172). Krais (1993: 173) emphasizes the value of Bourdieu's work in exploring the symbolic aspects of gender domination, arguing that "a socioanalysis of the social practice and thereby a denaturalization of the division of labor between the genders is a *conditio sine qua non* for the liberation of women." Harris, Bates, and Bennett, consciously or unconsciously, were carrying on a symbolic struggle over the appropriate forms of domination and, for Harris, the potential liberation of "their" women.

Conflicted Historical Foundations

The verbal battles between Harris and Bates and Bennett, as well as reflecting the historical context in which they took place, also exemplify long-standing contradictions present in the cultural foundations of the American Republic. Liberal beliefs in equality and freedom were asserted within firmly based economic and social structures dependent on the presence of patriarchal families and domestic slavery. In Bourdieu's terms, gendered and racial symbolic violence grounded the Republic. Recognizing the consequences of challenges to those foundations is critical in understanding the position of women, not only within the patriarchal family but also in relation to the legal and penal systems of the state that shaped the development and use of penitentiaries, refuges and workhouses, and women's reformatories.

Stanley, in her analysis, notes that the abolitionist movement for the emancipation of the slaves decried the destruction of family bonds in the slave markets while attacking domestic slavery as a violation of the right of every man to contract for his labor. Exemplifying Bourdieu's view of the "misrecognition" of symbolic violence, abolitionists remained unaware of the fundamental structural and legal tension between assuming the "gender rules of classical liberal theory, which defined men as masters of the household with proprietary rights to their dependent wives" (Stanley, 1998: 29), while firmly holding the liberal view that "idealized ownership of self and voluntary exchange between individuals who were formally equal and free" (1998: x). However, as Stanley emphasizes, opponents of the abolitionists as well as vocal supporters of slavery were aware of implications of the abolitionist position not only for the foundations of the patriarchal family but for the capitalist labor market. The clear absence of "equal and free" conditions for the white laboring poor easily gave rise to accusations of the presence of "wage-slavery" not only in the North, but also in the prisons.

The Reverend Samuel Seabury (1861: 65–66), a widely respected New York Episcopalian moral theologian writing at the time of the

Civil War, provides a classic statement of the linkage of slavery, prisons, and the position of women that reveals the patriarchal assumptions underlying legal structures that were differentially applied to wives and slaves. Seabury asserts "that in all human society, and under every form of government we find two general divisions of persons," those who have an "immediate" relationship to society, or to its governing power, and those with a "mediate" relationship. Minors are related to society only through their fathers or guardians, wives through their husbands, and servants and slaves through their masters. For Seabury, and many others, this distinction of persons is "founded in Nature and a necessary element of the social order" (67). The main principle on which the very being of the state rests for support is

> the subordination of wives to their husbands, of children to their fathers, and of slaves (in every community which has them) to their masters. . . . Their position is one of subordination and dependence; and men—freemen—whether they be "the lords of creation" or not, are in fact the lords and rulers of the political community to which they belong. (68)

Seabury argues that the slave's relation to the master is of the same form as that of wife and child—one of mutual responsibilities: care and protection on the part of the master, and subordination, service, and dependence on the part of child, wife, and slave (187).

Aware of the paradox in the abolitionist argument that Stanley's research explores, Seabury comments that in the North "the great body of the laboring class" also stands in "mediate" relation to the state and he will "quarrel with arbitrary power at the South when we get rid of jails and state-prisons at the North" (190). In response to the abolitionists' protest that slavery separates families, Seabury retorts: "Look to your jails and prisons . . . have the inmates of these dismal abodes left no relatives outside the walls that confine them to mourn over their disgrace, their incarceration and sufferings?" (205). Ultimately Seabury views his work as an ideological defense of patriarchal society against those who would "raise the *individual* above the State" and who demand that "not only must slaves have equal civil rights with their masters, but women must have an equal share in government with men, and the poor an equal share of property with the rich," in defiance of both the "law of Nature and of CHRIST" (314). He reaffirms the major slavery defenses of Bledsoe (1857: 223–225) and Ross (1857: 47–56).

Legal Embodiment of Patriarchy

The patriarchal social framework that Seabury defends was embodied in the legal system at the founding of the Republic. The critical question that arises is the degree to which this embedded social framework and the symbolic violence it masked continued to shape the position of women in relation to the legal system—particularly black and poor women—long after that founding. While the Thirteenth Amendment, with the abolition of domestic slavery, legally freed servants and slaves from dependency on and domination by their masters, wives and children remained firmly within the patriarchal relationships of the domestic family. In 1873 Maria Bradwell appealed Illinois's refusal to allow her to practice law to the Supreme Court, arguing that it was in violation of the Fourteenth Amendment's right to equal protection. The appeal was denied. Justice Joseph Bradley's concurring opinion is revealing:

> The civil law as well as nature itself, has always recognized a wide difference in the respective spheres and destinies of man and woman. Man is, or should be, woman's protector and defender. The natural and proper timidity and delicacy which belongs to the female sex evidently unfits it for many of the occupations of civil life.... The constitution of the family organization, which is founded in the divine ordinance, as well as in the nature of things, indicates the domestic sphere as that which properly belongs to the domain and functions of womanhood. The harmony, not to say identity, of interests and views which belong, or should belong, to the family institution is repugnant to the idea of a woman adopting a distinct and independent career from that of her husband.... It is true that many women are unmarried and not affected by any of the duties, complications, and incapacities arising out of the married state, but these are exceptions to the general rule. The paramount destiny and mission of women are to fulfill the noble and benign offices of wife and mother. This is the law of the Creator. And the rules of civil society must be adapted to the general constitution of things, and cannot be based on exceptional cases. (83 U.S. [16 Wall.] 130 [1873] quoted in Taub and Schneider, 1982: 126–127)

Equally essential to an understanding of women's position before the courts is the often-overlooked clause of the Thirteenth Amendment that "freed the slaves." The Thirteenth Amendment, reflecting the awareness of Seabury and other "lords and rulers of the political community" of the critical linkage between Southern slavery and Northern prisons, recognized and legalized involuntary servitude and slavery and established the state as the master over those duly convicted of crime. The public sphere of the state, rather than the private sphere of the family, might legally own slaves and servants. At approximately the same time that Justice Bradley was defining the "domestic sphere" as the proper place for "womanhood," the Virginia State Supreme Court rejected an appeal, based on the Bill of Rights, of a white inmate in the state penitentiary. The court succinctly defined his status as a slave:

> The Bill of Rights is a declaration of general principle to govern the society of freemen and not of convicted felons and men civilly dead. Such men have some rights it is true, such as the law in its benignity accords to them but not the rights of freemen. They are slaves of the State undergoing punishment for heinous crimes committed against the laws of the land. (21 Gratten [Virginia], 794–797, 796 [1871])

As Bourdieu and Wacquant (1992: 163 n) note, the law is "the form par excellence of the symbolic power of naming and classifying that creates the things named." The law "in its benignity" names and classifies the "heinous crimes" against it, and "creates" slaves of the state.

"Creating" and "Classifying" Women and Slaves

It might appear that these learned legal pronouncements by Supreme Court justices in the 1870s would have little bearing on the battles between Harris and Bennett and Bates. Yet it was precisely during this period that the women's reformatory movement began, grounded in the "reality" of the "women's sphere" that Harris defended in the 1930s (Rafter, 1983: 289–291; 1985: 23–51). Bates and Bennett's call for a maximum-security facility for "desperate and incorrigible" women who had committed "heinous crimes" was rooted in the gendered "naming and classifying" that founded the penitentiaries in the early days of the Republic.

In the process of defining criminal actions and penalties during this period the courts and legislatures debated women's position in the "civil society," and the "domestic" relationships of husband and wife, as well as the racial status that legitimated a master-slave relationship. While both women and men argued for women's right to membership in the new "civil order" as electors, office-holders, and jury members, no early state legislatures or courts upheld that right. Wertheimer (1977: 48), in summarizing the legal position of women, concludes that "through the revolutionary period the colonial woman enjoyed considerable more freedom than her European sisters, but the stricter adherence to Blackstone's codification of English common law by the new American states following the war ended that freedom."

In his authoritative *Commentaries on the American Law* written in 1826, Kent (1832) grounded U.S. law on Blackstone's interpretation of English common law. Blackstone recognized that married women retained their "personhood" under civil and ecclesiastical law in other jurisdictions, but argued differently for the common-law tradition:

> By marriage, the husband and wife are one person in law; that is, the very being, or legal existence of the woman is suspended during the marriage, or at least incorporated and consolidated into that of the husband, under whose wing, protection and *cover,* she performs everything . . . under the protection and influence of her husband, her *baron* or lord. . . . The courts of law will still permit a husband to restrain a wife of her liberty in case of any gross misbehavior. . . . In criminal prosecution, it is true, the wife may be indicted and punished separately, for the union is only a civil union. . . . In some felonies, and other inferior crimes committed by her, through constraint of her husband, the law excuses her; but this extends not to treason and murder. (Blackstone, in Sharswood, 1859, vol. 1: 442–444)

As a consequence of the general acceptance of this common-law tradition, the courts were faced with the difficult task of determining when a woman was, or was not, acting as a *feme sole,* rather than "under the cover" of a *baron,* as well as when a slave was property or a person. As *feme sole,* a woman became a person legally and morally responsible for her actions, capable of owning property, signing contracts, using the civil courts, and being charged in the criminal courts.

One persistent problem in the new United States was that many persons were either unable to understand or unwilling to form the proper civil unions of the English common law or held too little property for the man to assume the economic responsibilities of a *baron*. One ironic consequence, particularly among new immigrants and the urban and rural poor—which included many of the free blacks—was the presence of women who, while living in family relationships, were without a civil union. As these women were *feme sole* in the courts, the men and children in their lives were without legal "existence" (Bloomfield, 1976: 91–135). A less frequent but continuing problem, beginning in 1648 with Margaret Brent in colonial Maryland, was those women who "disturbed the peace" by protesting the denial of their right to vote and hold office when as *feme sole* their property was taxed (see Andrews, 1933: 123, on Margaret Brent's protests; see also Stanton, 1881; Lerner, 1993; hooks, 1981; Flexner, 1996).

An equally persistent dilemma for judges and juries occurred when wives accepted the common law and, in a status similar to that of slaves, "gave up" their "legal being." In an effort to respond to the questions arising from the "mediate" position of women, Kent (1832, vol. 2: 129–188) devoted an entire chapter to providing legal citations for the lawyers of the period to help them determine the "position" of women in various cases of the law. If the husband were unwilling or unable to provide sufficient care, should the wife or the husband be charged for any theft or fraud committed by the wife in supporting themselves and their children? Or if the husband and wife were engaged in illegal actions, should the woman be charged as a codefendant, judged as with "lessened responsibility" because of the presence of coercion, or commended and released as a loyal and obedient wife? What responsibility was incurred in cases where the husband, in the process of legitimately "restraining the liberty" of his wife, seriously injured or killed her? Was a wife's plea of "self-defense" in resisting him legitimate? Or with "equal justice before the law," should the judge and jury judge such questions of intent and responsibility irrelevant? Kent and his fellow lawyers attempted to traverse the administration of penal justice in the context of complex and conflicted symbolic perceptions of women's responsibility. Two paths were available that remain with us to the present day—the refuge and the penitentiary.

The State's "Dependent Women"

The historical roots of refuges or halfway houses, shelters for battered women, treatment centers, and other facilities for the "care" of women were based on the perception that women who violated the criminal law were dependent women who as victims, without the adequate or legitimate "cover" of a man, needed to be cared for by the state. The legal basis for this form of "penal justice" flows directly from the widely held proposition expressed by Blackstone that the protection and care of children and women were the responsibility of fathers and husbands. The consequent legal assumption was that in the absence of this protection and care, the state as *parens patriae* assumes that responsibility. Schlossman (1977: chap. 1) has traced the sources of U.S. usage of the state's power to "care and control" to the English common-law tradition that the king, as the "father of the nation," had the responsibility to function as a "guardian" of those who were unable to protect themselves. Even in the contemporary courtroom, the usage of *parens patriae* easily moves to include women. In a recent National Institute of Justice publication, Judge Kay Tsenin (2000: 16) notes that in the world of the sex trade, one is "dealing with people whose conduct is defined by the legislature as criminal but who are victims themselves—and often victimized over and over." Tsenin recommends "mandated intervention programs . . . acting in loco parentis—protecting the street worker from herself, her pimp and the ravages of her work" (20).

In Kent's time, as Dorothea Dix (1967) complained in the 1840s, these "interventions" included the whole world of asylums, poorhouses, and local jails, which housed the poor, the mentally ill, the retarded, and both convicted and unconvicted women and children. Both the state and concerned members of "benevolent societies," functioning *in loco parentis,* not only "cared for" the women and children under their charge, but also assumed, with Blackstone and Kent, that they might "restrain" them of their "liberty in case of any gross misbehavior." Always present, in addition to the controlling rules and regulations of the "house," was the threat in the face of "gross misbehavior" of either the denial of care or incarceration in the jails and penitentiaries of the day. In a later day, for Bates and Bennett the "care and control" of minimum-security facilities or halfway houses would be appropriate for dependent but not dangerous women. As Freedman (1981: 155) asserts, however, underlying the frequent practice of adult women being addressed as "girls" would be "the paternalistic view that women and children are inherently dependent," needing the control as well as the care of others, "while men, even when incarcerated, retain a degree of adult status."

Penitentiaries and Dangerous Women

In the 1830s, with the use of the legal fiction of *feme sole*, the courts placed women in the new penitentiaries. In the midst of conceptual struggles over if, or in what circumstances, both women and slaves were "persons" responsible for their actions and should be treated like men, de Beaumont and de Tocqueville wrote their famous report *On the Penitentiary System in the United States* in 1833. Francis Lieber, in his introduction to the report, "wished to invite the reader's attention [to] the imprisonment of women" since "it is a branch of administration of penal justice much and unfortunately neglected in our country" (xiii). While considering the neglect "unfortunate," he recognizes that it could be attributed to the fact that

> according to their destiny and consequent place they occupy in civil society, they are less exposed to the temptation or to inducement to crime; their ambition is not so much excited, and they are naturally more satisfied with a dependent situation. . . . They have not the courage or the strength to commit a number of crimes, [and] according to their position in society, they cannot easily commit certain crimes such as bigamy, forgery, false arrest, abuse of civil power and revolt. (xiii)

Lieber's analysis was an effort to explain why "in all countries women commit less crime than men, but in none is the disproportion of criminals of the two sexes as great as in ours," as in 1828, "in the state prisons of New York, Connecticut, Pennsylvania and Maryland, the women were in proportion as 9.34 to 100 of both sexes" (de Beaumont and de Tocqueville, 1833: 269). Significantly, this "disproportion" has been maintained, with fluctuations, to the present day. However, de Beaumont noted that "the proportion of women in the prisons of the Union must become more considerable the more you approach the South, where negroes are more numerous, because the coloured women commit more crimes than white women." Beaumont attributes this to the fact that "no provision for economic help is given to freed slaves" (223). In turn, the disproportionate number of Irish women prisoners was seen to be a result of their "excessive misery," their "violent habits," and the "singular inconstancy of their national character" (253, 257). While "inconstancy" of national character might not be directly related to their status as *feme sole,* clearly the propensity for theft and reputed violence of the Irish and "coloured" women would bring them into the courts.

For Lieber the need of penitentiaries for women was even more critical than for men:

> To this must be added the fact, known to all criminalists, that a woman, once renouncing honesty and virtue, passes over to the most hideous crimes which women commit with greater ease than a man passes from his first offense to the blackest crimes committed by his sex. (de Beaumont and de Tocqueville, 1833: xiii)

As a *feme sole* legally and morally responsible for her actions before the courts, a woman is not only "like a man," but according to "all criminalists" even more dangerous after "renouncing honesty and virtue." With confidence in the value of isolation from family, evil companions, and fellow convicts, and the use of terror, silence, and work as a means of total control, the penitentiary movement's leaders did not overlook its value for women. The inspector of Sing Sing reported that "no doubt is entertained, but the same discipline which now controls and subdues the male convict may be made equally serviceable with the female" (de Beaumont and de Tocqueville, 1833: xii). Ironically, the very assertion that, with "equality before the law," women should be treated like men obscured the heavily gendered perceptions of reality reflected in Lieber's assertion:

> A matron is quite indispensable if the Auburn system is applied to women as well as men; she alone can enforce the order of this system, whilst it is nearly impossible for male keepers. The whole system of opposition in womankind is raised against him. Besides, the moral management of female convicts must differ from male criminals, and even their labor requires total separation. (xiii)

Rafter's and Freedman's studies of this period (Rafter, 1985: 3–21; Freedman, 1981: 7–21) reveal that despite the presence of women in penitentiaries, their position was far from equal. Rafter (1985: 4) concludes that if the male historians of the penitentiaries had looked for the women, crowded into the corners of male institutions, "they would have found that in nearly every respect, it contradicted the usual picture of penitentiary discipline" as one of silence, isolation, and hard labor.

Rafter quotes Harriet Martineau's contemporary description of the reality for women at Auburn:

> The arrangements for the women were extremely bad. . . . [T]he women were all in one large room, sewing. The attempt to enforce silence was soon given up as hopeless; and the gabble of tongues among the few that were there was enough to paralyze any matron. . . . There was an engine in sight which made me doubt the evidence of my own eyes; stocks of a terrible construction; a chair, with a fastening for the head and for all the limbs. Any lunatic asylum ought to be ashamed of such an instrument. The governor [warden] liked it no better than we, but he pleaded that it was his only means of keeping his refractory female prisoners quiet while he was allowed only one room to put them all into. (Rafter, 1985: 6, quoting Martineau, 1838: 124–125)

Conditions varied in the Northern states, but Rafter concludes that while women found themselves in prisons based on the "masculine model" of "retributive purpose, high-security architecture, a male-dominated authority structure, programs that stressed earning, and a harsh discipline," within that model women were "vulnerable to sexual exploitation, easier to ignore because so few in number, and viewed with distaste by prison officials." Ultimately women were "treated as the dregs of the state prisoner population" (1985: 21).

The "New South": What Happened to Patriarchy?

A critical shift in analysis needs to occur when examining the condition of women in the prisons of the postbellum South. While the patriarchal assumptions of Blackstone, Kent, and Lieber play a key role in understanding the position of white women under the criminal jurisdiction of the state, precisely the absence of those assumptions in regard to slaves, both men and women, is fundamental for an understanding of black women's position before those courts. As Melish (1998) explores in her study *Disowning Slavery,* the North easily refused to recognize the presence of domestic or state slavery in its own history, while viewing the Thirteenth Amendment's purpose as the freeing of *Southern* slaves. The Southern states after the Civil War, however, had no difficulty continuing the practices of slavery in their prison systems. In his research,

Lichtenstein concludes that "the criminal justice system served as a prime means of racial control and labor exploitation." For "African-Americans, this same system became a powerful symbol of injustice, linking the punishment of crime and their former status as slaves as forms of white oppression," through an "obvious racial double standard" in the ways in which "white prosecutors, judges and juries enforced the law" (1996: 17–18).

Stanley (1998: 124–127) explores the significance, in the face of the understandable reluctance of the freed black slaves to sell their labor to their former masters, of the subtle shift in the abolitionist belief that working under a contract as an independent human being was a symbol of freedom, to the belief, expressed by members of the Freedman's Bureau and embodied in the Black Codes, that *not* to sell one's labor, to become "idle and vicious" or dependent by begging on the "benevolence" of whites, was itself a crime—vagrancy. Under the Black Codes and later "race-neutral" vagrancy laws, local sheriffs and the county jails provided a major source of the black convict labor force in the New South. Despite the Supreme Court's concern regarding wives working outside the home, the Freedman's Bureau "refused to discriminate by sex in enforcing the duty to work," holding that "the wives' labor must be equally as available as the husbands for purchase on the free market" (Stanley, 1998: 141). And by extension, as convicts their labor could be freely sold. Lichtenstein asserts ironically that while the Republicans affirmed a free labor ideology, they discovered that industrial slavery would build railroads and consequently "the political economy of Radical Reconstruction forged the chains that would bind [the South's] convicts for the rest of the century" (1996: 36). Under convict leases based on an awareness that "the language of the Thirteenth Amendment still allowed the southern states to use the criminal law to sell blacks into bondage," black women as well as men worked in the fields, the mines, and the railroads (Lichtenstein, 1996: 36; Rafter, 1985: 88–91).

With this understanding of "equality" for black women, a description of Mississippi's Parchman Penitentiary is revealing. Oshinsky (1996: 168–177) contributes a later Southern picture to supplement Martineau's view of a Northern penitentiary. He stresses that "from Emancipation to the swiftly imposed Black Codes and burgeoning jails, and then to convict leasing and labor, Parchman's reinvention of the old plantation system followed decades of forced black labor" (146). As in the North, fewer women were sent to the state penitentiary—"at no time between 1870 and 1970 did females comprise more than 5 percent of the state prison population." More critically, while the women's "numbers were low, their color never changed . . . [typically being] young, poor and black, [and] convicted of a violent offense" (169). Echoing Beaumont, a white Delta resident asserted that "Negro women exhibit a ferocity as bloody and as savage as that exhibited by the men" (169). Oshinsky provides this brief description of women's lives at Parchman:

> The women were separated from the men's quarters by acres of cotton fields and a high barbed-wire fence. Yet sex and rape were all too common in a camp surrounded by male sergeants and guarded by male trusties. . . . The women slept in a large dormitory, much like the men. They canned vegetables, ran the prison laundry, and worked dawn-to-dusk shifts in a sweat-filled sewing room, making clothes, bedding, and mattresses for the entire farm. One of their songs went:
>
> You talking bout trouble
> You don't know what trouble means (repeat)
> What I call trouble
> Is a Singer Sewing Machine.
>
> When cotton had to be planted and picked, the women helped in the fields. They worked in long, tight formations, surrounded by dogs and trusty-shooters. (172–173)

Significantly, black women at Parchman continued to play out gendered roles within the penitentiary—those of slave women on the plantation. No symbolic belief in women's "separate sphere" extended to black women.

Where were the white women? Patriarchy was not dead. Oshinsky (1996: 174–175) quoted local newspapers: "It is a fortunate thing for Mississippi that white women seldom indulge in serious crime. Probably half the counties would be embarrassed if they had to confine a woman in their jails." White women could be protected, even in the case of homicide, by the "care" of either the judge or the governor. In clear cases of murder, juries might feel the necessity of conviction—reflecting Blackstone's belief that the "cover" of a husband would not extend to treason and murder. However, an interesting application of a form of *parens patriae,* the governor's power to pardon, could be used to protect white women from imprisonment. Oshinsky cites a case where the jury foreman reported: "We hated to send a woman to prison, but we had no choice. It was either death or life imprisonment." However, "after being bombarded with mercy requests," the governor issued a full pardon (Oshinsky, 1996: 176–177). Some white women did enter Parchman. Oshinsky describes the refusal of pardon to one white woman:

> "We consider her one of the most daring and cold-blooded Robbers and House-Burners, male or female, within the state," said one of the signers of a successful petition to deny her a pardon, "and we consider her very presence a menace to the safety of our property and probably our lives. We believe that fifteen years is a light sentence for her crime, and the Penitentiary is the safest place for her." (175)

Clearly, an "incorrigible" and "dangerous" woman, regardless of her race, belonged in maximum security.

A variation of this dynamic occurred in the territorial prisons of the Far West, where neither the numbers, resources, nor institutional structures were present to construct either the penitentiaries of the North or the South's reproduction of slave labor (Klungness, 1993; McGinn, 1993: 37, 67–68). That they anticipated the imprisonment and recognized the "equality" of women is revealed in the "Rules and Regulations for the Government and Discipline of the Arizona Territorial Prison." The rules stated: "So far as practicable the rules governing male convicts shall apply to females" (Klungness, 1993: 15). Klungness recounts that when the first woman, Lizzie Gallagher, arrived in 1879 to serve a fifteen-month sentence of hard labor on a manslaughter conviction, the staff were faced with a dilemma. The rules required that new prisoners be stripped and clothed in prison stripes, and that their hair be cut. Lizzie was pardoned forty-two days later. With deeply gendered assumptions regarding the appropriate treatment of women, the use of the pardon to "solve" the conflicted "equality before the law" continued in Arizona through the last years of the nineteenth century. However, Klungness notes:

> By 1908 juries no longer felt punishment in the prison was too cruel or inhumane for women of the Territory. There was also no clamor to pardon them because of the terrible conditions under which they were held. That the women were now separated from

the men and had a good exercise yard of their own may have been one reason they were now expected to serve out their sentences. Or, it may have been the Mexican and Negro prisoners who were currently arriving did not enjoy the same status as prisoners. (1993: 179–180)

The symbolic violence of both race and gender shaped the lives of the women who found themselves sentenced to the "maximum-security" prisons of the United States.

"Fallen Women": Dangerous and Dependent

Mary Belle Harris's defense of her Federal Industrial Institution for Women at Alderson as a "demonstration here which had set a standard for the country" can only be understood in the context of the complex and conflicted symbolic perceptions of women's "place" that grounded the movement for women's reformatories in the postbellum North. While there was a continuing affirmation of the patriarchal family, with the dependency of the white woman and her sexual "services" reserved for her husband, at the same time the ability to sell one's "services" in the market as a commodity was hailed as the mark of "freedom." The prostitute, forced by poverty or "wantonly selling her body" in the market, posed a symbolic threat not only to the structures of the family but to the belief that assumed the foundation of human relationships to be an equal and free contract.

A major depression in the 1870s brought the same fear of "idle and dangerous" unemployed from the South to the North. Stanley (1998: 128) argues that "the lessons of emancipation quickly traveled north . . . for like the former slave, the Yankee poor had neither masters nor property, and both subsisted by selling their labor or by depending on alms." As a consequence, "just as the ideal of free labor was transported south, so its coercive elements—articulated in rules governing freed people—were carried back north" (130). Northern laws made vagrancy a crime, punishable by arrest, imprisonment, and compulsory labor. The 1881 New York vagrancy law included as one of the definitions of a vagrant, "a common prostitute that has no lawful employment whereby to maintain herself," while an 1882 disorderly conduct law "allowed the police to arrest women who annoyed city residents by loitering or soliciting in a 'public thoroughfare'" (Alexander, 1995: 54). Stanley describes the conflicting perceptions of a "fallen woman." Is she a woman driven by need to "sell her body" and therefore in need of care and protection? Or is she a woman who "by prostituting her body" was an illegal dependent, "someone with nothing legitimate to sell in the labor market, someone no different from a beggar . . . an 'idle and wanton person'" (1998: 262)?

Reflecting these alternate views of women's "condition," the beginnings of the women's reformatories in the 1870s reflect a paradoxical combining of the "benign" dependency of the refuge for white "fallen women" in need of the care and protection by other white women, with the control, discipline, and hard labor of the penitentiary required for "dangerous" women. The reformatories can be viewed as reaffirming not only the value of the domestic sphere in creating a homelike environment where "fallen women" would learn the values of domesticity, but also, as formerly "idle and wanton" persons, the provision of hard work to enter the "legal" labor market. In later "industrial" reformatories like Alderson, women would be "prepared at their release for the basically female-dominated and lowly-paid occupations of domestic service, laundry, sewing and secretarial work—the domestic labor of the office" (Heffernan, 1994: 41).

Zebulon Brockway's significantly named "House of Shelter," considered the first women's reformatory in the United States, was opened in 1868 (Rafter, 1985: 24–28; on Brockway, see Pisciotta, 1994). The policies for the House of Shelter were influenced by Brockway's visit to Massachusetts's Lancaster School for Girls, where girls were placed in small "family" groups supervised by female officers who served as maternal role models. Brenzel (1983: 45) outlines the gendered assumptions that structured Lancaster:

> It was generally held that the doctrine of *parens patriae* legitimated the State's assumption of the role of responsible parent for these girls. The staff of the school would then serve *in loco parentis* to the girls during the pre- and postpubescent years. Also sentences would be indeterminate regardless of age or offense. . . . Since *parens patriae* was considered protection rather than punishment, such compulsion was regarded as not only the girls' legal due but as an act of love. . . . Sexual experience . . . was a cutoff point; violence was abhorred in boys; wantonness in girls.

The Michigan legislature enacted, "as an act of love," the first indeterminate sentencing law that allowed women convicted of prostitution to serve up to three years, under the assumption that "with retraining they might be reformed." Rafter notes that with the additional provision for parole under the supervision of the state, "this piece of legislation marked a turning point in American penal policies" (1985: 25). In the 1960s this special application of indeterminate sentencing to women was still being challenged in the courts (Muraskin, 1993: 214).

Following the House of Shelter, the first completely separate, independent, and female-run institution was opened in Indianapolis. Sexual scandals—"women may be forced to minister to the lusts of the officers, or if they refuse, to submit to the infliction of the lash until they do"—and the stated desire of the warden of the Indiana State Prison to get rid of the "expense and annoyance" of women, were founding factors. The first superintendent of the "Women's Prison and Reformatory" proudly stated that Indiana "has taken the advanced step of assigning to women the privilege of caring for, elevating and reforming her own sex" (Rafter, 1985: 30–31).

Domination and Struggle: Women's "Reformation"

Rafter's history of New York's Western House of Refuge at Albion (1983) explores the ways in which the state sought to control "wanton and idle women" asserting their sexual freedom. Josephine Shaw Lowell, who played a key role in the founding of all three of New York's women's reformatories, asserted: "One of the most important and most dangerous causes of the increase of crime, pauperism and insanity is the unrestrained liberty allowed to vagrant and degraded women" (Rafter, 1985: 44). The control of women's bodies could be maintained at three sites: their initial incarceration, their parole revocations if "they showed signs of relapsing into impropriety," and ultimately by their lifetime transfer to the Newark Custodial Asylum for Feebleminded Women (Rafter, 1983: 291). It should be noted that Harris's Alderson itself was not without alternate sites of control. Despite Harris's insistence that there was no need of a maximum-security institution for women, after an "attempted riot" in 1936 twenty-five women were transferred by Harris to the cellblocks of the Cincinnati Workhouse—described as "the women's equivalent of being sent to Alcatraz." Its threatened use at Alderson continued into the 1960s (Heffernan, 1994: 54).

As a model for Alderson's later "model" reformatory, Albion is considered by Rafter (1983: 288–290) "a major development" in prison history:

> With establishment of this reformatory, New York extended the power of state control over a population of young, working-class women guilty mainly of "offences" such as promiscuity, vagrancy and saloon-visiting. It created a new arm of the criminal justice system with authority to incarcerate such women for a period of years, during which the reformatory tried to retrain them to become chaste, proper and domestic. The Albion reformatory, like other women's prisons founded in the late nineteenth and early twentieth centuries, became a means of increasing and legitimating sexual and class inequality. And, like other institutions of its type, it was founded and operated entirely by women.

The reformatory setting reaffirmed a dependency, not on a spouse or a *baron,* but on "benevolent" women, who were in turn under the control of the state. At the same time, reflecting the ambiguities of women's "position," the women's reformatory movement was part of the larger feminist movement that challenged those assumptions. Harris's battles can be viewed in that light. Her efforts to modify the "loss of freedom" in prison with forms of self-government, her questioning whether the "domestic sphere" should be gendered, and her assertions of women's ability to be autonomous were perceived as threats.

Maternal Love and Immoral Relations

The development of self-contained "women's spheres" in turn raised an additional challenge to heterogendered assumptions—the fear of homosexuality. Freedman (1996a: xiii) explores the ways in which accusations of "immoral behavior" within the Massachusetts Reformatory for Women were used to discredit Superintendent Miriam Van Waters and members of the wider women's reform movement who sought to replace punishment and isolation with "maternal love" and supportive relationships between and among both women and staff. In their effort to "minimize same-sex relationships rather than punish them," they were vulnerable to the charge that the reformatories "were a dangerous source of lesbian relationships" (263).

Despite the accusation, however, the networks of support that sometimes arose among the women in the form of "families"—mothers, daughters, sisters, brothers, husbands, wives—actually tended to reproduce the "care, protection, service, subordination and dependence" of the patriarchal family (Heffernan, 1972: 87–106; Giallombardo, 1966: 158–188). One inmate, at a later time at Alderson, provided this description of the husband-wife roles: "The masculine partner dominated the relationship, demanding and getting service. Their clothes were washed and ironed for them, their room cleaned, presents made or bought, and commissary provided" (Flynn, 1963: 160, quoted in Heffernan, 1972: 94).

Owen (1998) found the continued presence of these women's networks of meaning and relationship in her contemporary study of the 4,000 women at Central California Women's Facility. Present also was the problematic belief among many of these poor and frequently abused women that "a man will arrive to provide the care and support promised by the myth of motherhood" (12). For Bourdieu (2001: 1–2), this exemplifies his belief that symbolic violence "is a gentle violence, imperceptible and invisible even to its victims, exerted for the most part through the purely symbolic channels of communication and cognition (more precisely mis-cognition), recognition, or even feeling." Ironically, these imprisoned women were not "a dangerous source of lesbian relationships" challenging heterogendered assumptions, but rather women who envisioned a future that embodied those assumptions.

Correctional Institutions: The "New Equality"

At the same time that Harris was defending Alderson as a "standard" for the country, by 1935 "the women's reformatory movement had drawn to a close" Rafter (1985: 182) concludes from her historical research. In the face of the economic pressures of the depression and the absence of a "national alarm" over prostitution, states that had maintained women in two facilities—penitentiaries and reformatories—brought them together. For example, in Wisconsin in 1933 the Women's Unit at the Waupun Penitentiary was closed. On the grounds of the Wisconsin Industrial Home for Women, a new building with locked cells was constructed as the Wisconsin State Prison for Women. In 1974 the facility's name was legislatively changed to the Taycheedah Correctional Institution.

While often renamed with gender-neutral language as "correctional institutions," administered by both men and women, the fusion of institutions that reflected historically alternate views on the position and treatment of women occurred within correctional systems designed by and for men. Their marginal presence reaffirmed the view that women were an "expense and annoyance." While no longer "the object of intense rehabilitative efforts by women outside the walls," as a heritage from their reformatory pasts, women still "continued to be treated as children" with programs that seldom prepared them for independence on their release, but instead "stressed personal grooming and domestic skills" (Rafter, 1985: 182–183).

Rafter (1985: 186–188) in the 1980s could envision a future of "more equitable treatment" in the presence of a series of lawsuits that challenged "differential treatment" and "discrimination" against women in both the state and federal correctional systems, but she could not envision the gendered consequences of "equal treatment"—being "treated like men"—twenty years later. While multiple factors have played a role in the dramatic increase in the number of imprisoned women, ironically the "equal treatment before the law," embodied in mandatory and "truth in sentencing" legislation as a vital part of masculine "wars" on crime and drugs, obscured the gendered reality of who went to prison under that sentencing. Women, and particularly minority women, rather than the symbolic "violent black man," have been disproportionately sentenced under the laws. Like their foremothers—*feme sole*—they are poor, black, and Hispanic rather than Irish, and single, with many "invisible" children and men in their lives. Bennett's dangerous "madams" and "molls" have diminished, but not his "confirmed drug users." Perhaps their threat, as was that of their "idle and wanton" predecessors, is their perceived "withdrawal of services" from both the family and the legal market.

In the Federal Bureau of Prisons, Bates and Bennett have won the battle, although their successor as head of the bureau, Kathleen M. Hawk-Sawyer, is a woman, reflecting the long struggle for "equal opportunity." As inmates, women also have the "equal opportunity" to serve their time in facilities "specialized" by security level. Harris's Alderson, tucked in the "hollows" of West Virginia, is a minimum-security camp. While Alderson retains its original open lawns and cottages, the new construction, required to respond to the growing numbers of women, duplicates a male facility in both size and design. A former superintendent, in whose honor the new building was named, remains aware of the irony reflecting on the struggles against the Bateses and Bennetts of her day to retain Harris's vision of Alderson.

Now, at Marianna, Florida, Bennett finally has his "maximum-security" facility for women. The controversial documentary *Through the Wire* asserts that Marianna, isolated from the centers of population, houses not only "violent" women but "political prisoners" whose protests against existing structures of economic, racial, and sexual power are perceived as "endangering" the foundations of the state (Heffernan, 1994: 72–73). They perhaps are indeed the dangerous women—"desperate and incorrigible"—that Bennett feared.

Gender: Dependency, Domination, and Liberation

Bates, Bennett, and Harris can be viewed as struggling consciously and unconsciously for symbolic dominance over "their" dangerous and dependent women. Their struggle, and the struggles of others involved in shaping the lives of incarcerated women, have been played out in the face of deeply held beliefs of gender and racial domination and a complex and conflicted criminal law:

- Women have been named and classified as "dangerous women" based on gendered crimes of sexuality and threats to structures of property, contract, and racial dominance, and legitimately treated as "slaves of the state."
- Based on historically embedded patriarchal structures of dominance and subordination, responsibility, service, and sexual control, the state has assumed also the responsibility of "caring for" and controlling "dependent" women within facilities that embody those assumptions.
- Within a deeply grounded male order, an assertion of "equality before the law" assumes that for women "equality" is to be "treated like a man," and gender-blind laws and facilities reflect that reality.

The voices of women and men have been raised before and since the founding of the Republic to question the gendered, class, and racial structures of domination that were embodied in the law. Mary Belle Harris and others in the women's movement viewed the presence of compassion, love, and support as the most powerful of relationships among both women and men, though articulated in the language of the "women's sphere." As Bourdieu (2001: 4) asserts, liberation of women from the symbolic violence that legitimates relations of domination—both within and beyond prison walls—can come only from a "cognitive revolution" and the

> formulation of strategies aimed at transforming the present state of the material and symbolic power relation between the sexes . . . in agencies such as the school or the state, sites where principles of domination are developed and imposed. . . . A vast field of action is opened up . . . to take a distinctive and decisive place within political struggles against *all* forms of domination.

4

Women's Stories of Survival and Resistance

Kathleen J. Ferraro and Angela M. Moe

The ways in which women are disciplined to conform to social norms are gendered in both process and content. In the contemporary United States, processes of surveillance and social control of women are most often diffuse and invisible, disembodied forces that exert their influence through psychic projections and introjections of ubiquitous "enforcers." There are also active, embodied forces of social control, such as restrictive abortion laws, domestic battering, and sexual assault, which circumscribe women's choices (Deveaux, 1996). Adopting some of the theoretical insights of Foucault (1978), feminist scholars have articulated the ways in which women's incorporation of gender norms into their subjective sense of self, their identity, creates an ironic relationship between control and resistance (Diamond and Quinby, 1988; Fraser, 1989; Sawicki, 1996). Although many aspects of conventional femininity and heteronormativity are repressive, they simultaneously establish sources of resistance and power. For example, the patriarchally defined institution of motherhood imposes self-sacrifice and enormous social and financial burdens, yet also provides women a source of power, love, and dignity (Ferraro and Moe, 2003). These resources can then be called upon to support resistance to injustice and violations of women's self-determination. Thus, although gender norms have developed historically to benefit heterosexual men, with race and class stratifications of privilege, the subjective experience of femininity includes aspects of both oppression and liberation.

Feminist explorations of the control of women have emphasized the technologies of control located in socialization, discourse, and visual and textual media much more than the explicit force of state authority. In criminology, studies of "correctional" practices have almost always focused exclusively on men, since women compose such a small fraction of the "correctional" population (Davis, 1998). However, in the 1980s, the dramatic increase in the incarceration of women, which continued throughout the 1990s, catalyzed renewed attention to women, crime, and the apparatus of formal, embodied state control (Chesney-Lind, 1997; Kline, 1993). Studies of women's experiences with crime and incarceration through their own narratives (Arnold, 1990; Gilfus, 1992; Richie, 1996), and through program evaluations and analyses (Koons, Burrow, and Morash, 1997; Kruttschnitt, Gartner, and Miller, 2000), have begun to document the unique and complex relationships of gender, race, and class to carceral punishment. More recently, scholars have considered how incarcerated women negotiate gendered processes of social control in ways that both reinforce and challenge conventional femininity (Bosworth, 1999b; Ross, 1998). To date, most of the attention on incarcerated women has focused on the prison as the more long-term, totalizing institution. Jails are a more neglected location of the social control of women despite the fact that more women pass through these facilities than through prisons annually. Moreover, women may spend years in jail, awaiting sentencing or through repetitive incarcerations. Since jails are intended to provide short-term intervention, punishment for misdemeanants, and holding cells for felonious offenders, they neither develop serious programs nor receive the external scrutiny that sometimes exists for prisons (Pollock-Byrne, 2002; Koons, Burrow, and Morash, 1997).

Our purpose is to contribute to the literature on women's carceral experiences through an examination of narratives provided by jailed women during in-depth, topical life-history interviews at a detention facility. We begin by examining the women's descriptions of surveillance within the detention facility and the ways in which their privacy and autonomy are violated through various degradation ceremonies. We follow this with a discussion of the many concerns women raise with regard to the available programming and conditions in jail. We then discuss the limitations of the grievance process within the institution as a primary example of "stunted resistances." This is followed by an examination of the various aspects of jail culture that women employ as avenues for resisting and surviving the carceral experience.

Methods

Our interviews were conducted with the goal of obtaining information about women's experiences with violence. We relied on an open-ended interview schedule developed to explore the interconnections between neighborhood, family, and relationships in women's encounters with physical violence as offenders and victims. While we did not ask explicit questions on the conditions of the jail, women frequently spoke of the jail, staff, and other residents, as well as their coping mechanisms for surviving incarceration. Their numerous accounts of the carceral experience formed the basis of this analysis.

We conducted thirty interviews with women incarcerated in three custody levels within two facilities at the Pima County Adult Detention Center in Tucson, Arizona, during the spring of 2000. Jail administrators who explained the research to the women and developed a list of volunteers prior to our arrival recruited participants. The women were not screened by us or, to our knowledge, by correctional staff, prior to their participation. Our goal was to interview as many women as we could within budgetary restrictions.

The women ranged in age from twenty-one to fifty years, with an average of thirty-four years. Fifteen women (50 percent) were white, seven (23 percent) were black, three (10 percent) were Latina, two (7 percent) were American Indian, and three (10 percent) were identified as biracial. Almost all of the women had low or no incomes prior to their incarceration. Both sentenced and nonsentenced women participated. With each woman's permission, we audiotaped the interviews and later transcribed them. The interviews lasted between thirty minutes and four hours. Each woman was given an opportunity to choose her own pseudonym for purposes of confidentiality. Participants received stipends for their participation, which we put on their books in the form of money orders.

The Culture of Confinement

Several features of the carceral experience influenced the ways in which women coped with their incarceration. These included surveillance and privacy infringement, health care, counseling, education, work, and violence.

Surveillance, Privacy Infringement, and Degradation Ceremonies

Surveillance and lack of privacy are definitive of the carceral experience. Strict regimentation of activities, movement, diet, and interaction was one of the most problematic aspects of the jail experience for women. There were three security levels in the detention facility: (1) an admissions area, known as "H Pod"; (2) a highly controlled, thirty-day facility, known as "J Pod"; and (3) a longer-term, lower-security facility, known as "The Mission," where sentenced women were held and often obtained work furloughs. The levels progressed in safety, respect, and freedom, with the admissions area being the most degrading and The Mission described as "pretty good." Within the admissions area, guards were not only rigid, but also arbitrary and abusive. Lonna described the levels and emphasized that women were controlled by threats of being "sent down" to a higher security level. She also expressed the initial shock and confusion a number of the women described upon entering the facility:

> You have to spend 30 days over there [J Pod] and then you get to come over here [The Mission]. But where it's really bad is where you're at before this, at the main jail [H Pod]. They just talk to you like you're nothing. You spend 24 to 72 hours there I think. You can't even look at a guard, they lock you down. I went in there and she's like, "Don't you shake your head at me." She goes, "That's it. You're not coming out." It means that you're locked down for 23 hours out of 24 and they give you an hour to come out and play ball or eat or whatever. I didn't know that's what that meant.

Lonna clearly distinguishes between the security levels and their associated privileges, as well as the swiftness with which newly arrived inmates are made to feel like "nothing" while learning the interactional rules of the staff. Anne also expressed feelings of degradation as she described a typical day in J Pod:

> You're a caged animal. You're locked down until they tell you you can get out of your room. It's kind of degrading. They wake you up, make you clean, sweep and mop, tables, floors, walls, windows, showers, sinks, your room, whatever there is to clean. From like 9:00 until 10:00 you're allowed to come out of your room to make

phone calls, get a book, or whatever. After that you're in your room. You eat lunch in your room, on your bed. There is only one person allowed in the bathroom at a time. You're not allowed to step one foot out into the hallway or you get written up. You're confined in a little area about this big [motioning to the interview room, approximately six feet long and six feet wide] with two beds in it. There's no room to do anything. From like 12:00 to 2:00, you're allowed to come out of your room again to make phone calls and if you have money on your books, you're allowed to order coffee or whatever. You can't share with anybody. You can talk, but you have to be really quiet.

Not only did women struggle to understand the process of learning formal rules and procedures in the facility, they also struggled to understand and obey the quirks of particular correctional officers. Some officers seemed to opt for a rigid schedule, devoid of attention to individual needs, as a way of monitoring inmates. Such regimentation was perceived as degrading and unhealthy. In the following excerpt, Lonna articulated an appreciation of the need for rules and acknowledged correctional officers who followed procedures in a respectful manner. However, officers that exceeded necessary levels of control were perceived as deliberately cruel:

Those in here [The Mission] are really pretty cool. In "J" I don't understand. There's no reason to be that way. A couple of them are really nice. That just goes to prove that you don't have to be that way. [Q: So how do inmates handle it? Just learn to read the guards real quickly and figure out what their moods are?] Definitely. You know how there's these stairs? I was in this dorm up here—D dorm. Some guards will tell you to come down your own stairwell. Other guards will tell you to come down this stairwell and up this stairwell, or however. If you go down the wrong stairwell or up the wrong stairwell, you're in trouble. You get written up. I didn't talk to anybody because I didn't know anybody in here so I didn't know which way I was supposed to go. I never got written up but the guard would tell me, "Now I'm here." [Q: You mean for when the rules change?] Mmm-hmm. You don't know. You could ask but then they'd say, "What are you, stupid?"

In order to avoid increased regimentation and additional lock-downs, Orca explained the way in which some of the women monitored each other's activities:

> Got real hairy a couple nights ago up at the D-end dorm. Two girls were at it and they were yelling back and forth. It was like, "You shut the fuck up or the whole pod will be on lock-down for like two days." D-dorm is the quietest dorm. They are seldom hollered at. A, B, C, and the multipurpose room are constantly being yelled at. We're the quietest dorm. Everybody will start yelling and we'll go, "Shhh, we don't want to get yelled at."

Orca's description of the silencing of women mirrored the preincarceration experiences of women who had repressed their own voices in attempts to avoid verbal or physical assaults by parents, teachers, husbands, and boyfriends. Most of the women had indeed been sexually and physically abused prior to entering jail, and thus recognized the potential benefits of self-regulation in avoiding assault (Harlow, 1999; Rice, Smith, and Janzen, 1999). Certainly in jail, the less said, the better.

The stress of coping with strict regimentation was compounded by the constant surveillance, scrutiny, and lack of privacy the inmates endured, as Orca described:

> I have no privacy. I can't even take a shit in privacy. There's three showers and I had to take one today because I didn't expect to be starting my thing [menstruation] here and I did and it was torture. It made a mess and I had to ask for clean clothes. We're not allowed to wash these [uniforms] in the sinks. We can wash our underwear and our T-shirts and our sweatshirts in the sinks, but we can't wash these.

Orca went on to describe the fluorescent orange jumpsuit-uniforms the inmates were required to wear. She and others thought the uniforms were a dehumanizing expression of the state's ownership of their bodies. However, Orca also acknowledged the flexibility jail administrators have allowed the inmates in wearing their own clothing at certain times:

> I've got a white T-shirt and when I wear it I feel kinda' normal. They let me keep my bras. They let me keep my own underwear too. I got sweatshirts too so in some ways I can feel kinda' normal. We always have to have these on [orange pants], 24 hours a day,

7 days a week. We have to put these on [orange shirts] over our T-shirts if we're coming for a visit or something. We have to announce to God and everybody that we are prisoners of Pima County Jail. I am Pima County Jail property.

While wearing their own undergarments and shirts was a way in which women could feel a little less objectified, required jail clothing, stamped with the words "Pima County Jail," a constant reminder of their subjugated status, marked their physical bodies, which most immediately represented their personhood. In combination with rigid yet arbitrarily enforced rules and schedules, constant surveillance, and lack of privacy, the women struggled to maintain a sense of dignity and individuality. In this context, lack of attention to their physical health was particularly distressing.

Health Care

Health care for women has been consistently lacking in U.S. jails and prisons (ACA, 1990; Belknap, 1996; Ross, 1998; Shaw, Browne, and Meyer, 1981). While most jails and prisons provide basic health care services such as intake screenings and mental health appraisals, gynecological care, as well as prenatal, obstetric, and postpartum care, is frequently unavailable or inadequate (ACA, 1990; Ross, 1998). Only 53 percent of jails provide gynecological and obstetrical services, while 59 percent provide prenatal and postpartum services. In addition, prisons and jails do a very poor job of providing care for inmates in medical emergencies. Just over half have medical staff on site twenty-four hours a day. In emergencies, less than 20 percent of jails routinely call paramedics, and only 32 percent will provide transportation to hospitals (ACA, 1990).

The lack of adequate health care was a major concern for the women in our study (Ferraro and Moe, 2003). Even serious injuries received little attention. As Brina stated, "I fell and twisted my ankle. It was black and blue and swollen. It took three and a half days to get me emergency x-rays. That's how the system works here." Anne elaborated on the difficulty of obtaining care and the dismissive attitude of some correctional officers:

My bunkie, before she got in here she'd gotten into a fight with somebody and kicked a glass door. She has this big cut on the bot-

tom of her foot that still has glass in it. You can literally see it. So
she went and saw medical. Medical didn't give her Neosporin. They
didn't give her peroxide or alcohol or anything to put on this cut.
She's gone as far as to tell the surgeon that her foot is infected and
she needs to see somebody. She jumped off her bed, and her foot
like bursts open and all this puss and blood just splatter everywhere.
You would think that they would call medical immediately because
she's bleeding. "No, just wait until the nurse comes tonight at 7:00."
There's a lady next to me who has hepatitis C from doing so many
drugs. Her liver is all messed up. You can tell just by the color of
her. She's like yellow and green. She keeps telling them, she's put in
like seven medical slips, she's put in grievances, she's talked with
the sergeant. You know, "I need to go somewhere." She can't pee.
She hasn't peed in two weeks. They're not doing anything.

Requests for medicine were also frequently ignored, as Tamara described:

This is not the place to be if you're sick. The doctor hasn't paid
attention to any of my requests. They're not going to do anything. I
put in a request every so often. I give up. I don't want to see a doctor here no more. I'm supposed to be taking pain-killers anyway for
a surgery I just had and they don't care. [Q: What is the procedure
if you need something?] You have to fill out a medical slip and you
give it to them [correctional officers]. Usually by the time you're
feeling better, they'll try to give you something for it. I got a cold
and it took I think four days to get something to clear my nose up.

Kathy was a licensed nurse practitioner prior to incarceration, and she vowed to become an advocate for prisoner health care when and if she is released:

If I, by a miracle, win my case and get an acquittal and go before
the State Board of Nursing and get my nursing license straightened
out, I'm going to advocate for medical care for all prisoners and
people held in county jails and try to put a group of nurses together
with either a hotline or somewhere where you can write to get help
on the outside, because I've seen, in this jail, outlandish, horrible
situations right down to and including people dying in here without cause.

Clearly as a strategy of resistance, Kathy employed her professional knowledge to plan for positive social action in the future, as well as to assist women during her incarceration. Employing skills she used on the outside not only helped other women, but also helped Kathy to maintain a sense of dignity and purpose while in jail:

> They come in with bugs [lice]. What I've been doing for nine months is catching bugs on people's heads 'cause you have to actually catch the bug and put it on tape or they won't quell them. I've been doing it for everybody for nine months . . . and I help people fill out their medical slips. A lot of these people come in here and they don't know how to read or write and they can't really put it together and say what it is they want to say. . . . People in here need an advocate.

Pregnancy and aftercare posed significant concerns. As Kathy reported: "This girl went into labor and she was so scared and she screamed and cried and nobody came. Finally several of us started screaming and screaming and screaming until somebody responded because she was getting ready to deliver her babies, her twins, all alone."

Lisa was incarcerated the day after she gave birth by Cesarean section to her daughter. Although her doctor provided written orders that she not work, she was required to perform hard physical labor:

> My doctor told me six weeks not to work, and I been bleedin' like a lot 'cause I had my baby and I been getting real bad headaches, like spinnin', and they got us workin' downtown, moppin' parking lots. We were there four and a half hours today, moppin'. My back was hurtin'. I'm like, "If something happens, it's your fault." I told 'em, "By law you're not supposed to, if you have a doctor's excuse." They're like, "If you don't like it here, we'll throw you in H." I'm like, "No, that's okay." I wanna be able to see my kids, so I gotta do what I gotta do. Today I had tissue comin' out, it was weird, big chunks, and I'm like, "That's not right." I only get headaches when I work.

For Lisa, resistance was combined with compliance, as she acquiesced to the unreasonable demands to work in order to avoid being sent to a higher security level. Appeals to the authority of her doctor and the law were ineffective in the jail, since the staff knew she had no resources to effectively insist on her legal rights. In this fashion, women's marginality outside of jail was reflected inside the jail as they lacked the power to demand basic health care. While resistance was present, the possibilities for controlling their own bodies were limited.

On the other hand, some women expressed gratitude for the medical services they received, as they could not receive such care on the outside. Boo had been incarcerated on many occasions and was five months into her pregnancy at the time of her interview. She felt that her incarceration was a way to keep away from drugs and receive medical care during her pregnancy:

> I'm pregnant so this is my chance to get off of drugs. I'm kind of thankful for it, but then again, you know, who wants to get locked away? But it's nice, though. I mean, to me this is my home away from home, 'cause I don't have nobody on the outside. So, it's kind of hard for me, but then at the same time, I like it in here 'cause I get that special attention that I crave. They give us three pregnancy bags a day, which contain two cartons of milk, two orange juices, and two fruits and you get three pills three times a day during breakfast, lunch, and dinner. If I get a little thirsty in between our lock-downs, they let me get up and go get a juice, or eat one of my apples real quick. They're real considerate about things like that.

Boo's appreciation for the health care she received in jail reflects the abysmal state of health care for indigent women in Arizona. The Arizona Health Care Cost Containment System (AHCCCS) is Arizona's approach to health care for low-income people, but it is extremely difficult to qualify for benefits. Those who are able to enroll in the system receive only $1,670 per year in care services, compared to the national average of $1,874 (Caiazza, 2000). However, at least outside of jail women can wait in emergency rooms to be seen, while in jail they are at the mercy of staff to determine when and if they will receive care. A similar situation exists with regard to mental health services.

Counseling

The need for proper programming to address women's psychological needs is great, as about 16 percent of adult female jail inmates are categorized as emotionally disturbed (ACA, 1990). Approximately 10 percent report a current mental or emotional condition (Harlow, 1998) and

17 percent report having received medication for an emotional disorder (Greenfeld and Snell, 1999b). Specifically with regard to jail inmates, between 70 and 80 percent of female inmates suffer from at least one lifetime psychiatric disorder (Teplin, Abram, and McClelland, 1996; Koons, Burrow, and Morash, 1997).

Mental illness is not the only reason jailed women could benefit from counseling, as at least half of all female jail inmates have suffered physical or sexual abuse prior to incarceration (Harlow, 1998, 1999; Morash, Bynam, and Koons, 1998). Drug and alcohol addictions also affect a majority of incarcerated women (Belknap, 1996; Leonard, 2001). At the very least, most suffer from low self-esteem and depression, and some resort to self-mutilation or suicide as a response to untreated problems (Browne, Miller, and Maguin, 1999; Haywood et al., 2000; Pollock-Byrne, 2002).

Unfortunately, approximately 30 percent of women's jails do not provide any type of psychiatric care (ACA, 1990). A study of 1,272 jailed women found that only 24 percent of inmates received the mental health services they needed while incarcerated (Teplin, Abram, and McClelland, 1997). This is consistent with the most recent survey data from the National Institute of Justice, which indicates that only about 20 percent of female jail inmates receive mental health services after admission to jail (Harlow, 1998). Too often, facilities that do provide psychiatric care limit treatment to the use of psychotropic drugs (Ross, 1998). This is unfortunate given that women report psychological counseling as being the most important service they need upon being incarcerated (ACA, 1990). Given the vast amount of abuse many incarcerated women have suffered throughout their lives, provisions for counseling would be a resource for empowerment, and possibly a deterrence from crime. The need for such services was clearly indicated by the women we interviewed, such as Angel:

> I see so many girls in here that don't need to be in prison. They need to be intensively in some sort of therapy. They've been so severely abused that their personality is just splintered, they don't even know who they are. They're not in touch with who they are. They're just shells of people. They need to be put back together before they can begin to be expected to understand any kind of responsibility or consequences.

Fortunately, counseling services seemed to be fairly good in the

Pima County Adult Detention Center. Many women remarked that they had met with very understanding counselors and that efforts were made to address their common concerns, including violence in their homes and separation from their children. Perhaps the most prominent counseling service available was a program called PEP, which offered a range of supportive and self-awareness services, including domestic violence counseling, anger management, drug and alcohol counseling, and support groups. The women reported watching videos during PEP that helped them to think through their own lives and circumstances within a supportive environment. As Brina explained:

> It's anger management. It's counseling, group counseling. They show you videos. They showed that movie about Tina Turner's life and the violence, "What's Love Got to Do With It?" Tomorrow, we're going to watch the second half of the movie "Isaiah," which hits home for me because of losing my baby. I didn't necessarily put her in a trashcan but the consequences are still the same. I think it is a good movie to show. It brings hope to the women in here who have maybe not put their children in a garbage can but have lost them to circumstances. It gives you hope that you can straighten yourself out. You can get everything rearranged and on the right track.

Women also commented on the helpfulness of AA (Alcoholics Anonymous), NA (Narcotics Anonymous), and CA (Cocaine Anonymous), which were all readily available programs. In fact, as Marie stated, the effectiveness of these services was enhanced because they took place inside the jail:

> I'm taking advantage of the programs in here. I go to AA and NA. I like the AA meetings because they helped me when I got off drugs the first time. But in here, it's a lot different. The people in the circle are here. It's better. There are some hard-core addicts in here. They have hit rock bottom and they've hit rock bottom bein' here. So it's a lot more intense from the start.

Incarcerated women rate drug treatment among the top three types of services to which they desire access (ACA, 1990). However, some of the women in our study expressed concern that because of a lack in the variety of counseling services available, all inmates were expected to attend and benefit from PEP and the substance abuse programs, even if those services did not fit their individual circumstances. Lonna reported on this "one size fits all" approach:

> Mostly everybody is in here because of drugs. I experimented in high school and stuff like that, but it's not an issue for me. I don't do drugs anymore. I hate to sit here and say "I don't do drugs" because everybody looks at you like, "Yeah, right. Everybody does them." I have just totally different problems.

In addition, women awaiting sentencing for more serious crimes were held in maximum-security cells and excluded from participation in groups with the general population. They spent more time in jail than misdemeanor offenders, but received fewer interventions. Moreover, services for more severe mental problems that required extensive treatment and/or psychotropic drugs seemed to be lacking, similar to the way in which treatment for physical ailments was insufficient. Orca described a severe mental disorder that had gone untreated:

> I'm manic-depressive. I need to be on meds. I've been in denial of that. Maybe I've been self-medicating with cocaine because it made me feel good. I was like, "I have energy. I can clean. I'm not depressed. I don't sleep all day."

It appeared as if the only time inmates were successful at receiving attention for more serious mental problems was in response to suicide threats. The institution's response to a suicide threat involved putting an inmate on "suicide watch," which was not helpful and appeared to be abusive, as Orca described:

> They take you and put you in a holding cell that's smaller than this. There's a bunk in there and they chain you to it. They take away your clothes and your blanket, everything. You have nothing. You can't even get over to the toilet. If you have to go to the bathroom, you do it right there. I was on suicide watch for 48 hours. If I wasn't suicidal, that'll drive you to it.

In response to being placed on suicide watch, Orca deliberately chose not to express sadness or negative emotions. Her attempts to avoid being placed on suicide watch are another example of how the women resisted jail authorities through acquiescing to threats and employing strategies of self-monitoring developed through years of abuse. As many of the women learned prior to their incarceration, speaking out about their maltreatment only brought further punishments to *them,* not to their abusers. Likewise, discussing depression and suicide only resulted in worse treatment in the jail.

As is the case with physical health care, mental health care is almost nonexistent for indigent women in Arizona. The state has been under federal court order since 1972 to provide adequate mental health services, but the state has failed to provide the necessary funding. The suicide rate in the general female population in Arizona is 5.9 per 100,000, compared to 3.9 nationally, and for low-income women of color, it is even higher (Caiazza, 2000). Under these conditions, local jails have by default become mental health facilities for the poor and homeless. Clearly, the pressure and degradation of the jail experience are not therapeutic for women suffering from mental health problems. Even for those without such problems, however, the availability of programs that could assist women in leading crime-free lives is minimal.

Education and Vocational Training

Educational programming and vocational training can be very useful in helping women live productive lives upon release, but funding for it has suffered as a result of the trend toward prison and jail construction and heightened security (ACA, 1990; Davis, 1998). Arizona state law requires that inmates obtain an eighth-grade reading level; thus basic education and literacy services are provided to women in prison. However, due to federal legislation, public funds cannot be employed to support higher education. Hence the college classes that were once available are now only accessible to women with funds to pay tuition or through support from private foundations. Educational programming in jails is often limited to assistance with general equivalency diploma (GED) preparation. This is unfortunate, as the need for education is great. Only 55 percent of women in jails have a high school education; 12 percent have completed eighth grade or less (Greenfeld and Snell, 1999b). Given these figures, it is not surprising that educational programming was ranked by the American Correctional Association (ACA, 1990) as the most beneficial service to adult female inmates.

Few jails (approximately 27 percent) have vocational training available for female inmates. While this may be because of the high inmate turnover in such facilities, vocational programming is greatly desired among jailed women (ACA, 1990). Unfortunately, much of the career development training available to incarcerated women may not help them develop skills for gainful and sustainable employment upon release. Many such programs are gendered, offering training in female-dominated occupations such as cosmetology, secretarial skills, sewing, and homemaking, not unlike the past when incarceration was seen as a means of resocializing women into gender-appropriate roles (Belknap, 1996; Davis, 1998; Rafter, 1990; Ross, 1998).

The women in our study had little desire for such gendered vocational training. In fact, a good number of them had job experiences in nontraditional fields or aspired to such. As India commented:

> I've been workin' for two years in construction and landscaping. I've been doin' good, my boss likes the way I work. He tells me, "You know, you're pretty strong for being a girl." I mean who can take the center block off of a two-ton truck in a matter of minutes without even being fazed? I don't even need anybody to help me. Shit, I put a lot of work on myself but I learned how to do a lot of things too. I'm proud of myself for coming this far.

The most basic forms of educational programming were available to the women we interviewed. Many reported earning their GEDs after taking the preparatory classes in jail. However, any further education was unavailable and many expressed a concern about their lack of vocational training and work experience.

Work Experiences

Aside from educational and vocational training programs, many incarcerated women could benefit from work experiences that provide them with marketable skills, as most are poor and have dependent children for whom to care upon their release (ACA, 1990; Belknap, 1996). Approximately 60 percent of incarcerated women have received welfare assistance in the past and while many are unemployed at the time of their arrest, those who are working are predominantly employed intermittently or temporarily in the service industry (ACA, 1990; Chesney-Lind and Rodriguez, 1983; Haywood et al., 2000). Poor work records and minimal skills, combined with a criminal record, make the future earning potential for released inmates very bleak. While work furlough and work release programs can be very helpful in assisting inmates in finding work despite their records, women have historically been excluded from such programs (Janusz, 1991).

Unfortunately, there are few work programs available for female jail and prison inmates. Less than 50 percent of jails require inmates to perform institutional work assignments. The work assignments that are available, which include groundskeeping, janitorial services, food service, clerical or administrative tasks, and laundry services, rarely translate into marketable job skills that will garner sustainable income upon release (ACA, 1990). Despite such problems, job assignments are highly sought after. According to Ross (1998), however, the best jobs, usually those paying over two dollars a day, are offered to minimum-risk inmates and white inmates first.

Job skills and experience seemed to be a concern for the women we interviewed. Fortunately, work assignments were readily available in the least restrictive area of the facility, The Mission. Tamara described some of the work opportunities:

> There's four different crews you can work on. One is the commissary. That's the good one. Then there's a night crew that goes at like 10:00 at night and they come back at about 4:00 in the morning. They go to the main building over there. They scrub lots of bathrooms in the jail. That's a nasty job. I used to be on this crew. You have to do the "bookies," where they first bring the people that are booked. All the cells over there, you wipe them down. It's just nasty. It's terrible.

While some work assignments were more desirable than others, most of the women we spoke with appreciated the opportunity to work. As Gillian commented, "I'd rather be over here working. I don't mind it. I'll beg to go out on the front fence work crew. To me it's not punishment. It gives me something to do."

In addition, a work furlough program was available as one of the privileges awarded to women in The Mission who successfully completed thirty days in the facility. It allowed women to leave the detention center to look for jobs and work for their own wages. The women looked forward to furlough and were immensely proud of themselves for receiving it. Tamara explained:

The far side [of the unit] is where we stay, those who work here for the jail. This dorm on this side, that's work furlough. That's for the people that get to go out to their own jobs. [Q: So you're literally just pointing to the next door down as where you want to be next?] Yeah, because then I can go out. This is much better.

The possibility of receiving more privileges was a strong incentive to refrain from rule infractions, particularly violence. However, the potential for violence, from both staff and other residents, was still a major concern for the women.

Violence

Prior research has found that, relative to incarcerated males, female inmates are much less violent toward each other. The most recent jail survey indicated that 57 percent of inmates said that jail was safer than or as safe as their outside residences, and only 10.5 percent of women reported being involved in a fight, or being hit or punched after admission (Harlow, 1998). Alternatively, correctional institutions pose a threat of violence in a confined situation where staff have the potential for abusing authority. The constant surveillance and lack of privacy described earlier facilitate a context in which women are vulnerable to sexual harassment and intimidation by staff, nearly 35 percent of whom are male (ACA, 1990; Chesney-Lind and Rodriguez, 1983; Ross, 1998; Human Rights Watch, 1996; U.S. General Accounting Office, 1999).

The totalizing character of jails results in the normalization of scrutiny by staff, who can observe everything women do, including showering, changing clothes, and using the toilet. This situation places women at great risk of assault by male guards. Rapes, unwanted sexual fondling, and sexual harassment are common, although few inmates report such incidents (Chesney-Lind and Rodriguez, 1983; Owen, 1998; Ross, 1998). Such abuse by staff is devastating for female prisoners, many of whom have been abused in various ways throughout their lives (ACA, 1990; Chesney-Lind and Rodriguez, 1983; Sargent, Marcus-Mendoza, and Yu, 1993; Ross, 1998).

Fortunately, we heard of few instances of physical or sexual abuse by correctional officers toward inmates. However, the violence inflicted by staff, as well as violence between inmates, seemed to be associated with the level of security in the various housing units. As Lonna described, violence overall was less prevalent at The Mission, where inmates were allowed much more autonomy as compared to J and H Pods, where inmates were more highly monitored: "A lot of verbal but no fight fights. There's too much to lose here [in The Mission]. In J nobody cares. In H there's nothing to lose. I'm talking physical things. I've seen them [correctional officers] throw people against walls for no reason at all." In the higher-security units, we primarily heard stories of violence arising from the carceral atmosphere. As Orca described: "This place can actually make one violent. It's almost like a territorial thing. Somebody stole somebody's underwear and I said, 'I catch any bitch with anything that belongs to me in their cubicle, fuck the COs 'cause they don't do anything about it. I'll break your fuckin' fingers.'"

For women whose experiences outside of jail consisted of routine violence, the use of defensive and reactive tactics was a pattern that was difficult to control, given the close quarters and lack of privacy. The environment actually seemed to facilitate the view that violence was a necessary survival strategy (Dobash, Dobash, and Gutteridge, 1986). As Boo explained:

> To this day, I have those habits and ways. I'm a fighter. I don't like to, but I will defend myself, and I don't know how to take no bullshit from nobody. Even pregnant, I almost got in a fight the other day 'cuz this girl got in my face and I told her, "Don't do that. Back up, please back up." I'm the type of person that don't even speak. I'll give you the opportunity to leave me alone and I'll tell you nicely to get away. If you make me stand up, I will hit you. I don't know, I've always been like that.

Boo went on to explain that she resisted the temptation to hit another woman because she wanted to preserve her chances of moving to The Mission. Women have control over their initiation of violence, and as mentioned earlier, usually assert control over each other to prevent group punishments. However, the formal grievance process was the only means with which the women could protect themselves from staff abuse.

The Grievance Process—Stunted Resistance

Grievance procedures have been criticized for serving administrative and bureaucratic interests rather than inmate interests (Bordt and Musheno, 1988). This appeared to be the case at the Pima County Adult Detention Center, as none of the women reported filing a grievance. In fact, most discouraged it, believing such action would only make things worse. As Orca stated, "If you grieve something, the COs make it hard on you. If you say something about COs and it gets back to them, oh God help you." As a result, some women have developed innovative ways for addressing their concerns, like Lonna:

> I saw so many things, I borrowed a pencil and I started writing down dates, times, incidents, and who was involved in the incidents. I've got this long list. I'm not going to let this go when I get out of here. I've seen some pretty abusive things, mostly from the guards toward the inmates. I will not fill out a grievance because if you fill out a grievance, forget it. They even tell you, "That's a nongrievable issue." So I've got my list. I figure when I get out I'll go to some congressmen, legislators, whoever I can think to contact. I'm going to make flyers with addresses and stand right outside that gate and hand them out so everybody else can write too. That's the only way that things are going to change. Things like that do not need to happen.

Lonna expressed the common perception that nothing could be done from the inside without generating retributive actions. While her plan to make flyers was never implemented, it allowed her to maintain some sense of agency and hope that "things are going to change." Women's plans for specific, political actions, however, were less common than women's reliance on other forms of survival and resistance.

Survival and Resistance

The women utilized a variety of measures as a way of surviving incarceration and resisting its effects, including religion, motherhood, relationships, and management of perceptions regarding incarceration. Their strategies reflected gendered experiences prior to incarceration, as well as their invocation of and resistance to gendered oppression within the institution.

Religion

As Ross (1998) asserts, religion may be both another mechanism of control and a vehicle of strength and cultural pride for women prisoners. There is, perhaps, no other aspect of the carceral experience that is so paradoxical in terms of perpetuating women's subordinate status while simultaneously providing a resource for resistance. The role of religion in jail culture is determined by the kinds of services and individuals permitted into the facilities. In contrast to the paucity of health, counseling, and job training programs, Christian services were widely available and accessible to inmates. As Buckwheat noted, prayer groups and formal religious services occurred routinely: "All of us pray here. All of us, every night. On Sundays we go to the yard and get a little prayer circle together."

While Christian-based ceremonies were readily accessible, there did not appear to be similar accessibility for non-Christian inmates. As Angel, a Muslim, reported:

> You find more men in institutions that become Muslims. My son converted to Islam when he got to prison, and they seem to be very well organized. Of course I guess when I get to prison, I'd find other women that are Muslims, but not in the county jail. They provide you with a Koran here and there is a chapel, but there is nobody to run the Islamic service.

Ross (1998) documented the difficulty American Indian women have encountered in trying to practice indigenous spirituality within prisons. Fortunately, the Pima County Adult Detention Center did offer weekly sweat lodge ceremonies for women incarcerated there, and these ceremonies provided an important source of strength. However, not all Southwest nations involve women in sweat ceremonies, and other forms of American Indian spirituality were not accommodated within the jail.

The majority of women, including African Americans and Latinas, utilized Christianity as a means of coping with their circumstances. A common theme throughout our interviews involved women rationalizing, or attempting to rationalize, their experiences through references to God. For example, some reasoned that arrest and incarceration were messages from God that they were not following the right path in life. Their spirituality and faith helped them endure incarceration and hold on to the belief that their futures would be better. A number of women commented that they had "turned their lives over to God" and that they had "put it in the Lord's hands." The following excerpt by Linda is illustrative of such feelings:

I used to think of it as something bad, you know, coming to jail, but each time I came to jail I've had a spiritual enlightenment in my life. I'm just wanting to let God control me as much as I can so that I can have a better life and don't have to keep coming back and forth in here. My faith is stronger than it's ever been. I just want to take my family and anybody else who wants to go with me into the spiritual world with Jesus.

As Ross (1998) points out, the embrace of Christianity in many ways endorses the racist, sexist, and classist nature of U.S. culture, which has resulted in the marginalization and criminalization of low-income and nonwhite women who populate the jails. While women perceive Christianity as providing comfort, it is also a convenient ideology for staff and society at large, since it focuses women's attention on their own transgressions and "the spiritual world with Jesus," rather than the injustices they have suffered within and outside of jail. Yet the terms are set by the jail staff, and participating in Bible study and prayer circles helps women demonstrate that they are good prisoners and potentially good mothers who deserve to be reunited with their children.

Mothering

Consistent with prior research, almost all the women we interviewed had dependent children (ACA, 1990; Belknap, 1996; Schafer and Dellinger, 1999; Greenfeld and Snell, 1999b). The vast majority of incarcerated women (72 percent) retain legal custody of their children while incarcerated and most return to care for them upon release (ACA, 1990; Hairston, 1991b; Pollock-Byrne, 2002). Separation from children, either temporarily or on a long-term basis, is one of the most overwhelming and difficult aspects of incarceration (Pollock-Byrne, 2002; Ross, 1998). During their mother's absence, children are most often cared for by maternal grandmothers or great-grandparents (ACA, 1990; Owen, 1998). However, some are placed in foster care, which increases the likelihood that Child Protective Services (CPS) will become involved in the situation, thus endangering women's parental rights (Pollock-Byrne, 2002; Ross, 1998). A number of the women we interviewed had already lost custody of their children or feared losing custody of them. The possibility of maintaining a normal relationship with children is circumscribed by restrictive visitation policies and a lack of supportive kin who are able to bring children for visits. For those who do come to see their mothers, visitation is often limited to noncontact interaction. Only 38 percent of jails allow contact visits between mothers and children and only 14.5 percent allow extended child visits (Snell and Morton, as cited in Chesney-Lind, 1997). However, the majority of imprisoned women with dependent children report never receiving a visit from them (Hairston, 1991b; Snell and Morton, as cited in Chesney-Lind, 1997). In addition, some women refuse to tell their children where they are because they do not want their kids to see them incarcerated (Hairston, 1991b; Pollock-Byrne, 2002). For women who do see their children, incarceration may become even more difficult to endure, as they are more blatantly reminded of what they are missing in the outside world (Owen, 1998).

On the matter of child visitation and the need for fostering mother-child relationships, Angel articulated the plight of incarcerated mothers poignantly:

> The United States isn't responding to the needs of mothers with children. There's only one prison in the United States that will allow a woman to keep her baby up to five years old with her while she's incarcerated and I think there should be more facilities like that because a lot of kids are getting thrown to the relatives or getting thrown into foster care when it would be so much better for everybody to make the facilities. If they're going to keep putting us in prison like they are instead of spending that money to help rehabilitate our lives, then at least they can make it available to use to have our children with us.

Women used various strategies for maintaining a connection, if not communication, with their children. For example, Angel constantly wrote to her son, who was also incarcerated:

> My son and I write letters every week to each other. We've been doing some wonderful communication since I've been here. I try to make each letter to him some kind of a lesson. I feel like I'm still teaching him and so I use the letters as an opportunity to put that mothering in there for him and try to keep him on track and keep his spirits lifted and, you know, make sure he's growing.

Of course, in order to write to their children, women must be literate and have money to pay for postage. While the jail used to provide stamps as well as send letters between institutions via interagency mail, it no longer does so. Inmates must purchase postage for all of their written correspondence or complete an "indigent form" for each item they wish to send. Moreover, phone conversations are also limited for inmates, as they must be made collect and cost the responding party $1.90 per fifteen-minute call. One woman reported that she stopped calling her mother, who was caring for her fourteen-year-old daughter, after her mother incurred a $300 phone bill from accepting the collect calls. Phone conversations may also be tape-recorded and used as evidence against the women who are awaiting trial or sentencing, and thus represent a risky form of communication.

Despite these barriers, some women did maintain contact with their children. In these cases, it was primarily the woman's mother or another relative who brought the children for weekend visits. Many of these women expressed concern for the welfare of their children, particularly the impact their incarcerations were having on them, as Lonna described:

> My son's in a lot of trouble. He'll leave in the middle of the night or he won't come home from school. He's hanging out with bad little kids and stuff. I write to my kids and stuff and I made Jessica a little birthday card. She was all happy. I didn't want her to have nothing so my mother-in-law sent her balloons from me at school so they know that I'm not forgetting about them. They don't have a mom or a dad. My mother-in-law asked my son, "Why are you acting this way, Frankie?" He says, "Why do I have to come home? I don't have a family." My older daughter says, "It's true. My mom's in jail and my dad's out partying." Damn.

Even for women who had no contact with their children prior to incarceration, maintaining some notion of a connection was extremely important. For Orca, who no longer had custody of her son, writing children's stories served this purpose: "I write a lot. It's the only way I can cope. I write things for my son, children's poems and books." Later in her interview, Orca heard a baby crying in a nearby visitation room. She grew silent and began weeping. Others, like Julianna, held out hope that one day they would be reunited with their children:

> I believe in my heart of hearts, once you birth a child, they can take your child from you for so long but that child will come back. I

have a dream that we will reunite and be together. That's my strong belief. I can see me back with my family very clearly. As a matter of fact, that's what got me out of bed.

Other women, however, had lost all communication and hope for the future. Our shortest interview was with T.T., whose parental rights to her four young children had been severed by the state. T.T. had conquered her alcohol problem and performed the numerous requirements set by CPS for over two years. A weekend visit from her violent former husband, however, caused CPS to file for permanent severance. After this, she resumed drinking and was arrested for driving while intoxicated. T.T. appeared to be in a state of shock and blankly said that she had no reason to live. The interview was ended when it was obvious that it was painful for T.T. to discuss her situation, or even to think about her children. For most women, the loss of children was equivalent to a loss of self and meaning (Chesler, 1991). Relationships with other women provided some comfort and support in this regard.

Relationships with Other Women

Our findings substantiate prior research findings that intimate and non-intimate relationships are very important means by which women cope with incarceration and meet their emotional, practical, and material needs. These relationships often take the form of a pseudo-family or intimate dyad (Alarid, 1996; Owen, 1998). We found that women in the Pima County Adult Detention Center did bond closely with one or two other inmates in relationships that resembled a pseudo-family, but they primarily took the form of mother-daughter or sisterly relationships, which were built on trust and emotional support.

Intimate dyads also seemed relatively common, but there was widespread denial of such behavior. As has been documented in prior research, the women who engage in such relationships may not necessarily identify themselves as lesbian or bisexual (Owen, 1998; Ross, 1998). The lack of privacy and rate of inmate turnover prohibit the development of committed lesbian relationships in jail, and many do not involve sexual intimacy. These relationships may last for long or short periods of time and may be consensual or exploitive (Owen, 1998). Buckwheat's comments are illustrative of the existence of same-sex relations:

> There's too many women who are "he/shes" and, you know, they fondle each other in church and stuff. They just do a bunch of crazy stuff in jail. I'm just not for it. Even my bunkie, she's into stuff too. I don't mind 'em, you know, 'cuz that's their stuff, as long as they don't bring it on me. It's too much of a, how do you say the word, blasphemy, that they do here.

Such comments concerning same-sex relationships reflect the general societal homophobia, which is reinforced by Christian teachings as well as staff in the jail.

With regard to correctional officers, Morash, Bynum, and Koons (1998) found that the need for positive role models and supportive relationships with female correctional staff were extremely important for women offenders. They particularly recommended the presence of female staff within rehabilitative programs who have similar experiences as jail residents, such as prior drug or alcohol addictions and domestic abuse. Unfortunately, we saw little evidence of such relationships. A number of women actually reported avoiding relationships with other inmates and guards altogether. These women did not perceive that they had enough in common with anyone to merit the development of friendships. Such sentiments have been found in other institutions (Kruttschnitt, Gartner, and Miller, 2000). Given all of the problems we have described, it was surprising that some women still defined jail in positive terms.

Perceptions of Jail

Overall, the women viewed their incarceration negatively. They yearned for freedom and their everyday lives, despite the stresses they contained. Daydreaming about their release from jail seemed to help them cope with the time they had left in the facility. Orca described both her disdain for the facility and her dreams about leaving:

> I hate this place. I go outside here and I can almost *[pause]* for two seconds the sun is so bright. You look up through the chain-link fence to the sky, but you can't see anything. I have a window above my bunk. If I climb up on it, I can see the highway and whatever the street is over here. I can see where you leave, relieved to get out of jail. I watch people leave. I watch them lock the gates.

We also found that for many women, jail served as a safe haven from the circumstances they faced on the outside. As Linda stated, "Not always but most of the time I think jail is a safe haven for those who are about to kill themselves without even realizing it." A number of women reported feeling relieved that they were facing the issues that resulted in their incarceration and expressed hope that their current imprisonment would mark the end of their legal troubles. As Angel stated, "It's a good thing because now all of these bad things from my past will be cleared up and when I get back out into my life I'll be able to start fresh without anything hanging over my head."

For some, jail was regarded as a vital time in which they received the services and counseling they needed but to which they would not otherwise have had access, as Gillian described:

> When I wrote the judge I told him I dropped [tested positive] on purpose hoping to get help and I didn't. He said right there, six months in county jail or until rehab comes and gets me. He knows this is what I want. I'm tired of this life I have. I really am. Being broke all the time. It gets old. I used to have nice things but once I started doing that crack, I lost everything. That's why I say this is a blessing in disguise for me.

For one woman in particular, incarceration was regarded as a respite from her daily obligations as a single mother of seven children. Angel saw her incarceration as time in which she could better prepare herself to provide for her children upon release:

> In the event that I'm given a significant amount of time, like up to three years or more, then I have several things to keep me busy. I feel like my life is being started all over again, and especially because I've always known I had a book in me. I want to try to take this time and use it the best that I can to prepare myself for a career as a writer. If I'm paid to write and that's all I have to do, well then I can do that at home when my kids are at school.

When life outside of jail includes gendered responsibilities and burdens, and there are restrictions on access to resources to meet those responsibilities, jail may be seen as a respite. It is also a relatively safe place to take refuge from life on the streets, easy access to drugs, prostitution, and the violence that accompanies street life.

Conclusion

Few people know the types of abuses and mistreatment incarcerated women endure. As Davis (1998) writes:

> Women prisoners represent one of the most disfranchised and invisible adult populations in our society. The absolute power and control the state exercises over their lives both stems from and perpetuates the patriarchal and racist structures that for centuries have resulted in the social domination of women. (351)

This is particularly true within jail and detention centers, where women's access to programs and services, visitation, and health care is substantially worse, relative to prison (Gray, Mays, and Stohr, 1995). While our study found many commonalities between women's jail and prison experiences, important differences also existed, which were aggravated by the frequent turnover of inmates and relative inattention to long-term services. In this way, our findings contribute to the small but developing body of research on women's jail experiences, as well as women's imprisonment experiences more generally.

While many of our findings are perhaps not surprising, what is particularly alarming is the fact that despite the problems the jailed women in this study faced, incarceration provided a much needed break from their daily lives. While perceiving incarceration in a positive way may have been a strategy of resistance, it is hard to deny the fact that spending time in jail provided a welcome respite for many women. It allowed them to dry out from constant alcohol or drug use, heal from violent victimization, and plan for the future (Pollock-Byrne, 2002; Owen, 1998). This troubling fact is a testament to the lack of resources and concern dedicated to assisting women who are consumed with day-to-day survival within drug-infested, poverty-stricken, and violent homes and neighborhoods (Belknap, 1996; Owen, 1998).

The control of women through pervasive and routinized mechanisms of feminine subjectification, combined with institutionalized racism, sexism, and classism, is extremely effective. Despite extraordinary levels of violence against women (Tjaden and Thoennes, 2000), maternal poverty (Caiazza, 2000), and glaring disparities in wealth and resources, the vast majority of women continue to play by the rules and not seek vengeance or justice through violent crime. However, increasing numbers of women are being ensnared in the prison industrial complex, where control becomes much more explicit and repressive, reflecting gendered patterns of control outside the jail in a magnified fashion. Yet repression within the jail is far from complete, and even in this most restrictive environment, women find ways to resist and transform their experiences in ways that support their own goals. As survivors of rape, incest, battering, prostitution, and drug addictions, jailed women find ways to make use of the minimal services available, as well as the respite from life on the streets and within their families.

However, women's success in negotiating this hostile terrain should not detract from awareness of the utter unsuitability of incarceration as social policy for reducing women's participation in crime. The resources that the women in our study did find helpful (e.g., counseling and substance abuse treatment) could be provided in community facilities, which would not cut off contact between mothers and children or provide an environment in which women are routinely subjected to violence and degradation. The few strategies for political mobilization that were discussed by some women receive scant support from the community of feminist and prison activists, as women in jail remain an invisible population. Resistance from within the jail is extremely difficult, as discussions of the grievance process suggested.

Statutes that have accelerated the rate of incarceration for women, such as three-strikes laws, which mandate incarceration for third-time drug offenders regardless of the type of offense, have combined with decreased social spending and increased unemployment to swell the number of women in jail. These stories of survival and resistance suggest that incarceration of women for drug and minor property offenses may provide a brief respite from harsh conditions and a small chance for gaining access to resources. Incarceration does not, however, address those harsh conditions in a manner that would help women negotiate the world without drugs, check forgery, or welfare fraud. Successful intervention into the problems identified in these stories requires dual attention to social policy influencing poverty, violence, and a reliance on incarceration as well as simultaneous efforts to create humane, responsive conditions for those who are in jails and prisons. Coalitions of activists concerned with housing, poverty, violence, and prisons hold the potential for destroying the barriers of invisibility and forging an abolitionist politics informed by women's needs and experiences.

Note

This research was funded in part by a grant from the Center for Urban Inquiry, Arizona State University. The authors would like to thank the administration and staff at the Pima County Adult Detention Center in Tucson, Arizona, as well as all the women incarcerated there who so openly shared their stories.

5

Abused Women and Incarceration

Lori B. Girshick

Domestic violence and physical and sexual abuse in the home and control of women in prison are linked (Davis, 1998). As gendered modes of punishment—one in the private realm and one in the public—the movements concerned with private battering and state incarceration of women should be more closely connected. Threatened and actual violence is one of the strongest patriarchal modes of controlling women. The sexualized nature of this violence begins as early as infancy and extends without limit. Females of every age are subject to possible sexual abuse, reinforced by gendered sex roles in a culture where women are sexualized in the media and throughout every societal institution.

When women enter the prison system, despite leaving all their possessions at the door, they walk in with a history that includes their emotional and psychological abuses stored in their bodies. These abuses affect their sense of self and how they view and respond to the world. The experiences of incest, battering, rape, and assaults from strangers—experiences that have not been integrated to allow the survivor to deal with everyday life events—result in a myriad of significant consequences. These include, but are not limited to, posttraumatic stress disorder (PTSD), lack of personal boundaries, low self-esteem, depression, suicidal impulses or attempts, mental illness, sexual dysfunction, and fear and distrust of others (especially men). The sexual and physical abuses of women begin when they are young girls and adolescents and continue into their adulthood. While males experience a range of abuses, their abuses, particularly by people they know, do not continue throughout their lifetime, making revictimization a gendered issue. This gendered distinction regarding abuse contributes to a disparate context for women's experiences of doing time compared to men.

Analytically, impacts of abuse of women create circular links. Girls who are abused are at higher risk of engaging in adolescent and adult criminal behavior. Girls and adults who are abused often turn to drugs to cope with their abuse. Drug use is connected to criminal acts to procure more drugs. Incarcerated females are revictimized, creating the survival need for further problematic coping behaviors. This is not to say that without abuse there would be no females committing crimes or abusing substances. But it is probably safe to say the rates would be dramatically lower.

In this chapter, I discuss how the abuse histories of women clash with the sexualized environment of jails and prisons. Experiences of touching (such as in pat and strip searches), containment (when handcuffed or restrained, and when locked in isolation), and invasion of personal space (through room searches or visual surveillance) are examples of how institutionalized power reinforces gender-specific victimization. Given the disproportionately high rates of victimization of women in prison, their punishment is doubly gendered—through their abuse as females outside of jail or prison and through their revictimization throughout the control process of incarceration.

Abuse Rates

Rates of rape and sexual assault prevalence are difficult to determine because of the vast underreporting of these crimes. The FBI's Uniform Crime Report, which is based only on rapes reported to law enforcement, documented approximately 96,000 forcible rapes in 1997 (FBI, 1997). The National Crime Victimization Survey, which is a survey of U.S. households, estimated 311,000 rapes and sexual assaults in 1997 (Rand, 1998). Only one rape in eleven is reported to authorities (Beattie and Shaughnessy, 2000). There is one rape or one attempted rape committed every 1.6 minutes, with most survivors knowing their assailants (BJS, 1994). In 1990 the national rate for incest was reported to be one in four females sexually abused by the time she is eighteen years old (Finkelhor et al., 1990), a number believed to hold today. Blume (1990) thinks that the number is likely closer to 50 percent, because many women do not remember their childhood sexual trauma until late in life, if at all. Due to repression, incest is dramatically underreported.

Estimates of battering range from 1 to 4 million women victims each year (BJS, 1995; APA, 1996). More than half of all married women will be battered by their husbands during their marriages (Landes, Squyres, and Quiram, 1997). The American Medical Association (AMA, 1992) asserts that more than 12 million women will be battered by an intimate partner at some point in their lives.

Studies of women in prison show higher rates of childhood and adult abuse than in the population at large. According to a Bureau of Justice Statistics special report (BJS, 1999), nearly six in ten women in state prisons have experienced physical or sexual abuse in the past. Over a third of incarcerated women have been battered, and just under a quarter have been abused by a family member. Women inmates are almost four times as likely to be physically or sexually abused before prison compared to men (Morash, Bynum, and Koons, 1998).

Singer and Bussey (1995), studying women in jail in Cleveland, Ohio, found that 48 percent of the women had been sexually victimized as children and 68 percent had been sexually assaulted as adults. A study of women inmates in Texas revealed that more than half had been abused growing up and nearly three-fourths had been victimized as adults (McClellan, Farabee, and Crouch, 1997). In a study of women in a minimum-security prison in North Carolina, 68 percent reported abuse as a child, 85 percent had been battered as an adult, 83 percent had been emotionally abused as an adult, and 43 percent had been raped as an adult (Girshick, 1999). Leonard (2000), in her study of battered women inmates in California, found rates of 55 percent of childhood sexual abuse and 48 percent of childhood sexual assault. A study on inmates at the Federal Correctional Institution for Women in Dublin, California, showed that 47 percent had been physically abused in childhood, 39 percent sexually abused as children, 66 percent battered as adults, and 43 percent raped as adults (Schaefer, 1994). Browne, Miller, and Maguin (1999) interviewed 150 women at the Bedford Hills Maximum Security Correctional Facility in New York. Their findings demonstrated that violence across the life-span of incarcerated women inmates is "pervasive and severe" (316). Seventy percent of the women reported experiencing severe physical violence in adolescence; 75 percent experienced severe physical violence by intimate partners in adulthood. Fifty-nine percent of the women experienced some sort of sexual molestation as children, while 33 percent were raped or sexually attacked as adults. Virtually every study shows high rates of revictimization, with single women frequently experiencing multiple types of abuse. Once incarcerated, women with abuse histories are subject to environments that replicate the same challenges to their autonomy and self-concepts, with negative consequences to how they experience "doing time."

My focus here is on illustrating how incarceration retraumatizes women with a history of previous abuse, thus adding another layer of punishment to loss of freedom. I argue that often imprisonment recreates the abuse experiences, hence revictimizing the inmate. Rapes and sexual abuses also occur within prisons. There are implications to this for the women, not only in their suffering over and above their loss of freedom, but in specific program needs and in policies that the prison system must reexamine and change. Applying our knowledge about abuse and trauma to women in prison will make a significant difference in the women's lives while they are incarcerated and when they are released, as well as a significant difference to prison management.

Childhood Abuse and Later Criminality

Abuse in childhood—physical and sexual abuse, and neglect—appears to be connected to many types of maladaptive coping behaviors such as truancy, running away from home, drug use, and later criminal behavior (Gilfus, 1988; Lake, 1993; McClellan, Farabee, and Crouch, 1997). From the standpoint of the adolescents, these may be coping mechanisms for situations from which there seems to be no relief—for example, the girl who runs away to escape an abusive stepfather, or the child who skips school so that bruises won't be detected. In the eyes of the adult community, these individuals may be seen as unruly children with discipline problems. Additionally, the link between early sexual abuse and later prostitution is particularly strong (Chesney-Lind, 1989; Widom, 1995).

Longitudinal research by the National Institute of Justice showed that childhood victimization increased the likelihood of delinquency, adult criminality, and violent criminal behavior. The institute studied 1,575 children through young adulthood, finding that "being abused or neglected as a child increased the likelihood of arrest as a juvenile by 53 percent, as an adult by 38 percent, and for a violent crime by 38 percent" (Widom, 1992: 1). A study of 908 individuals by Widom (1995) showed that sexual abuse seemed to be the variable with most impact on later criminal behavior. Widom (1995: 6) speculates that "the trauma and stress of these early childhood experiences or society's response to them" is what affects later criminal behavior rather than the sexual nature of the incident per se.

Lake (1993) points out that women's illegal behavior and their victimization by intimates and strangers are intertwined. Escaping to the streets to avoid sexual abuse at home leads many women into high-risk environments. Pimps and johns often brutalize women engaging in prostitution. Other women are battered by boyfriends in order to force them into committing crimes.

Understanding Posttraumatic Stress Disorder

The trauma impacts resulting from childhood sexual abuse and adult rape, sexual assault, and battering affect a person's sense of self and ability to function in the world, and are related to the likelihood of revictimization. Root (1992) points out the difference between stress and trauma. With stress, there is inconvenience and distress, which is alleviated when the stress is removed. Traumas, on the other hand, "represent destruction of basic organizing principles by which we come to know self, others, and the environment; traumas wound deeply in a way that challenges the meaning of life. Healing from the wounds of such an experience requires a restitution of order and meaning in one's life" (229).

The most commonly cited trauma impacts of rape found in the literature include fear, vulnerability, depression, negative impact on sexual satisfaction, promiscuity, prostitution, suicide attempts, loss of trust, loss of self-esteem, loss of a sense of control over one's life, loss of confidence, drug abuse, and flashbacks. Many concrete losses may be experienced, such as loss of jobs, relationships, and the ability to drive or to leave the house (Kelly, 1988). When rape survivors do not successfully reorganize their lives, they often are diagnosed with disorders without taking trauma into account; in other words, something is deemed to be wrong with the survivor for not recovering (Root, 1992).

Resick's 1993 overview of the psychological impact of rape points to fear and anxiety as the most frequently noted symptoms. She cites a study by Kilpatrick, Edmunds, and Seymour (1992) wherein they estimated that 3.8 million adult women have had rape-related PTSD and that 1.3 million women currently have rape-induced PTSD. Many studies in Resick's review noted depression as likely, and suicidal thoughts and attempts were found to be much higher among rape victims than nonvictims. In looking at social adjustment, work adjustment suffered the most compared to marital, parental, and family adjustment.

Studies of battered women show similar posttraumatic stress symptoms such as nightmares, flashbacks, numbing, hypervigilence, intense anxiety, difficulty concentrating, and heightened startle response (Dutton et al., 1990; O'Keefe, 1998; Saunders, 1994). Neurophysiological theories suggest that trauma and high levels of chronic stress affect brain structures involving alarm and fear centers that trigger freezing, cognitive and behavioral shutdown, and startle responses (Root, 1992).

Battered women who killed or seriously harmed their abusers have been found to evince more severe trauma symptomatology than a clinical sample of battered women (Dutton et al., 1994). O'Keefe (1998), in her study of battered women incarcerated for killing or seriously harming their abusers compared to battered women in prison for other offenses, found that women in both groups had experienced severe battering and had significant trauma symptoms. Battered women in Kentucky who were convicted of killing, seriously injuring, or of conspiracy to murder their abusers, portrayed in the book *Sisters in Pain* by Beattie and Shaughnessy (2000), shared histories of severe and brutal abuse. Their trauma symptoms included inability to cope "normally," distorted perceptions of what was happening in their marriages, denial, and dissociation. They had histories of incest, physical beatings as children, sexual torture by their husbands, miscarriages caused by beatings, drug abuse to self-medicate, and feelings of helplessness and hopelessness.

Theories of revictimization generally rest on the assumption that unresolved trauma is part of the process in increased risk of revictimization (Arata, 2000). Finkelhor and Browne (1985) propose a model of traumagenic dynamics in order to understand the impact of childhood sexual abuse. The four factors of this model are traumatic sexualization, betrayal, powerlessness, and stigmatization, which when they all act together differentiate sexual abuse from other types of childhood trauma such as parental divorce. These factors distort the child's sense of self and sense of the world, with serious consequences.

In traumatic sexualization, a child's sexuality develops inappropriately as a result of sexual abuse. She may learn to manipulate sexual behavior to get gifts, attention, and privileges. There is confusion between sexual behavior and sexual morality, as well as learning behavior that is inappropriate to her age. The second factor, betrayal, refers to the circumstance when someone whom she trusted has harmed her. The betrayal of trust may be because of the offender's actions or because family members do not protect or believe her (Finkelhor and Browne, 1985).

A common outcome of child sexual abuse is the feeling of powerlessness, when the child feels a lack of efficacy. She may be unable to stop the abuse from happening or understand why it is happening. And last, she feels the shame, guilt, and badness that result from inappropriate sexual behavior, which results in a self-image that includes stigmatization. These factors help us understand how the child could easily be revictimized later in life (Finkelhor and Browne, 1985). Other theories look at vulnerability that arises out of child sexual assault. As adults, these women often have liberal sexual attitudes and increased levels of sexual activity, placing them at risk for further abuse (Koss and Dinero, 1989). Chu (1992) focuses on the coping mechanisms of dissociation and numbness that might lead a woman to deny when she is in a vulnerable situation, hence being open to revictimization.

The different theories are not mutually exclusive, and all of these factors may play a role in future victimization. Of course, not all children are victimized in the same way, with the same frequency or severity. The variables are many. However, unresolved abuse seems to be one of the most complicated factors. New abuses compound the trauma symptoms. An incarcerated woman will be "inundated" with situations that can trigger her past boundary violations and re-create scenarios of power and powerlessness, devaluation, and betrayal of trust (Heney and Kristiansen, 1998).

It is not only cumulative traumas that impact us. Living daily in a traumatic environment such as poverty, when there is constant threat to life, or *incarceration* will impact the ability or inability to reorganize life. Coping strategies that seem unusual or disorganized are often normal responses to trauma and should not be pathologized. In these contexts, our focus needs to shift from the individual to the traumatic environment (Root, 1992). Structural problems such as racism, classism, sexism, and violence are all too often ignored when individuals are pathologized. Shifting this focus depoliticizes how we understand abuse and decontexualizes women's lives (Kendall, 2000a, 2000c).

It therefore becomes important to examine the institutional context within which women inmates live their lives, where daily and cumulative violence impacts them. It is in this exploration that we see the contradictions inherent in incarcerating individuals we seek to simultaneously punish and rehabilitate without taking into account both the society we removed them from and the subculture we lock them within.

The Security Mandate

Total institutions like jails and prisons take on a certain life of their own. The total institution is characterized by top-down rules and regulations, with inmates dressed uniformly and following a rigid prescribed daily routine (Goffman, 1961: 6). Depersonalization is a way of life and a mechanism of control. Because the inmates' lives are regulated and controlled, a forced dependency emerges (Watterson, 1996). The prison becomes the substitute parent in its "caretaking" activities as the authorities have "total power over the lives of the people they govern" (Watterson, 1996: 79). Inmates are dependent on prison authorities for their basic needs of food, medical care, showers, and items such as tampons, and for "privileges" such as mail, phone calls, visits, and attending programs.

The security mandate of prisons is contrary to any sense of rehabilitation or individuality on the part of an inmate. Since treatment requires change, this control undermines the possibility of effective programming (Leventhal, 2000). In this context of intimidation, isolation, and constant surveillance, it is a struggle for inmates to maintain any personal dignity and individuality. Aspects of positive mental health and maintaining self-respect include autonomy, intimacy, responsibility, mastery, and dignity, yet coercive environments undercut these elements (Kendall, 2000a; Watterson, 1996). Instead, women find prison a place of humiliation, claustrophobia, boredom, anxiety, loneliness, lack of privacy, abuses of power, no choices, uncertainty, and the constant overstimulation of noises and arguments (Faith, 1993). The stresses of incarceration exacerbate the low self-esteem and feelings of worthlessness most women walk in with. They frequently experience depression, anxiety, nervousness, weight gain, and a host of physical symptoms such as trouble sleeping, backaches, and headaches (Fogel, 1993).

In fact, the risks and needs of women in prison resulting from their experiences and external environments have been turned into "risk factors" in many prison systems. Their needs resulting from dependency, low self-esteem, low educational levels and poor work histories, prostitution, homelessness, suicide attempts, substance abuse, and so on, which are rooted in social problems, are now discussed in terms of criminogenic risks. With this semantic turn, it is the offender who must change, not the institutions of society (Hannah-Moffat, 2000). Prison risks are assessed in terms of security issues, meaning, for example, that a history of self-injury can be seen as violent behavior and hence a risk for the security of the institution. An inmate concerned for the welfare of her children may be viewed as an escape risk, while if she were not incarcerated she would be a caring mother. Furthermore, these needs, now defined as risks, are interpreted as predictors of recidivism risk. "Needy" women may require increased supervision, without having their true needs met (Hannah-Moffat, 1999, 2000).

Male Guards in Women's Prisons

The passage of Title VII of the Civil Rights Act of 1964 had an enormous impact on where male and female guards worked. While males have always guarded female inmates, the reverse had not been true. Title VII changed that. As equal opportunity in employment was opened up for female guards to move into male prisons, male guards were able to move to women's prisons. Today male guards outnumber female guards by two or three to one in women's facilities (Human Rights Watch, 1996; Pollock, 1998). The only legal discrimination allowed by an employee's sex is if a qualification is "reasonably necessary" to perform the specific job (referred to as a bona fide occupational qualification).

Male inmates and, to a lesser extent, female inmates have pressed litigation challenging that having officers of the other sex guarding them has violated their right to privacy. According to Miller (2000), the Supreme Court has not adequately addressed the issue of cross-gender searches. She documents rulings by federal judges that are "wildly inconsistent" about the role that sexuality plays in searches and surveillance (294). This inconsistency is critical because surveillance, as the most common form of search, is the "cornerstone" of punishment (334). For example, in *Gunther v. Iowa State Men's Reformatory* (612 F.2d 1079, 8th Cir.) in 1980 and *Timm v. Gunter* (917 F.2d 1093, 8th Cir.) in 1990, officer employment opportunities were seen to outweigh privacy rights of male or female inmates. In other litigation on the issue of pat searches and privacy rights, one ruling went in favor of female inmates against male guards conducting pat searches, while in another case, female officers could conduct pat searches on male inmates. The rulings differed because of the perceived retriggering potential for women based on previous sexual abuse by males (Pollock, 1998).

Whether male or female, inmates usually try to get along with guards. While all officers hold control over daily life routines and discipline may be rigid or flexible depending on individual officers, many inmates try to work with them to keep life bearable and get their needs met. However, the self-esteem sacrifice on the part of inmates who out of necessity must obey unreasonable orders or tolerate demeaning treatment is also part of this complexity of accommodation within the context of control.

Guards represent access to many goods. They supply information, passes, sanitary products, and a host of other material items. Good rapport can make the difference between getting what you need and going without. Female officers in particular tend to administer more from a social-worker perspective and often show interest in the inmates' concerns. But conflicts are ever present and many inmates find staff petty and overly intrusive, or feel them to be egotistical. Some inmates prefer male officers, while others feel it doesn't matter—except for the near-universal discomfort with male guards in housing, shower, and toilet areas (Girshick, 1999; Owen, 1998; Zupan, 1992).

The controversies that have arisen with males guarding female inmates draw primarily upon legal protections found in the Eighth and Fourth Amendments to the Constitution and in international human rights law. The Eighth Amendment prohibits cruel and unusual punishment, meaning "unnecessary and wanton infliction of pain." The pain must violate contemporary standards of decency. A prisoner would have to prove that the prison official acted maliciously and sadistically. Cases related to sexual abuse have been brought using the Eighth Amendment. The Fourth Amendment provides for the right to privacy and to be secure in one's person. Lower-court rulings have found some limitations to these rights when prisoners have litigated about issues of male officers in shower areas and conducting pat and strip searches. Courts have upheld the security rights of institutions if these actions are done "respectfully." When not reasonably necessary for security, these actions have been seen to violate privacy rights. A complex maze of enforcement jurisdictions and criminal codes exist at state and federal levels and in the U.S. Department of Justice (Human Rights Watch, 1996).

The United States is also signatory to several international conventions that apply to the human rights of prisoners. These are the International Covenant on Civil and Political Rights and the Convention Against Torture and Other Cruel, Inhuman, or Degrading Treatment and Punishment. The United States is also bound to the Universal Declaration of Human Rights on torture and cruel, inhuman, or degrading treatment or punishment. When the United States ratified the two international conventions, it did so with attached reservations, trying to limit accountability to the standards by not passing enabling legislation. Hence the government cannot be sued for noncompliance (Human Rights Watch, 1996). This becomes important when the protections that exist at the state and federal levels are not enforced and prisoners are effectively left without any recourse.

Supervision Issues

Women inmates are daily confronted with situations that trigger feelings and memories of previous abuse from childhood and adulthood. They rely upon coping mechanisms that can put them at even greater risk of abuse. The frequent occurrence of routine pat searches, strip searches, room searches, and surveillance in shower and toilet areas can prompt inmate responses with the end result of disciplinary write-ups, further harassment, or being placed into solitary confinement. Pollock (1998) points out that some inmates overreact to any physical touching by a male guard. Their seeming defiance or hostility may escalate into an altercation and result in their being restrained. Many inmates internalize their stress responses with suicide attempts, eating disorders, or withdrawal. Other women experience a contradictory mix of tension, anger, submission, and passivity as they cope with officers' control mechanisms. Disobeying an order as a result of any of these external or internal responses can be interpreted as a security risk and women can find themselves put into administrative segregation.

Control over women inmates results in sexualized and retraumatizing behaviors. Women are touched against their will in pat searches, made to stand naked during strip searches, and are restrained by handcuffs and tying. They are locked in isolation. When their rooms are searched for contraband their beds are stripped, lockers ransacked, and personal items confiscated. Visual surveillance is constant in every conceivable area. Abusive and degrading language is rampant. The dependence of the women upon the guards for their every need makes the situation ripe for sexual abuses. Women will do what they need to do to get their needs met. Without adequate grievance procedures, without protections, the sexualized environment results in sexual abuses (Bill, 1998; Heney and Kristiansen, 1998; Human Rights Watch, 1996).

Some states, such as California, prohibit male guards from strip-searching female inmates. However, this protection is meaningless if male guards watch the process, which has been alleged (Human Rights Watch, 1996). In New York, videotaping of strip searches of women entering segregation was allowed in the mid-1990s. Male deputies and others then reviewed these tapes. The tapes showed that many of the procedures regulating searches were not being followed. Male officers were present and the inmates reported being forced to stand naked while portions of their bodies other than vaginal and anal areas were searched. Regulations call for no removal of undergarments until necessary, rooms to be warm and well lit, and the search to be conducted professionally. However, the humiliation of the women continued when they were not given their clothes to wear back to their cells but were forced to walk in undergarments or transparent paper robes (Human Rights Watch, 1996).

In Michigan, male officers are trained to use the back of their hands during pat searches when they are around chest and genital areas of the body. But women have reported that males grope or grip their breasts, nipples, vagina, buttocks, anus, and thighs with open hands and fingers. Women who have resisted this treatment have received disciplinary write-ups for disobeying a direct order (Human Rights Watch, 1996).

Physical touching and groping along with the incidents of forced stripping, handcuffing, or shackling that occur when handling prison-unit disturbances are easily interpreted as assaults, triggering inmates' traumatic sexualization (Heney and Kristiansen, 1998). The lack of privacy in housing areas when undressing and the powerlessness the women experience to stop surveillance of themselves while they are in shower and toilet areas compound their traumatization. In many prisons, inmates are allowed to cover their cell windows while they undress, or regulations call for partial curtains or walls in showers and toilet stalls. However, a study by Human Rights Watch (1996) found that these rules are frequently ignored. Male officers routinely enter these areas under pretext of searches or patrolling for misconduct. They do not announce their presence and they often make derogatory comments to the women about their bodies. Design of bathroom areas often allows for maximum viewing and therefore lack of privacy. Male guards are also sometimes present when inmates have gynecological exams or are delivering their babies.

Another invasion is that some male guards use sexually abusive and degrading language when speaking to or referring to inmates. While contrary to state prison rules of conduct, this language may stand alone or be a prelude to inappropriate touching and observing. Inmates report being called degrading names such as "slut" and "whore." Other times, comments about "getting a piece" or talk about "how big do you like them?" and other sexual innuendos—"you shouldn't bend over like that in front of me"—accompany touches or take place when women are in the bathroom (Human Rights Watch, 1996: 80). There is also harassment about how women look, especially if they are overweight, and name-calling of women whom guards perceive to be lesbians. Comments about body parts are constant. Other taunting occurs when women must ask for tampons or menstrual pads. Officers might throw sanitary items on the floor or say things about the women's hygiene. Women have been told to use their clothes or toilet paper instead, or to turn pads over. Women prisoners feel powerless to confront this pervasive degrading language and humiliation in the hostile environment of prison (Human Rights Watch, 1996).

Inmates' sense of powerlessness is enhanced when they attempt to speak out about these abuses. Their reports are given low credence (they are, after all, "criminals and liars") and they face retribution if they speak up. They risk losing the goodwill of officers, who are their link to information and goods. Another aspect of traumagenic dynamics is betrayal. Heney (1996) reminds us that incarcerated women may feel that prison is a type of victimization and that society has betrayed them. First they were not rescued as children and now the prison has become a persecutor.

A last aspect of traumagenic dynamics is stigmatization. Survivors of childhood abuse are different from those not abused, particularly in that they are "damaged goods." Prisoners are also "abnormal and bad." This social stigma of prison retriggers the stigma of the abused child. After release, secrecy about time spent in prison also exacerbates the secrets that had been kept about abuse (Heney and Kristiansen, 1998).

We can see from the above discussion that there are two major types of power that reinforce previous abuse experiences—power that is physical, such as touching, groping, or handcuffing, and power that is symbolic, in terms of degrading women through verbal taunts and threats, resulting in feelings of powerlessness due to lack of recourse regarding the violence against them. The importance of symbolic violence cannot be overstated, particularly given the sexualized context of surveillance in prisons. According to Thomas (2002), symbolic violence can be more devastating than physical attack because it distorts ways of thinking and seeing, and it reinforces social harms.

Sexual Misconduct Within the Prison

Sexual abuse, including oral, anal, and vaginal rape and other criminal sexual misconduct, is widespread in women's prisons. There is no way to escape the offenders, and grievance procedures often do not work. Human Rights Watch documented sexual misconduct in five states (California, Georgia, Illinois, Michigan, and New York) and the District of Columbia in its report *All Too Familiar* (1996). It found that the system itself sets up a forced dependency of inmates on guards that encourages the sexualization of interactions. Indeed, it is not only actual physical and verbal sexual abuse but also the *potential* for this abuse that makes it so powerful a form of control over women inmates. Like the battering relationships and other abuse they may have experienced, "walking on eggshells" waiting for the abuse to occur is a potent aspect of the process of power and control.

Many inmates have little or no financial resources. Some states, such as Georgia, do not pay inmates for their work while others pay less than one dollar a day. Yet women need to buy their hygiene products, clothing, and items of comfort. In this way, an underground economy develops, part of which is trading sex for cigarettes, gum, candy, food, and so forth. This can hardly be seen as voluntary participation but reflects the power that guards have over the inmates. At times, guards might demand participation for goods and "favors." Officers also have access to inmates' personal files, which give information about their vulnerabilities and past abuses. Officers are able to take advantage of this knowledge and target particularly troubled women. Previously abused women have difficulty stopping further abuse and do not know their rights. Many inmates are either accustomed to sexual exploitation or do not know how to respond to males in nonsexualized ways. As Human Rights Watch (1996: 64) points out in its report, these are women unaccustomed to having recourse against abuse.

All of the abuses mentioned above occurred in the states studied by Human Rights Watch. They interviewed women who said male correctional officers had raped them. Some women were repeatedly harassed for sexual intercourse, groped, followed into the showers, and so forth. Sometimes guards would manipulate a situation so as to be left alone with the woman inmate during her work shift. In attempts to carry out their work duties, inmates may find themselves forced to comply with sexual requests to get a signature or pick up supplies. Assaults occurred by prison doctors. For example, in New York, a doctor was known as "Dr. Feelgood," as he frequently fondled women's breasts and fingered women during medical exams (Human Rights Watch, 1996: 292).

Sexual abuses by guards sometimes results in pregnancies. Women are then harassed and often pressured to abort. In one case in California, the inmate wanted an abortion. Prison officials used her wish for an abortion as a way to pressure her to disclose who had impregnated her. She was put into administrative segregation in an attempt to force her to reveal his name, which she did not (Human Rights Watch, 1996: 78–79). An inmate in Georgia became pregnant after being raped by a guard. She was then forced to have an abortion that she did not want after being told she would not get parole. She was literally dragged to the abortion clinic (Human Rights Watch, 1996: 144–145). In New York, inmates with pregnancies resulting from improper sexual behavior from guards are similarly harassed. They may be denied medical care, placed in segregation, or denied placement in the mother-child nursery program after they give birth (Human Rights Watch, 1996: 298).

The grievance process can be difficult for inmates to access. It is a risky step more likely to lead to harassment and retaliation than redress for a wrong done to them. Officers always know when a grievance has been filed and the inmate will still be at the mercy of that officer for further sexual abuse or hassles in daily living. This serves as a serious disincentive for coming forward and making reports. Inmates report that sometimes the grievance is thrown into the trash right in front of them or that the word of the officer is always believed against the word of the inmate (Human Rights Watch, 1996). Investigations lack confidentiality and are rarely open to outside monitors, thus undermining the integrity of the investigation. Harassment such as being "thrown in the hole," being handcuffed for repeated interrogation, cell searches, and having one's jacket labeled "snitch" is common. Other forms of retaliation include losing work assignments, being pulled from programs, being targeted for disciplinary reports, and placement in administrative segregation (Human Rights Watch, 1996).

Overall, few officers seem to lose their jobs due to grievances filed against them. They may be temporarily transferred or even suspended, but if so, they are often rehired. Women see the officers back at the prisons and realize they are powerless to confront and stop the abuse. Even the occasional officer who loses his or her job still does not face criminal prosecution. The effect of lack of accountability and almost certain harassment and retaliation is that women keep quiet about sexual abuse and continue to be subjected to it. System betrayal is yet one more confirmation of their powerlessness, inappropriate sexualization, and stigmatization.

Trauma Coping Strategies

The coping strategies in response to physical and sexual abuse include dissociation, self-medicated "numbing" through use of drugs and alcohol, suicidal ideation, bulimia and anorexia, self-mutilation such as cutting or burning, running away, compulsive behavior, and hyperaggression. The goals are either escape or control. These strategies are highly problematic not only because they are often harmful but also because they are liable to be misdiagnosed for what they are, adding layers on top of the original issues that need to be addressed but remain hidden. Because incarceration mimics in many ways the past traumatic experiences most inmates have had, their coping strategies kick in (Heney and Kristiansen, 1998). Root (1992: 250) suggests that these survival behaviors should be viewed "as a reflection of a healthy capacity for self-defense" given the context inmates are forced to function in. Similarly, Dutton (1992) suggests that these coping strategies be viewed as strengths rather than as stable personality factors.

Patterns of substance abuse indicate that women in jails and prisons are likely to use more drugs more frequently and to use more serious drugs than their male counterparts. Males, on the other hand, tend to have serious alcohol-use patterns. More females than males are also under the influence of drugs at the time of their arrest, and more females than males commit their crimes to get money for drugs (Pollock, 1998). Many studies show a link between childhood victimization and later drug and alcohol abuse particularly in order to self-medicate and alleviate depression, with the substance use continuing into adulthood (McClellan, Farabee, and Crouch, 1997; Pollock, 1998). Battered and raped women also often turn to drugs and alcohol as a means of coping with their victimization and sense of entrapment (Bill, 1998; Singer and Bussey, 1995). This self-medication is functional when viewed in light of their trauma experiences (Dutton, 1992). In fact, getting clean from drug abuse can often precipitate a new emotional crisis because the pain of sexual and physical abuses comes into focus without a means to cope.

Consequently, it is no surprise that women in jails and prisons with high rates of physical and sexual abuse in childhood and adulthood also have high rates of addiction. Their substance use, along with other problems of low education levels, poor work histories, and single parenting, makes them likely candidates for drug dealing or other economic crimes in order to get money for living expenses and drug purchases. In Leventhal's interviews with women in a drug treatment program in jail she found that "abuse was almost always a precursor to drug use, which often began in a relationship with a man who used drugs, and addiction was almost always a precursor to the crimes that brought these women to jail—crimes like retail theft, prostitution, and repeated violations of probation" (2000: 44). This pathway to crime begins with victimization and substance abuse (Bill, 1998). These circumstances show the need for drug programs to cover issues related to abuse, relationships, and self-esteem.

Research reveals high rates of mental illness among jail and prison inmates. According to the American Correctional Association (ACA, 1990), more than one in ten women receive inpatient psychiatric care before being incarcerated in state prison, one in eight women receive medication for emotional or mental health problems while in prison, and up to two-thirds of women in jail require mental health services. Beck (1991) reports that almost a quarter of women in jails had taken mental health medication prior to their incarceration. More recently, a Bureau of Justice Statistics special report (BJS, 2001) notes that while incoming female inmates have slightly more physical impairments than incoming males (34 percent compared to 30 percent), they have about 60 percent more mental impairments than males (16 percent compared to 10 percent).

Subjected to increased control, women in prison report more suicidal thoughts than when they were on the street. Suicide attempts are seen as a means to gain some element of control in escaping their feelings and the reality of incarceration (Heney, 1996). Yet the response to suicide threats—suicide watch—can be an especially degrading and abusive experience. Wan and Ferraro (2000) report that jail inmates in

Arizona are chained naked to a bunk in an otherwise empty room for forty-eight hours. Women prisoners deemed a suicide risk in Georgia have been forcibly stripped, placed in restraints, and sometimes left hog-tied in their cells for days (Human Rights Watch, 1996).

Another particularly degrading experience that compounds women's depression is the treatment of pregnant inmates. An estimated 4 percent to 9 percent of women in jails and prisons are pregnant. According to Acoca (1998), pregnant inmates are in high-risk positions both medically and psychologically. There is a near-universal lack of prenatal care, insufficient nutrition in their diets, lack of information regarding pregnancy and parenting, and poor preparation for the mother's separation from the infant after birth. There are reports of women being denied abortions when they request them and, in other cases, women being forced to abort (Barry, 1989; Holt, 1982). Other concerns of pregnant inmates include body cavity searches, which may irritate the pelvis (Holt, 1982), and the use of shackles and restraints when being transported, with some women shackled even during delivery of their babies (Albor, 1995; Barry, 1989; Mills and Barrett, 1990).

The mental health symptoms that present in imprisoned women—depression, stress, trouble sleeping, anxiety, feelings of "going crazy," and the like—may be more linked to their posttraumatic stress symptoms from abuse and the exacerbating stresses and traumas of prison life than to mental illness of psychopathology, split personality, or borderline personality disorder (BPD). Walker (1993) writes that PTSD is likely to be a more accurate diagnosis for the battered woman than a personality disorder. The fact that the woman is often misdiagnosed shows that battering is not taken seriously. When focusing on psychopathology, practitioners stress the internal state of the inmate rather than the external factors that caused the inmate's problems, very possibly missing the battering, incest, or rape that led to the trauma symptoms (Saunders, 1994). When diagnosed with BPD, a woman inmate is seen as both bad and mad (Kendall, 1993). A diagnosis of BPD results in a focus on present thoughts and feelings to the exclusion of past experiences. It views the woman's state as a result of biological imbalance (Kendall, 2000b). While this may be a factor, what might be overlooked completely is her suffering from posttraumatic stress. Diagnoses that pathologize and stigmatize individual women are highly questionable. These approaches support the stigmatizing and traumatic environment of incarceration especially in terms of avoiding the role of external factors in women's lives.

There are other types of coping strategies in prison. While relationships in prison—pseudo-families and same-sex romantic coupling—are often written about in terms of inmate subculture, I believe there is also a strong coping component to them. In these pseudo-families, inmates take on family roles complete with kin terms of "mother," "father," "sister," "cousin," and so forth. In a study by Huggins (2000) of women inmates in Texas, the overwhelming reasons why women entered into pseudo-family relationships included to substitute for family on the outside, to feel accepted by other inmates, to feel love or to love someone, to not feel alone, and to talk and share problems. These relationships substitute for the nurturing that women miss or never had. In North Carolina, "state families," as pseudo-families are called, are quite common in medium-security prisons but diminish once women are in minimum-security facilities and receive home passes (Girshick, 1999).

Pseudo-families among women inmates establish a social order in the prison. These relationships provide support for resistance against other women who might try to harm or cheat a family member (Miller, 2000; Pollock, 1998). Another indication of how these relationships function is shown in the fact that in those where role relationships involve sexual intimacy, this intimacy is consensual rather than sexually violent (Miller, 2000).

Huggins (2000) found that about one-quarter of the inmates in her Texas study were involved in love relationships and another one-quarter in sexual relationships. Affection, care, and love were the major reasons for these relationships. According to Owen (1998) in her California study, these same-sex relationships are common, though many inmates insist they are unnatural. Girshick (1999) also found that many women in North Carolina prisons disapproved of both state families and same-sex relationships, yet they were apparently common as well. While these relationships held the possibility of exploitation (e.g., for canteen goods), sexual relationships tend to be consensual.

Coping with trauma while in prison is especially challenging for two reasons. First, abuses as a result of incarceration are in addition to the substantial trauma the women are coping with when entering prison. Second, there is a contradiction between available resources such as programs for battered women, which offer support, and access to protections such as grievance procedures, which utterly fail the sexually abused women. Perhaps the biggest obstacle to coping is the enormous strain of prison life, which by its very nature is oppressive. Even if there were no outright sexual abuse and rape, inmates would still be retraumatized by the other aspects of imprisonment. Dutton (1992) suggests that it may take a lifetime to completely transform trauma, especially with the occurrence of retriggering experiences. Root (1992) proposes that it is reasonable and normal for someone to take ten years or more to reorganize her shattered life, especially if she is in a setting with many cues that threaten her sense of security. In a prison setting, unless there are significant changes, I suggest that this may be nearly impossible.

Implications

When we as a society incarcerate women, we do not intend to solve every life problem or internal conflict that they enter prison with. However, it is in society's interest to acknowledge particularly glaring aspects of women's lives when these aspects have an impact not only on the well-being of the individual women but on how the prison system operates. Discipline issues, staffing effectiveness, programming, and our overall analysis of why people commit crimes and why they stop committing crimes can benefit by more closely examining abuse and its traumatic impact.

Departments of correction and prison administrators must acknowledge that the women in their charge have been substantially affected by their abuse histories. The implications of this suggest policy and program changes. The main policy changes relate to four areas: appropriateness of male and female guard duties; officer training regarding the impacts of abuse; officer training and enforcement about prison regulations; and effective grievance procedures for inmates.

In theory, male and female officers should be able to equally carry out their duties in any area of corrections. However, given the privacy rights of male and female prisoners, it does not seem unreasonable to limit supervision of housing areas (especially during third-shift hours), shower areas, and toilet areas. Most prisons already limit the conduct of strip searches to officers of the same sex as the inmates, yet this is often meaningless if male officers watch. Strictly enforced regulations about surveillance and strip and pat searches seem especially important in regard to the abuse histories of women and the privacy rights of both women and men in prison (Miller, 2000).

All correctional officers should be trained about the impacts of sexual and physical abuse so that they may more correctly assess inmate behavior. Coping strategies of women with posttraumatic stress disorder may appear to be aggressive or disrespectful when in reality they may be more about self-protection. Furthermore, officers will hopefully be less inclined to overreact by "throwing women in the hole" or placing them in restraints that traumatize them.

Human Rights Watch (1996) found that while states have rules in place regulating officer behavior, those rules are regularly disregarded. Guards are supposed to behave professionally but they often do not. Abusive and degrading language should not be tolerated. Guards should be disciplined for their unprofessional behaviors rather than having this behavior overlooked. Guards are prohibited from sexual contact with inmates, but many are apparently coercing women into sexual acts. Ambiguous policy and procedure language must be strengthened and women inmates must be informed of their rights.

This issue relates to the grievance process. In all cases, Human Rights Watch (1996) found that inmates are intimidated through lack of confidentiality, retaliation, and the futility of complaining against officers. Investigations must be thorough and sincere. Inmates should not be placed in administrative segregation, which is inherently punitive, during investigations. Inmates should be informed of how to file grievances and forms should be available for them. Filing a grievance should not be tantamount to loss of privileges for the inmate. If an investigation shows an officer has raped or otherwise abused an inmate, criminal charges should be filed. No pregnant inmate should be punished in order to coerce her to name her abuser, and abortions should never be forced on an inmate nor withheld if requested by the inmate. Clearly, the inability to act on her own behalf with the real possibility of redress duplicates the powerlessness experienced in the past. She has been—and continues to be—abused, controlled, and silenced. The repetition of this cycle is the crux of the problem.

In the programming arena, female inmates can benefit from the explicit interconnection of issues. Domestic violence, drug addiction, childhood abuse, and low education levels and poor work histories are interrelated problems. These issues should not be addressed in isolation from each other; rather, each program type should have components of the other issues within them. Abuse groups, for example, while focusing on the dynamics and impacts of battering and other forms of violence, would involve discussion of addiction, goal setting, self-esteem, and the like. Programs focused on assertiveness or empowerment would likewise refer to the issues the women are forced to come to terms with. A holistic approach is essential to relate to the women as they actually are. Programs where inmates are treated with respect are essential.

Even before programming begins, inmates need accurate assessment of their problems. An assessment should be done for PTSD, and mental illness diagnoses should be carefully screened rather than assumed. Medication can be helpful for women with PTSD but should be reevaluated regularly as programming begins to ease some of the trauma symptoms. Prisons should avoid overmedicating inmates. It is questionable whether any programming can be effective in an environment where inmates are dependent on officers, where inmates have so little control over their lives. In a program evaluation of therapeutic services for the Correctional Service of Canada, inmates pointed to these key needs: "A space to be themselves (a respite from a sense of constant surveillance), to be in control of their own lives and/or an opportunity to value and be valued by others," aspects of incarceration that prisons "inherently suppress and deny" (Kendall, 1994: 8). In fact, Kendall (1994) suggests that, given the antitherapeutic environment of prisons, perhaps the best we can offer inmates in terms of programming is to be sympathetic listeners, to assist with communication with their family and friends on the outside, and to help with preparing for parole and housing upon release.

One approach to this problem is to use more community corrections options whereby women are placed in intensive case management programs but live in their communities. It not only is less expensive for the taxpayer, but the potential benefits for the supervised women are greater. Simultaneous to working on reestablishing safety and security in dealing with their PTSD, women could be studying for their general (high school) equivalency diploma (GED), participating in job training programs, taking parenting or anger management classes, and so forth.

The insidious nature of abuse is seen clearly by the fact that violence against women is portrayed as a "woman's" issue when it is males who commit the vast number of battering and sexual crimes. Advocates in the community need to continue their work on women's rights issues to press for attitude shifts, changes in the laws, and greater resources for women and children in need. Addressing the external factors of abuse of women is crucial so that social problems are not seen and responded to as individual pathology.

Conclusion

A worthy goal for any department of corrections is that women leave prison stronger than when they came in. "Stronger" means they have a sense of efficacy in their lives, that they have healed some of their wounds, and that they can try to rebuild their lives. The stories of inmates' abuses relate an oppressive feature of women's experience; however, these women are never "only" oppressed. There are always aspects of resistance (Stewart, 1994). We should build on women's resilience. Within programs women form bonds and receive support (Leventhal, 2000) and feelings of isolation are disrupted (Heney and Kristiansen, 1998).

As long as we continue to incarcerate women, we must continuously look for ways to be more aware of the gendered aspects of our lives—the abuse histories of females being one. Prisons do not have to be managed in a way that leads to the revictimization of inmates. We can reduce the behaviors that retrigger trauma. Treating women inmates with respect and compassion would alter the entire atmosphere in women's prisons. Their reactivity would diminish. While guards will always hold power over inmates, there is no reason why this power needs to be abusive. Prisons could explore to what extent decisionmaking can be shared by inmates, or in what realms inmates could have more control over their lives. Short of stopping abuse before it begins, the next best measure is treating the survivors of abuse so that they can heal from the trauma impacts. It must become a goal of corrections policy to stop the retraumatization of inmates. While security will obviously remain a top priority of prison administrators, so should guarding the well-being of inmates. A shift in this mandate could result in a less abusive prison environment, a move toward healing for incarcerated women, and a safer society overall.

6

Imprisoned Mothers and Their Children

Susan F. Sharp and M. Elaine Eriksen

The United States is waging war on poor women and their children. Over the past two decades, the United States has been incarcerating increasing numbers of women, with the "war on drugs" being the primary cause of the explosion in the female prison population. When determinate sentencing for drug possession moved into the forefront of criminal justice policy during the 1980s and early 1990s (Wonders, 1996), the female prison population increased fivefold (Ekstrand, Burton, and Erdman, 1999). Indeed, the growth of the female prison population has far surpassed that of the male prison population in recent years (Greenfeld and Snell, 1999a), and the imprisonment of women is still growing. These women have become the latest focus of the carceral system (Foucault, 1977). Their actions are now closely supervised and monitored within U.S. prisons. Furthermore, the prison system has become a depository for marginalized women. As Turk (1976) has argued, the law is a weapon that is often used by one group at the expense of another group. Through formalization of the legal system, the illusion of impartiality and lack of bias is created (Trevino, 1996).

Clearly, the bias in criminal justice policies disadvantages many poor women. Even more disturbingly, the women themselves are not the only ones affected. Their children, who remain invisible, are largely overlooked by the prison industry. However, a mother's imprisonment may have devastating effects on her children that must not be ignored. This chapter is devoted to an examination of some of the most dominant and harmful consequences of imprisoning mothers.

Although prisoners are largely male, the number of women affected by current policies is not inconsequential. By midyear 2001, 94,336 women were imprisoned (Beck, Karberg, and Harrison, 2002). These women were not primarily violent or dangerous offenders. Instead, they were convicted of nonviolent offenses, primarily drug possession and, to a lesser degree, larceny. Indeed, according to Chesney-Lind (1997: 95), "Women's crime, like girls' crime, is deeply affected by women's place. As a result, women's contributions to serious crime, like that of girls, are minor."

With the advent of determinate sentencing of low-level drug offenders, women were caught up in America's attempt to stop the drug trade by punishing those at the lower end of the spectrum of drug offenses. Indeed, as Chesney-Lind (1997) has observed, the war on drugs became a war on women, especially women of color. What is less obvious, however, is that we are engaging in a war on the families of these women, primarily their children.

With large numbers of mothers being imprisoned, it is imperative to explore the effects of our current policies on their children. Because women compose only 7 percent of all prisoners (Beck, Karberg, and Harrison, 2002), the effects of the incarceration of women are often overlooked or deemed inconsequential (Flavin, 2001). However, as Flavin (2001) suggests, by closely examining the realities of female imprisonment, we can readily see that the effects are devastating.

The vast majority of the women sent to prison are mothers of minor children, and in most cases these children lived with their mothers prior to the incarceration. According to a recent government report, nearly two-thirds of the women in U.S. prisons were mothers of children under age eighteen; 64 percent of them reported living with their children prior to incarceration (Mumola, 2000). To put this in perspective, in 1999 approximately 115,500 minor children had mothers who were incarcerated in state prisons and an additional 10,600 children had mothers incarcerated in federal prisons (Mumola, 2000). In our haste to "punish" these women for what are primarily drug offenses and thefts, we are punishing their children as well, despite our lip service to the importance of maintaining families. Indeed, rather than strengthening families, the U.S. criminal justice apparatus appears to be weakening them. Research has documented a strong negative correlation between incarceration rates and good environments for raising children. Using a number of indicators to rank the child-raising environments, including the percentage of children allegedly abused or neglected, infant mortality, and juvenile arrests, states with the highest incarceration rates were determined to be the worst places to raise children (Ferrari et al., 2001). While the report drew no causal conclusions about the relationship between imprisoning mothers and the well-being of children, the findings suggest that there is ample reason to be concerned about the long-term effects of locking up mothers.

Not surprisingly, the children of women of color are the most likely to be adversely affected by current policies (Pollock, 1998). Two-thirds of the state female prisoner population and more than 70 percent of the women in federal prisons are nonwhite (Greenfeld and Snell, 1999a). These women are often mothers of dependent children. Statistics indicate that African American children are nearly nine times more likely than white children to have a parent in prison (Mumola, 2000). Thus almost 7 percent of black children under age eighteen, or nearly 800,000 children, have at least one parent incarcerated (Mumola, 2000). Although the majority of incarcerated parents are men, women of color are vastly overrepresented in the incarcerated female population. African American women are five and a half times more likely than white women and three times more likely than Hispanic women to be incarcerated (Beck, Karberg, and Harrison, 2002).

The prison system has evolved from society's need to somehow separate from the population at large those who were deemed dangerous to society (Foucault, 1977). In the twenty-first century, men are sent to prison because society perceives them as "dangerous" (Barak, Flavin, and Leighton, 2001; Shelden, 2001; Steffensmeier, Ulmer, and Kramer, 1998). In essence, the prison system serves as a place to keep those who appear to threaten the social order. Marginalized groups become redefined "as either 'bad' or 'mad'" (Barak, Flavin, and Leighton, 2001: 242). The assumption is made that repressive enforcement of the laws will somehow maintain the stability of society (Barak, Flavin, and Leighton, 2001).

Women who come under the jurisdiction of the criminal justice system, however, are not necessarily perceived as dangerous. Instead, they threaten the moral conscience of the dominant group, and thus the social order, by failing to meet proscribed standards of "appropriate womanhood." Despite the political focus on "family values," women who do not conform to middle-class cultural standards are more likely to be imprisoned (Belknap, 2001; Culverson, 1998; Erez, 1992; Humphries et al., 1995; Kruttschnitt, 1981; Sharp, Braley, and Marcus-Mendoza, 2000; Wonders, 1996). Even the courts have been used to control the behavior of those who do not meet rigid gender roles for women and mothers (Lynch, Michalowski, and Groves, 2000), and their children become innocent victims in the process.

The Madonna/whore dichotomy is used to view women (Feinman, 1986). Those who conform to the prescribed societal role are seen as "good girls." Those who do not meet the standards are seen as "bad girls," thus deserving of punishment for violation of social norms. This is particularly pertinent for nonwhite women, who are seen in general as violating cultural standards of femininity. Indeed, it has been suggested that for black women there is no "good girl" category (Young, 1986). Looking at the composition of the female offender population, the results are apparent. Not only are minority women more likely to be sentenced to prison, but they are also more likely to receive longer sentences. A recent study reported that black women were more likely than white women to receive sentences of five or more years, regardless of the offense or prior legal history. In contrast, white women were more likely to receive deferred adjudication (Sharp, Braley, and Marcus-Mendoza, 2000). Logically, then, we would expect the children of women of color to be even more adversely affected than white children.

It is readily apparent that a significant number of children are the invisible victims in the U.S. war on drugs. For that reason, several problems resulting from these incarceration policies must be addressed. One of the most pressing problems is the placement of minor children when the mother is sent to prison. A related issue is dealing with pregnant prisoners and the children born to them. Maintaining contact between female prisoners and their children is a problem resulting from incarceration of mothers. Finally, we must realistically and determinedly deal with the problems imprisoned mothers and their children face. Currently, little attention is paid to the needs of women in prison, but even less is paid to the needs of their children. Ideally, we should address these needs *before* sending the mother to prison. Interventions such as drug courts are potential alternatives. However, it is important to note that current diversionary responses can be cost-prohibitive. If we are unwilling to stop the mass incarceration of marginalized women, then we must work diligently to help them be successful upon release as well as work to ensure that the needs of their children are met.

Where Do the Children Go?

The criminology and criminal justice literature is predominantly andocentric, leaving the impression that "criminals" and prisoners are all alike—like men, that is. Because the information is based on men, the disparities in the experiences and backgrounds of women prisoners are often overlooked. This is extremely important in any study of the effects of incarceration on families. In 1997, Susan Marcus-Mendoza and I (Sharp) were commissioned by the Oklahoma Criminal Justice Research Center to do a study on the effects of incarceration on families of drug offenders (for more information, see Sharp et al., 1999; Sharp, Braley, and Marcus-Mendoza, 2000; Sharp and Marcus-Mendoza, 2001). As background information, we were referred to the proceedings of the Vera Justice Institute (1996; cf. Clear, 1996; Hagan, 1996; Moore, 1996; Watts and Nightingale, 1996). It was immediately apparent that the research focused on the families of male prisoners, with virtually no attention paid to female prisoners and their families. Family, the research suggested, consisted of the wife and children left behind when the father goes to prison. In our research proposal, we successfully argued that the project should instead focus on *gender differences* in the effects of incarceration. The research was framed in the argument that "family" quite often meant something different for female offenders (Sharp et al., 1998). For men prisoners, their family is one of two things: their parents or their wife/partner and children. However, most of the women who go to prison do not have a husband or partner in the home. Instead, their family is composed of their children as well as their parents and siblings. With the family composition different, the effects would thus be different and in need of research.

When a father goes to prison, the children usually remain with their mother. The family may experience turmoil and economic difficulties, but it remains intact, sans the father. However, the situation is quite different when a mother goes to prison. Unlike the children of incarcerated fathers, children whose mothers are in prison rarely remain with the other parent (Mumola, 2000). Female prisoners are three times more likely than male offenders to have been the only parent living with the children immediately prior to arrest (Mumola, 2000).

So, where these children go when their mother is sent to prison must be addressed. Statistics indicate that these children are usually sent to live with the mother's family members (Bloom and Steinhart, 1993; Mumola, 2000; Sharp and Marcus-Mendoza, 2001). Indeed, more than half of the mothers in state prisons reported that their children were living with a grandparent, and another one-fourth reported that their children were living with other relatives (usually the mother's sibling or an adult child). Sometimes family members are unwilling or unable to take the children, so an additional 10 percent were being cared for by foster parents or by agencies (Mumola, 2000). For children of women in federal prisons, family caretaking is even more important. Almost 90 percent of federal women prisoners reported that family members were taking care of their children (Mumola, 2000). Race is a factor is placement as well. Children of incarcerated white women were more likely to live with the children's fathers or in foster care. On the other hand, children of black and Hispanic women were more likely to be with the children's grandparents or other relatives (Enos, 2001).

Simply determining where the children live only addresses part of the problem, however. Often, family members can take some but not all of the children. Thus, many children are separated from each other as well as from their mothers (Belknap, 1996; Sharp and Marcus-Mendoza, 2001). Because one of every five incarcerated women has three or more children, the likelihood that the children may be separated from each other during the mother's incarceration period is high (Mumola, 2000; Sharp and Marcus-Mendoza, 2001). Furthermore, placement is not always constant. Many children are moved from one family member to another during the mother's prison term, further disrupting any sense of stability (McCarthy, 1980).

The most common placement is with the mother's own parent or parents (Bloom and Steinhart, 1993; Enos, 2001; Mumola, 2000; Sharp and Marcus-Mendoza, 2001). Mothers who are in prison often hope to regain custody upon release. Loss of the relationship with their children is the greatest fear of many incarcerated mothers (Enos, 2001; Sharp and Marcus-Mendoza, 2000, 2001). The maternal role is one of few positive options open to many of these women, so loss of that role may have negative consequences on a woman's emotional stability upon release (Correctional Service of Canada, 2001a, 2001b). Therefore, women often resist nonfamily placement, fearing it might lead to permanent loss of custody (Gaudin and Sutphen, 1993; Enos, 2001). The fear is realistic. It is not uncommon for parental rights to be involuntarily terminated during the mother's imprisonment (Bloom, 1993), and it may also be difficult for the mother to track her children's movement through the foster care system (Reed and Reed, 1997). Again, despite the emphasis on developing and maintaining healthy families, the punitive nature of the carceral system appears to work in quite the opposite way, further disrupting families of women prisoners.

While placement with family members may be the mother's first choice, it, too, has a downside. The families of most women prisoners face economic and emotional obstacles of their own, making it difficult to take on the added burden of caring for the children (Belknap, 1996; Enos, 2001; Sharp and Marcus-Mendoza, 2001). Moreover, more than 60 percent of women prisoners have been victims of childhood sexual or physical abuse (Greenfeld and Snell, 1999a), yet the children of women prisoners are living in the same homes in which their mothers' abuse occurred. One study reported that grandparents with a history of family violence were as likely as nonviolent grandparents to become primary caretakers for children of incarcerated mothers. Furthermore, 11 percent of women prisoners reported that their children were living with family members with a history of violence (Sharp and Marcus-Mendoza, 2001).

Recent statistics suggest that the percentage of female prisoners with abuse histories is increasing. Almost half of the women prisoners in 1997 reported that they had been physically abused, and more than one-third reported sexual abuse (Ekstrand, Burton, and Erdman, 1999). Clearly, the family members of women prisoners may not always be the safest caretakers for their children. The problem is exacerbated by the added stress that children may add to the family, making the potential for the children's abuse unsettling. However, because these children are "invisible," little attention is paid to whether or not they are placed in safe environments. Furthermore, the policies that promote loss of parental rights may be placing children in dangerous situations.

The scant research that addresses this issue does not alleviate these concerns. When the quality of care given to infants and preschool children by familial caregivers was compared with that given by foster caregivers, significant differences were found in the care of preschool children. Higher quality of both material and emotional care was found in foster placements than in family placements. Family members "offered significantly less verbal attention and positive social reinforcement to the children in their care" (Gaudin and Sutphen, 1993: 143). Overall, the research clearly indicates that prisoner mothers are faced with a distressing choice: between the risk of permanently losing their children and the risk of placing their children in potentially harmful situations. Girshick (1999: 116) suggests that these women experience distress as a result of having no good option. Obviously, policies of terminating parental rights need to be reexamined and perhaps changed. One alternative would be the development of policies that work toward reunification of mother and children, regardless of where the children may live during the mother's imprisonment.

Babies Born in Prison

More than 1,400 children were born to incarcerated mothers in 1998. However, most prisons are ill-equipped to deal with pregnant women and their offspring, leading one researcher to conclude that existing programs are "inadequate at best" (Daane, 2002: 61). In some cases, the prison's policies are even dangerous. According to a 1999 Amnesty International report, only one state banned outright the shackling of pregnant women while moving them to the hospital to give birth, and twenty-nine states allowed restraints to be used during labor and even during delivery. These policies could compromise the health of both the mother and the child. The loss of time to unshackle the mother may be a matter of life or death if complications arise. This is particularly serious when one considers that pregnancies of imprisoned mothers are far more likely to be high-risk than average pregnancies. The low socioeconomic status, drug use, and histories of domestic violence common among women prisoners increase the likelihood of problems during pregnancy and delivery (Acoca, 1998; Amnesty International, 1999; Kitzinger, 2001). However, correctional policies unnecessarily place women and their babies at risk, in order to "protect" society from these nonviolent offenders.

Better prenatal care is essential to ensure healthy birth outcomes (Markovic, 1995). An interesting program that has developed in England for pregnant prisoners should be considered in the United States. In London, volunteers assist women prisoners during labor and delivery. These *doulas* help the incarcerated woman develop a birth plan, support her through the birth process, and act as intermediaries with health care professionals (Parkinson, 2001). The emphasis on becoming proactive in her pregnancy and birthing can encourage the pregnant prisoner to take steps that increase the likelihood of more positive birth outcomes.

Additionally, facilitation in obtaining temporary child care is needed (Belknap, 2001). According to Daane (2002), the health needs of pregnant prisoners are just one facet of the problem; these women also face the related issues of child placement and separation grief. The punitive stance of most U.S. prisons, however, does little to address these concerns. Additionally, mothers have little if any contact with their newborns in many jurisdictions, thus allowing little chance for mother and child to bond (Kitzinger, 2001; Owen, 1998). In order to ensure adequate maternal and infant health, women should not be incarcerated during all or at least part of their pregnancies (Acoca, 1998). Probation or community-based alternatives may be a better option. If we as a country are indeed concerned about the health and safety of children, it is essential that we reconsider our current stance. Current criminal justice policies may be causing harm, even death, to the babies born to incarcerated mothers. The "just desserts" doctrine is thus being applied to those who are the most vulnerable and innocent.

Arranging for custody of babies born in prison is also a major issue. In many cases, a woman may have little opportunity to notify relatives who could take custody of the child. In some jurisdictions, if the family cannot arrive at the birth location within a designated time period, the baby is taken into the custody of the state (Sharp and Marcus-Mendoza, 2000). One of the difficulties with this policy is that many families live at a distance from the hospital. Their ability to gain custody of the newborn is contingent on both the prisoner's ability to notify them she has given birth and on their own ability to get to the prison quickly. Due to distance and their own obligations, the latter may simply not be feasible.

Historically in the United States, separation of women prisoners from their newborn infants has not always been the policy. The emphasis on traditional female roles in early women's reformatories encouraged the bonding between mothers and newborns. Infants, therefore, remained with mothers, often for extended periods (Belknap, 2001). Other countries, such as Canada, also allow time for bonding. In Canada, pregnant prisoners may apply for compassionate release to community sentencing (Correctional Service of Canada, 2001a, 2001b). It is interesting that despite the U.S. emphasis on the importance of maintaining intact families, we have policies designed to further the disruption of families. On the one hand, we decry family disruption, equating it with the genesis of criminal behavior. On the other hand, U.S. penal policies seem designed to create and further disruption of families. Perhaps Reiman's contention (1998) that the purpose of prisons is to fail at crime control is not a far-fetched explanation. The marginal classes and their children are expendable, and cycling them through the criminal justice system serves its own purpose, fueling the private prison industry while diverting attention away from "less serious" corporate crime (Lynch, Michalowski, and Groves, 2000). Regardless of the reasons, the results of current penal practices separate mothers from their children, even immediately following birth.

There are a few important exceptions. New York's Bedford Hills program allows mothers to keep their infants with them until the first birthday, but infants are allowed to remain until the mother is released if that date is within eighteen months. Women rotate working in the nursery, caring for the children. The program promotes healthy parenting skills, with inmates teaching other inmates. This involvement of other prisoners as sources of peer counseling and support is essential (Morash, Bynum, and Koons, 1998), with research on men prisoners indicating that this involvement increases the potential for success upon release (Hairston and Lockett, 1985).

The Bedford Hills program also runs a summer camp program for older children. During the camp, children stay with host families, attending the on-site program during the day. Bedford Hills is widely acclaimed as a model program, allowing mothers to bond with their newborns while also learning healthy and effective parenting skills (Boudin, 1998; Morash, Bynum, and Koons, 1998).

There are other "babies behind bars" programs that allow infants to remain with their mothers in eleven states as well as in the Federal Bureau of Prisons. Seven states accomplish this through community-based programs, while the four remaining states incorporate nurseries into the prison setting (Ekstrand, Burton, and Erdman, 1999). The Federal Bureau of Prisons program includes prenatal classes, social services, and life-skills training. At least two months before anticipated delivery, mothers are moved to a community facility. There, they remain with their newborns for three months after birth. At that time, the mother is returned to prison (Ekstrand, Burton, and Erdman, 1999). The way in which this program operates has both positive and negative features. While it does allow early bonding between the mother and infant, after the brief period of bonding the mother and infant are separated. Research has not yet indicated the degree to which this abrupt separation may be harmful for the baby as well as the mother.

There is no consistent agreement about the benefits of allowing pregnant prisoners or other imprisoned mothers to keep their children with them. Some have raised the issue of the potential of harm to infants from living in a prison setting. They cite the lack of stimulation and normalcy as potential problems (Drummond, 2001). Furthermore, not all prisoner mothers want their children with them. Indeed, some do not even want visits from their children. These women say they do not want their children to see their mother in the prison environment and fear the pain of watching their families leave but not being able to leave with them (Owen, 1998).

The debate over infants in prison is far from being settled. While, advocates cite the many benefits, opponents cite the negative results. Again, the best option would be to not imprison pregnant women, in most cases. However, as we have seen, the well-being of women and their children is not a primary concern of the system.

Mother-Child Contact

For women prisoners who have been the major caretakers of young children, incarceration affects their relationships with their children while they are imprisoned (Bloom, 1993). It also can create problems upon release (Sobel, 1982). Thus the level of contact maintained between imprisoned mothers and their children is of utmost concern. However, the U.S. prison system is not conducive to maintaining strong mother-child relationships (Bloom, 1993).

Three types of contact between incarcerated mothers and their children are noteworthy: mail, telephone calls, and visits. Most mothers in prison report some sort of weekly contact with their children (Mumola, 2000). However, mail contact appears to be the most common, with almost two-thirds of the women in state prisons and three-fourths of those in federal prisons reporting they received mail from their children at least once a month (Mumola, 2000). It is important to remember, however, that many of the children of incarcerated mothers are too young to read or write, and mail contact may provide little comfort to toddlers who miss their mother.

Telephone calls provide more personal contact for the mother and her children, and almost half of imprisoned mothers have telephone contact with their children at least weekly. However, telephone contact with individuals in prison must be collect, and the cost can be financially devastating for already impoverished families. A fifteen-minute telephone call can cost more than thirteen dollars (Sharp and Marcus-Mendoza, 2000). The cost of maintaining this more personal type of contact, in addition to the cost of supporting the women's children, may compound problems faced by the family members who are caring for the prisoner's children.

There may be other restrictions on telephone contact (Bloom, 1993). Telephone contact is sometimes considered a privilege that must be earned. For example, in Oklahoma, telephone contact in the early stages of incarceration is limited to clergy and attorneys. It may take weeks or even months for the mother to be allowed to call others, weeks when her children may feel abandoned by their mother. At a time when the relationship has been suddenly disrupted, contact is not allowed. This can increase the stress of both the mothers and their children, who are unable to verbally reassure each other (Sharp and Marcus-Mendoza, 2000).

It may also be difficult for mothers to call at times convenient for the family. Although the woman may have a general idea of when telephone time is allowed, she must also wait her turn to use the telephone. Additionally, the prison is not run to benefit the prisoners but rather to facilitate the job of the guardians. Telephone time may be curtailed by inmate count times or by events that disrupt the regular flow of prison life.

The most intimate type of contact, visitation, is often not possible for women prisoners and their children. Indeed, the majority of the women in state prisons never receive visits from their children (Ekstrand, Burton, and Erdman, 1999). The physical locations of women's prisons are a major factor. Females compose a small percentage of total prison populations. Consequently there are fewer correctional facilities for female prisoners. The end result is that prisoners may be housed at considerable distance from their families (Bloom, 1993). Indeed, most women prisoners are housed over 100 miles from where they lived immediately prior to incarceration (Beck and Karberg, 2001). It is even worse in the federal system, with more than half of the women imprisoned more than 250 miles from home and nearly 30 percent more than 500 miles from home (Ekstrand, Burton, and Erdman, 1999). Hence, taking children to visit their mothers is a costly and time-consuming endeavor. Since women prisoners and the family members taking care of their children frequently come from lower socioeconomic strata, it is easy to see how the problem of distance can translate into no visitation. Furthermore, many women's prisons are located in rural areas with limited public transportation available. Conversely, many of the women come from urban areas, often far away. If the family does not own an automobile that is trustworthy, it may be impossible to take children to visit their incarcerated mother.

The use of private prisons to incarcerate women can also create visitation problems. Because of the rapid growth of the female prisoner population over the past fifteen years, adequate facilities have not been available to house them in some states. These states have thus turned to private industry for solutions. However, private prisons are not under the same constraints as public prisons. Unlike the public sector, which must garner taxpayer approval prior to construction of new prisons, the private prison industry faces fewer restraints. Furthermore, private prisons are not under the same disclosure requirements as the public sector (Barak, Flavin, and Leighton, 2001). They serve as warehouses, providing inmate beds to any willing payer. In Oklahoma, for example, a research team went to a facility to administer a survey, only to discover that more than eighty women had been suddenly transferred without notice to a privately operated facility in Texas (Sharp et al., 1998, 1999; Sharp and Marcus-Mendoza, 2001). This problem has been solved with the construction of a new private prison in the state. However, the private prison now houses women from other states, currently Wyoming and Hawaii. It is obvious that the distances from their home states will result in few children being able to visit their incarcerated mothers.

The problem of limited visitation with children is not just a question of "pampering" women prisoners, despite conservative outcries to that effect. Parent-child visitation has been found to have many positive benefits for both children and parents. Children who can visit their parents are more able to express their feelings about separation. Their fears about what has happened to their mother can be reduced when they see where their mother is living. Similarly, mothers whose children visit are more able to work through their separation anxiety and grief. Finally, visitation increases the chances for successful family reunification through maintenance of ties (Gabel and Johnston, 1995; Henriques, 1996). Maintaining relationships with family while in prison is a strong predictor of reduced recidivism. While there is scant research about the role of visitation and women's successful releases, one can draw some conclusions by examining research with male prisoners. One study of male inmates reported reduced recidivism for men who had three or more visitors in the year prior to their release. Furthermore, furloughs and overnight visits from family were also predictors of success (Hairston, 1991a). Given the importance of children to women prisoners (Owen, 1998), women should benefit from visits at least as much as men, if not far more.

Maintaining contact between the imprisoned mother and her children is essential in order to minimize the disruption to the family. Imprisonment disrupts the family in two ways. First, family cohesion is threatened. The sense of being a family may become fragile, and maintaining consistent contact is one way to minimize the harm. Second, the relationship between the mother and her children becomes strained

(Clear, 1996; Hagan, 1996; Hairston and Lockett, 1987: 162). The degree to which parent-child separation is problematic is a "glaring difference between the male and female prison experience" (Harris, 1993: 53). Furthermore, contact with loved ones outside the prison helps prisoners to maintain mental health (Hairston, 1991a), but women prisoners sometimes cope by not thinking about "outside." This can then further harm the already tenuous relationships with children (Owen, 1998), which in turn affects the prisoner's mental health even more, and so the cycle continues.

Both the mother and the children may experience depression as a result of her imprisonment (Koban, 1983; Henriques, 1996; Siegal, 1997; Sharp and Marcus-Mendoza, 2000, 2001). For women offenders, their relationships with their children may be the only positive thing in their lives (AIM, 2001; Girshick, 1999; Owen, 1998; Sharp et al., 1999). Loss of these relationships can be devastating, leading to depression (Girshick, 1999; Owen, 1998).

Children are also negatively affected. Depression is a common response to a mother's incarceration (AIM, 2001; Bloom and Steinhart, 1993; Moses, 1995; Sharp et al., 1999; Sharp and Marcus-Mendoza, 2001). The children of women prisoners have often lost not only their caretaker but also their homes. They may be afraid for their mother, and they are frequently separated from siblings (Belknap, 1996; Bloom and Steinhart, 1993; Markovic, 1995; Sharp and Marcus-Mendoza, 2001). School performance may be affected, often leading to dropping out (Hagan, 1996; Moses, 1995; Sharp et al., 1999; Sharp and Marcus-Mendoza, 2001). Finally, imprisoning mothers perpetuates the cycle of crime and incarceration. The children themselves begin getting arrested (AIM, 2001; Bloom and Steinhart, 1993; Clear, 1996; Hagan, 1996; Owen, 1998; Siegal, 1997; Zaplin and Dougherty, 1998).

The large numbers of incarcerated mothers and children affected by current incarceration policies indicates that there is a significant need for addressing their problems through prison programming (Bloom, 1993; Bloom and Steinhart, 1993). However, to date there has been little done to acknowledge this pressing issue, much less to curtail the negative impact on incarcerated mothers and their children. There are a few programs currently in place that are designed to increase mother-child contact. Almost half of the parenting programs examined in a recent national study fit this category (Morash, Bynum, and Koons, 1998). However, "contact" is somewhat loosely defined, with programs ranging from long-distance relationships to extensive visitation. Reading

Family Ties, a Florida program, uses computers in an innovative approach to maintaining contact between mothers and children (Drummond, 2001). Other programs encourage personal contact, including a North Carolina program that offers home passes and occasional family retreats in conjunction with a local church. Priority for the overnight retreats is given to women whose children are unable to visit regularly (Girshick, 1999).

However, most prison systems do not go to great lengths to facilitate mother-child contact. Ekstrand, Burton, and Erdman (1999) undertook an in-depth analysis of women's needs and available programs in California, Texas, and the Federal Bureau of Prisons. Of the three, only California offered overnight visitation. In other states, available programs included regular visitation, overnight visitation, special programs for mothers and children, parental education, and residential mother/child programs (Zaplin and Dougherty, 1998). Additionally, some states offer "Girl Scouts Beyond Bars" (Moses, 1995). The program, initiated at the Maryland Correctional Institution for Women, has spread to other states. Supporters contend that the program benefits both mothers and daughters by providing more than visits. Prisoners attend two Girl Scout meetings per month with their daughters on the prison grounds. In these meetings, mothers and daughters work together on projects and crafts. The program has other requirements that may benefit the prisoner mothers. Each woman must attend a monthly one-hour group with a social worker. However, the program is not without flaws. First, the program provides contact between mothers and their daughters but not between mothers and their sons. Furthermore, although the women are involved in the groups with the social worker, no mental health services are afforded their daughters or the children's caregivers. The program also has a serious downside in some locations. When the mother is transferred to prerelease, her participation is ended. Shortly before release, when logic dictates that contact between the prisoner and her children should be increased, it is instead decreased (Moses, 1995).

Others programs have evolved that help maintain contact between imprisoned mothers and their children. MATCH (Mothers and Their Children) programs, which originated in a federal institution, have spread to other locations. In MATCH programs, Children's Centers for play and learning allow the mothers and their children to work and play together, developing healthy bonds. Support and referral services for child custody issues are also part of the programs. MATCH programs also provide services that are indispensable to success upon release, including individual and family counseling, transition services, and referrals (Boudouris, 1996). Another program, the Mother-Offspring Life Development (MOLD), uses five visitation days per month as a reward to prisoners for good behavior (Zaplin and Dougherty, 1998).

While these programs do increase the contact between some inmate mothers and their children, taken alone they cannot undo the harm caused by imprisoning mothers. Remember, many women's families live too far away to participate. Even when the family can participate, most programs merely offer slightly more frequent visitation. The programs that offer additional elements, especially counseling and transition services, have the most promise. However, these programs are few and far between, and for the most part the children of women prisoners remain invisible, out of sight and out of mind as far as the criminal justice apparatus and the general public are concerned.

Postrelease Services and Alternatives to Incarceration

If we are to continue imprisoning mothers, postrelease and transition services are essential to successful outcomes. Most programs provide minimal transitional services. The few existing programs that do provide postrelease assistance are an exciting development. However, because they are costly, it is unlikely that they will be adopted on a widespread basis. The Women's Prison Association (WPA) in New York City is the most promising. During 1996–1997, WPA programs placed 99 women in permanent housing and aided 344 mothers and 286 minor children (Conly, 1998). The programs are structured to help women work toward reunification with their children after incarceration. First, women learn skills necessary to successful reintegration into society. For many women, the program is their first opportunity to learn how to perform simple daily tasks like budgeting. Next, women are placed in an apartment while they work toward regaining custody of their children. When the mother and children are deemed ready, they get their own apartment. The program provides social services, including psychological screening and referrals for the children (Conly, 1998). In the final phase, mother and children receive assistance in obtaining permanent housing, locating suitable employment for the mother, obtaining financial and social services, peer support groups, life-skills training, parenting education, and extensive follow-up and case management (Conly, 1998).

The WPA program provides a solution when the mother has been imprisoned. However, researchers and activists alike have argued that instead of after-the-fact attempts to undo the damage of maternal incarceration, finding an alternative to prison is a more fruitful direction (Acoca, 1998; Chesney-Lind, 1991; JusticeWorks Community, 2001). The PACT (Parents and Children Together) program is dedicated to keeping nonviolent women offenders and their children together. The program provides medical care, child care, and counseling services to the family. It is not administered by the state department of corrections, which is unusual. And unlike many programs, there are no limitations on age or number of children (JusticeWorks, 2001). Similarly, the California Mother-Infant Care program allows mothers and infants to stay together in a community-based facility (Siegal, 1997). Mothers can eventually earn the right to have work furloughs, better preparing them for a return to the community (Ekstrand, Burton, and Erdman, 1999).

Conclusion

The machinery of the criminal justice system has caught women and children in its grip, with little thought or planning for the consequences. The "gender neutrality" of the war on drugs has not been neutral. As Girshick (1999: 24) observes:

> One problem with "get tough" policies is that nonviolent offenders are treated as if they were violent criminals. The "war on drugs" imprisons both petty dealers and drug lords. Women, who commit more nonviolent crimes, are paying disproportionately for society's response to violent offenders, who are primarily men.

Girshick's assessment is correct, but it does not go far enough. She failed to mention the dependent children of these women. Children of women offenders are the invisible victims of the "wars" on crime and drugs. For the most part, their plight is ignored. These children and their mothers are "throwaways," persons of little consequence. Indeed, in some states the correctional system does not even track what happens to the children when the mother is imprisoned.

While some programs and pilot programs have been developed for offender mothers and their children, these reach few of those affected. If we are to stop this injustice of the criminal "justice" apparatus, it is imperative that we focus on the effects of maternal incarceration. Ideally, we should rethink our current approach and refrain from imprisoning women for crimes that are the consequence of their marginalization. Developing programs that combat poverty and its related problems would benefit these women and society far more. Clearly, Girshick is correct when she argues that "our questions need to be about women, not about crime or prisons, and about who women are and how they become what they are" (1999: 26). By acknowledging who these "new women criminals" really are, we can more clearly address their needs.

However, the machinery of the criminal justice system currently pulls women into its clutches. For that reason, we must develop programs that help women and their children who are caught up in the system. In particular, programs that offer alternatives to incarceration and postrelease transition services have promise. There is, however, a caveat. Many alternative programs require that the offender make restitution. Given the obligations to support a family and the low earning ability of most women offenders, this may set the women up for failure rather than success (O'Brien, 2001). Further evaluation of what works for women offenders *and their children* is needed. We need to examine the degree to which programs affect the life chances of mothers and children alike.

As long as the United States continues its love affair with incarceration, marginalized populations will remain at risk. Clearly, poor women, especially women of color, are endangered. These women are the casualties of the war on drugs, their children the "collateral damage." Until the illusion of impartiality of the criminal justice system (Trevino, 1996) is made apparent, it is imperative that feminist and critical scholars continue to depict the consequences—for both mothers and children—of imprisoning women. Likewise, it is imperative that we continue to search for programs to ameliorate these consequences.

7

Gender, Race, and Sexuality in Prison

Mary Bosworth

Prisons are, by nature, sites of inequality, control, and oppression. They are the means by which society regulates, and on some level hopes to transform, its criminal, its poor, its unwanted, its disturbed, and its sometimes-violent members. Increasingly, prisons have become the destination for growing numbers of minorities and women. Despite the undeniable restrictions faced by prison inmates, however, much literature suggests that relations of domination and subordination in penal institutions are not completely fixed. Rather, within certain boundaries that are dictated by the practicalities of daily life, power relations are constantly negotiated.

In order to engage actively with the regime and with one another, prisoners must successfully construct themselves as agents, despite the restrictions placed upon them. They must, in other words, transcend their stigmatized identities as prisoners to present themselves as individuals with rights and the ability to "get things done." To do this, they draw upon their lived experiences outside the prison walls, laying claim to their experiences and preincarceration identities. Such characteristics, which are generally representative of their race, gender, class, and sexuality, in turn underpin and help structure their means of coping with confinement.

In this chapter I shall trace the relationship between power and identity by describing research I conducted in three women's prisons in England in the mid-1990s.[1] I hope to clarify how sociocultural identities are imbricated in daily prison life by examining women's accounts of incarceration. In this way, I shall discuss how power relations in the prison, as outside, rest on ideas, experiences, and representations of race, gender and sexuality. I shall consider, in other words, how power is shaped by identity politics. Radically updating Erving Goffman's analysis of total institutions (1961), I hope to demonstrate how power relations in prison are negotiated through the presentation of self.

Methodology: Doing Feminist Research

In my research, I visited a "closed" medium-security and an "open" minimum-security establishment as well as a remand center where women were held awaiting trial or pending sentencing. I stayed in each prison for an average of about four weeks, conducting detailed, semi-structured interviews. In total I recorded discussions with fifty-two women, who ranged in age from eighteen to fifty-eight years, and in sentence length from a matter of weeks to life. These prisoners, the majority of whom were white, were doing time for crimes from shoplifting to murder. Most of them were drug (ab)users of some sort, mothers, and unemployed. Many were survivors of physical and sexual abuse (for greater detail, see Bosworth, 1999b).

Like many feminist researchers, I tried to break down barriers between myself and the women I interviewed (Fonow and Cook, 1991; Gelsthorpe and Morris, 1990; Reinharz, 1992). I endeavored to destabilize some of the methodological traditions of prison studies by creating an ongoing dialogue between my empirical and theoretical research as well as with the women. To do this, I used a variety of interview techniques, from group discussions to one-on-one sessions. I distributed written questionnaires to some, and spoke informally to others. To tie the interviews together, I collected standardized information about a range of topics including the women's socioeconomic background, previous times in prison, and other issues related to their experiences in prison (see the appendix to Bosworth, 1999b). Such continuity later helped me identify patterns among the prisoners' testimonies.

Rather than looking for a fully "representative" sample, I aimed for diversity. Similarly, instead of representing the women as the final arbiters of truth, I sought to weave their stories with secondary literature on punishment, imprisonment, and gender. Most important, I strove to join theory and practice, applying ideas from feminist debates about identity and subjectivity to what I saw, and to what the women told me.

Identity Politics: Destabilizing "Woman"

In the 1990s, following the demise of Marxism and in response to the political gains made by many social movements in the previous decades, identity or the "self" became *the* topic of contemporary theorists in a range of fields. Scholars everywhere discussed how "self-identity is not something that is just given, but something that has to be routinely created and sustained in the reflexive activities of the individual" (Giddens, 1991: 52). Most people agreed that who we are and who we perceive ourselves to be are subject to a dialectic of control that is both internally driven and externally defined. We are always at the same time audience and actor. We view others while they look at us. As a result, the formation of our subjectivity is continually "in process" (Braidotti, 1994: 98) and dependent upon repetitive performativity (Butler, 1990).

Feminists, in particular, were often obsessed by identity, and their ensuing debates over essentialism and difference were heated (see, inter alia, Fuss, 1989; Butler, 1990; Young, 1990; Braidotti, 1994; Schor and Weed, 1994; Benhabib et al., 1995). Much of their discussion rested on the definition of "woman." While liberal feminists had traditionally invoked an undifferentiated figure of "woman" as the subject and object of their political goals, since the 1980s other feminists had queried this construct. In particular, women of color and lesbian feminists had argued for a long time that the "woman" in whose name feminists fought often excluded their needs and experiences (hooks, 1981; Wittig, 1981). A sense of self lay at the heart of this argument since, as bell hooks put it, "Contemporary black women could not join together to fight for women's rights because we did not see 'womanhood' as an important aspect of our identity" (hooks, 1981: 1).

When combined in the early 1990s with the effect of postmodernism, which everywhere declared the death of man, history, and "truth," such a rejection of essentialism led to a radical reconsideration of the (literal and figurative) subject of feminism. While some, like Judith Butler, excitedly wondered "what new shape of politics emerges when identity as a common ground no longer constrains the discourse on feminist politics" (1990: ix), others were less sanguine. Seyla Benhabib (1995: 29), for example, wondered how it could be possible for someone to act, and others to organize, if there is no longer a belief in "a self-reflective subject, capable of acting on principle."

At the same time that feminists were arguing over the impact of postmodernism upon the goals of the women's movement, many male theorists were also discussing the meaning of identity and subjectivity, albeit in a somewhat different form. A range of scholars, from Anthony Giddens (1991) to Nikolas Rose (1989, 1996), proposed that identity and agency were the most crucial challenges of the late twentieth and the twenty-first centuries. According to this view, a defining characteristic of our time is the fluidity of our sense of self and the fundamentally restricted nature of our agency. No longer part of well-defined community groups or other social organizations, people are able to move much more freely through time and space than ever before. Most of us, however, have limited ability to control the shape of our own lives. Whether subject to the whims of global capitalism, anachronistic electoral systems, or entrenched race relations, we are constantly confronted with our own powerlessness.

Although sometimes seemingly divorced from "real" women's lives due to their philosophical density, such debates over identity provide a fruitful source of inspiration for the analysis of imprisonment. Prisons, after all, are based in large part on the regulation of identity. Not only do penal institutions offer numerous courses in dealing with offending behavior, drug addiction, alcoholism, and other matters, but prisoners also have to change their behavior and sense of self to deal with their term of confinement.

Similarly, prisoners, by virtue of their punishment, are denied most of the qualities associated with full adult status in a liberal democracy. Most important, they have little independence or autonomy. All aspects of their daily lives are decided for them, including what they may eat and what they may wear. As feminist philosopher Iris Marion Young points out, we are usually trained to place much weight on such issues. It is generally thought, according to Young (1997: 126), that

> respecting individuals as full citizens means granting and fostering in them liberties and capacities to be autonomous—to choose their own ends and develop their own opinions. It also means protecting them from the tyranny of those who might try to determine those choices and opinions because they control the resources on which citizens depend for their living.

Despite the apparent benevolence of such views, they also serve to deny certain people the benefits associated with citizenship. Focusing on single mothers, for example, who are frequently dependent on the state for many things, Young (1997: 127) claims that those who are not fully independent "often have their autonomy limited in many ways," making them "second-class citizens."

In other words, those people, like prisoners, who have their choices and freedom severely curtailed may find it difficult to appeal to the generalized ideas of rights and justice. They may, as a result, turn only to their "concrete" needs, stressing the qualities that spring from their embodied selves rather than their universal identities as citizens.

In the following sections I will discuss how gender, race, and sexuality underpinned the women's sense of who they were. I will further demonstrate how they provided the basis for the women's interpretation of prisons and for their attempts to get things done. By drawing on theoretical literature outside criminology I will suggest how identity and agency are linked in women's prisons.

Gender: Femininity as Entrapment or Resistance

According to feminist theorists and others, gender is crucial to a person's sense of self. As Butler (1990: 25) writes: "It would be wrong to think that the discussion of 'identity' ought to proceed prior to a discussion of gender identity for the simple reason that 'persons' only become intelligible through becoming gendered in conformity with recognizable standards of gender intelligibility." Gender, is, in other words, a fundamental aspect of identity and, as a result, a profound source of self-identification (Goffman, 1977: 304). It is not, however, something fixed. Rather, as Simone de Beauvoir (1953) recognized so long ago, our identity as women is something we become. In the language of more contemporary feminists, it is a quality we act out, or, more accurately, an identity or role that we constantly try to perform. Categories like "woman" or "man" are, in other words, labels we hope to merit through consistently conforming behavior patterns.

The inherent flexibility accorded to gender by feminist theorists like Judith Butler is intriguing for interpreting prison life since it may offer new ways of understanding women's experiences of incarceration that can take account of their agency. While the existence of hegemonic notions of gender in any society mean that individuals usually conform to certain types of behavior, Butler and others suggest that at certain times, people may also misperform their gender. The potentially destabilizing effects of such activities, evident in the variety of ways in which normative gender identities are enforced throughout society, demonstrate the inherent power of gender, and its centrality to social relations. The question arises, then, whether women in prison may somehow harness this power of gender to "get things done."

Feminist criminologists commonly analyze how experiences of imprisonment for women are conditioned by discourses, or "regimes of femininity," which seek to regulate behavior through policing women's appearances, labor, and behavior (Carlen, 1983; Hannah-Moffat, 2001). Such scholars frequently discuss how female prisoners are offered predominantly gender-specific tasks and activities like sewing, cooking, and cleaning courses, and tend to be disciplined more harshly for minor infractions of prison rules. Likewise, they point out that women tend to be overmedicated both in the community and in prison if they are perceived to be refractory (Sim, 1990; Liebling, 1994; Auherhahn and Dermody Leonard, 2000).

However, criminologists have been less interested in the ways that the women themselves interpret the gendered restrictions they face, and their means of dealing with or resisting their control. In particular, they have tended to ignore the manner in which female prisoners often recognize the gendered machinations of power and punishment and how they are, at times, able to use similar ideas to attain their aims (however, see Bosworth, 1999b; Shaw, 1992). Without wishing to discount the very real paternalism of prison regimes, or the well-documented ways in which women are constantly taught outmoded feminine skills and behaviors instead of practical or employable ones, it may be possible, using ideas from feminist theory, to investigate how gender works in a more nuanced way that does not always fully restrict the agency of prisoners themselves. After all, as Erving Goffman (1977: 324) observes, "every physical surround, every room, every box for social gatherings, necessarily provides materials that can be used in the display of gender and the affirmation of gender." Consequently, unlike other aspects of their identity, particularly those associated with practical tasks, women are able to draw on their gendered identity while incarcerated. It may even be possible that women are able to lay claim to certain ideals of femininity for their own benefit.

First, it is important to recognize that many of the women themselves are cognizant of the dominant ideas of gender by which they are judged. As T. put it, "You get sentenced to prison and you get categorized, don't you? You're a woman, so you get this. You do dress-making, you do sewing. Because you're a woman." Some, like D., traced these ideas earlier within the criminal justice system, commenting that "it's seen as a man's thing to commit a crime, but women are supposed to be barefoot, chained to the sink, and pregnant. They are the mother figure." These same woman, many of whom, like J., claimed not to have "noticed" or been "bothered" by gender stereotypes in their lives outside prison, were often more attuned to them inside.

At least part of the reason for the women's newfound sensitivity to sexism may have been related to the manner in which each of the three prisons included in this study offered only highly gender-specific classes and employment. Other than a limited amount of maintenance work and gardening to keep the institutions going, women were instructed all but exclusively in activities involving traditional feminine skills like sewing, cooking, and cleaning. Many extracurricular courses or training reflected old-fashioned "women's skills" as is evident in classes in hairdressing, flower arrangement, and beauty. Although many women appreciated any further education offered to them, like D., they generally agreed that "they're not very practical things," asking, "Who's got the time to do silk painting on the outside?"

Another gendered characteristic of each regime that generated a lot of frustration was the experience of living in a community made up solely of women. In contrast to the situation in many U.S. prisons, where women may be at risk of sexual abuse from prison staff, most women appreciated the presence of male guards and personnel. Some, like J.A., exclaimed, "Can you imagine if there weren't male officers?!"

Despite their criticisms of the restrictions placed upon them as women, the prisoners themselves were clearly influenced by fairly rigid gender norms. Thus they commonly asserted that the most important need of women in prison was increased access to children, even if they themselves were not mothers. Just as outside the prison walls, for most prisoners, women were "supposed" to be, or at the very least should want to be, mothers. Similarly, most prisoners found the notion of "women's needs" a little mystifying as a category of analysis. Despite their criticism of specific examples of sexist treatment or behavior, the general category of "gender" as a basis for either judgment or action was, on the whole, unfamiliar to most. Few women self-identified as feminists. Given this situation, it is interesting to reflect on what role gender played in their negotiation of power relations in prison.

In my research experience, a gender identity enabled some women to recast themselves as more than just "prisoners." It even sometimes enabled them to reject some of the more negative associations with which they had become stigmatized as a result of their lawbreaking.

K.'s claim that "I'm a 100% mother. I've never spent a night away from my kids before" provided a buffer to the self-image she would otherwise have to adopt, that of a prisoner. Being a mother suggested that she had responsibilities, legitimacy, things to do. The implication was that she deserved a little respect. By insisting, moreover, that she was a "good mother" despite being in prison, K. raised the possibility, however fleetingly, that this loaded term may be more elastic than is usually thought.

A crucial result of confinement and punishment is that prisoners are disqualified from many rights and expectations associated with full agents. They have, in other words, lost their legitimacy. Though (usually) protected by certain legal, minimum standards of care, they are rarely constructed as, or encouraged to be, reasoning agents deserving to participate freely in their own decisionmaking. While feminist criminologists have long pointed out that traditional ideas of femininity tend to exacerbate this situation, they also paradoxically sometimes provide women with a means of resistance.

Women spoke frequently of attaining goals by representing their needs as being associated with their biology and their gender identities (see Bosworth, 1999b). For example, the final prison I visited, Winchester, was attached to a men's prison. As a result, all of the food and other services were generally produced in the men's side and brought over to the women's annex. The women, who wanted to be able to prepare and choose their own food, were engaged in a lengthy dispute about this situation. While in fact arguing for increased autonomy and choice, both supposedly gender-free attributes of adulthood, their strongest bid for reform rested on that traditional feminist enemy— good old-fashioned biological determinism. As M.C., a woman of color, put it, "Women's bodies are different from men's bodies, we have different needs. We lose blood every month, they don't. They don't seem to understand that. They don't seem to think that we need supplements for things like that."

Finally, it is worth noting that, for some women, prison seemed to offer them and their families an opportunity, however limited, to recognize how their lives outside were structured by gender. In a discussion about how their male partners were coping while they were incarcerated, three women, all of whom had young children, mentioned that their boyfriends or husbands were having to engage in the feminine tasks they had never before conducted. J., for example, said her partner was complaining about having "the kids all the time [because] they can be little monsters." Another woman, J.A., described her partner as initially "put[ting] this hard front on." He wrote in his first letter to her in prison: "'I miss you—I miss your cooking, I miss your cleaning.' It was all the things I actually do . . . at the end of it he just put 'ha ha,' but he meant it!" Over time, however, her boyfriend apparently reflected on her absence: "It made him realize though. Because in his last few letters he's been saying, 'I promise I won't come home from work late. I promise I won't go out for a drink.' . . . 'Cos now he knows what it's like to be at home on your own all day. . . . Now he realizes."

Agreeing with these two accounts, T. similarly talked about how difficult her husband was finding the responsibilities of full-time child care, a task that she normally did. According to her, his reaction was due to the fact that "half the time they [men] think, 'Oh, kids are no problem,' because they only see them for a few hours a day." Like J.A.'s boyfriend, however, her husband had somewhat revised his masculinity while she was in prison. Thus she reminisced:

> He doesn't want to show his feelings in front of anybody else. But the first day he came and visited me, he walked past the gates with his mates and I shouted "See you!" and he shouted "I love you!" and I, like, stepped back in shock, because he'd shouted it to me in front of his mates. . . . He'd never done that before. Ever.

For these women, the gender relations of their normal lives were disrupted by imprisonment, perhaps in some cases for the better. While most of the women resented the restricted range of options inside because of the traditional femininity that was forced upon them, time away from their everyday lives also provided some with a more critical view of how their lives had already been structured by particular assumptions about gender identity. Above all, the examples suggest that categories of identity function in a variety of ways and that, as Gayatri Spivak (1994) suggested, in a much different situation, there may be some mileage to be gained from strategic essentialism or identifying as "woman." As the next section will demonstrate, however, any attachment to gender identities may be complicated by race.

Race: Disrupting the Color Line

Most societies organize themselves around mutually exclusive sets of binaries: white or black, man or woman, heterosexual or homosexual, citizen or alien. In this binary construction of difference, the first term is always privileged over the second. Such duality maintains an entrenched system of power relations. Just as some feminists have sought to disrupt gender binaries, so too has critical race theorist Paul Gilroy (1993) argued that, in any analysis of race or ethnicity, we must be open to the possibility of change and subversion.

Using the notion of "double consciousness," Gilroy shows how race always exists in a web of relations, traditions, and histories beyond the individual, which are related to the geopolitical relationships between Europe, the Americas, and Africa. In these relations there is always some movement from oppressor to oppressed and back again. Not only have many black cultural forms and expressions greatly influenced white ones, but due to immigration and intermarriage there has been continual intermingling of ideas and identities. To conceive of the world in opposites is therefore reductive and ultimately misleading. Once again, this move away from simple essentialism has many implications for understanding the prison. In particular it opens new possibilities for considering how race and gender intersect in constructing prison life, relations, and opportunities.

The role played by race and ethnicity in the negotiation of power in prison is rarely considered. Given the overrepresentation of people of color in all prison systems as inmates, and their vast underrepresentation as prison officers, it seems that color and culture are indices of certain positions within a power hierarchy. While many, like Biko Agozino (1997), would argue that such power relations are fixed, I found in my own research that race relations were frequently structured in part by class and geography. England is a country with an entrenched class system that is underpinned by sharp geographical boundaries. As a woman from Manchester put it, HMP Risley (a prison in northern England) was fine because

> I had family in there, and there were lots of girls from my estate and that. So that weren't a problem. Styal—easy—right next door to Manchester airport, so still again girls that I knew from on the out. Holloway [in London] was different, because that was 500 women I'd never met before in my life, and there is a North-South divide.

Indeed, throughout my research, I found that women of all ethnic backgrounds formed alliances and friendships with others from similar areas and backgrounds, rather than simply with those of a similar ethnic or racial background. All of these relationships could and did shift, suggesting that power and allegiances were somewhat transitory (Bosworth, 1999b: 136–137). Of course, my findings on this matter were undoubtedly influenced by a number of factors, including my own status as a white woman from part of the British Commonwealth. Similarly, the prisons I visited had relatively low numbers of women of color, particularly when compared to prisons closer to London like Holloway.

Despite the influence of geography and class, race and ethnicity were frequently described by prisoners as sites of localized debates over identity. In the women's prisons, such discussions took many forms, and were complicated by the presence of many foreign nationals who practiced cultural and social mores very different from those of all British prisoners. For the most part, of course, foreign nationals were greatly disempowered. Miles from home, often unable to speak the language of their fellow prisoners, they were, even more than the others, cut off from the rest of the world and dependent upon the prison system. Where groups of women from similar cultural background coexist, however, their difference can at times be a source of strength and unity. Thus in Winchester, which had an unusually high proportion of foreign prisoners, women from Nigeria offered one another support, observing traditional forms of courtesy and respect to one another based on age and class. Despite being housed separately, they all knew each other and met up in church. Here, in fact, they dominated, attending all services irrespective of denomination, and dancing and singing together (Bosworth, 1999b).

Another example of the possible power of difference was expressed by A.S. in a story about the prison she had been at last. According to her:

> We had some Bosnians in Styal . . . and we thought that they couldn't speak English. One could speak broken English, and I was informed that she would be able to help me with my French and I'd help her with her English. It was funny, because when it actually came down to teaching I was told that her friend who was with her couldn't understand English, and I remember saying something, she was asking why I was here, and when I told her, she looked up, and she was listening, and she was listening to what I was saying, so she could. But she was pretending that she couldn't. It's a good protection.

In this story, difference becomes a mask and a possible shield to hide behind. Refusal or inability to speak the dominant language both separates one from the rest, as well as serves to block them out.

Once again, as with the example above about motherhood, these women were able to emphasize their racial and ethnic identities to supersede their identities as prisoners. Unlike those prisoners who self-identified as mothers, however, the Nigerian and Bosnian prisoners incurred at best the suspicion and sometimes the wrath of both the prison administration and their fellow inmates. In Winchester, for example, racist ideas about "Africans" intertwined with assumptions about women's tendency to be overemotional or hysterical in the guards' accounts and treatment of the Nigerian prisoners. In particular, they heavily guarded the foreign prisoners in church, in case their energetic singing and dancing got "out of hand." Outside of church these same women were often patronized and/or assigned to the more menial tasks in the prison.

Some of the women identified a broader connection between gender and race in the English criminal justice system. According to D., for example, "Women and blacks are on about the same level because they get treated unfairly by the court." Such overt recognition of the interconnected nature of race and gender oppression was rare. Instead, race and ethnicity generally featured in debates about seemingly banal and everyday issues such as when S., a young Afro-Caribbean offender, explained that having a black personal officer would help because the officer would understand her need for special hair-care products.

When asked directly about racism, some of the women of color demonstrated the difficulty often associated with identifying the source and form of institutional racism. C., a young offender of mixed descent, for example, struggled to articulate her experiences, saying that the officers "haven't said anything, but it's the way they go about things. They act right, 'cos they'd get the sack, but it's the way they go about it." In response to the murder of Steven Lawrence and the subsequent inadequate response by the London Metropolitan Police Service, criminologists in England are currently paying greater attention to institutional racism. The Stephen Lawrence inquiry best expresses the subtle and insidious nature of such prejudice by defining institutional racism as

> The collective failure of an organisation to provide an appropriate and professional service to people because of their colour, culture, or ethnic origin. It can be seen or detected in processes, attitudes

and behaviour which amount to discrimination through unwitting prejudice, ignorance, thoughtlessness and racist stereotyping which disadvantage minority ethnic people. (MacPherson, 1999: §6.34)

That such behavior exists demonstrates the limited efficacy, as compared to gender, of laying claim to a racial or ethnic identity as a means of coping with imprisonment.

In addition to "institutional racism" emanating from the prison administration, racist beliefs were expressed by a number of the prisoners. Typical of such views, one white woman said: "I always used to think racism was white people against black, but the colored girls here do tend to stick together. . . . Apparently . . . West Indian girls do have a slight attitude problem, but then again, I don't know, because I don't know anyone on the outside who is West Indian." Another white woman, J.U., broke into an aggressive denunciation of the hygiene of "Pakis" during a group meeting of prisoners and staff. No staff member intervened despite her racism, which contravened prison service rules. This same woman later described in an interview stealing chocolate from "Paki" babies on the mother-and-baby wing of a previous prison. Given that she herself was married to and had children with an Afro-Caribbean man, and had described receiving racist treatment from guards and in her hometown as a result, her outbursts point to the complexity and irrationality of racist beliefs. England, like other European countries, has a particular mistrust of those thought to be immigrants (Gilroy, 1987). Given the sociohistorical tradition, individuals of South Asian descent, irrespective of their actual citizenship, often fit into this category.

The fact that the women themselves espoused racist beliefs should be of no surprise. The presence of prejudice, however, warns against any overly simplistic celebration of prisoner rights and agency, since it is clear that prejudice limits the liberationist effects of race as a form of identity management. Likewise, as the next section will demonstrate, prejudice may restrict the capacity of prisoners to form intimate relationships with one another, which may otherwise help manage some of the pains of imprisonment.

Sexuality: Challenging Gender and the Prison

Recently, outside criminology, feminist theorists like Judith Butler and Diana Fuss have sought to include sexuality as one of the main topics of analysis within feminism. According to them, sexuality is important because it provides a means of subverting gender relations. Lesbian relationships in this view profoundly destabilize the dominant organization of society. They provide an alternative way of being in and of interpreting the world, which is in stark contradiction to the norm. Men do not play a part in this vision, and as a consequence it may be possible to imagine and enact new ways of being, both sexually and as women.

Whereas the resistance to heterosexist arrangements of power posed by same-sex relationships may be open and identifiable, so too can it be more subtle and hidden. Intimate relations in prison, both those of a sexual nature and more platonic ones, fall under this second category. Although early sociological studies describe lesbian and homosexual relations in great detail (Ward and Kassebaum, 1965; Giallombardo, 1966; Sykes, 1958), sexuality in prison today is often overlooked (however, see Freedman, 1996b; Pollack, 2000). Such silence over intimacy even from feminist criminologists has further limited an understanding of the effects of gender in prison, since sexual orientation and sexual practices are vital to constructions of masculinity and femininity (Ingraham, 1994). Lesbian and homosexual relations in prison can be understood as strategies of resistance not only to the pains of imprisonment as traditional sociologists would have us believe, but also to constructions of gender put forward by the institutions themselves.

In the prisons I visited, many women claimed that prisoners engaged in sexual and intimate relations. Such relations were interpreted in many ways. For some, like S., who self-identified as a lesbian, they were understood as the basis for their harsh treatment. Thus, when asked why she had been sacked from working in the laundry, she claimed that it was because "me and my friend were lying on the sofa. I had my arms around her and she had her arms around me." For others, like Y., sexual and physical intimacy were positive experiences. Still others, like M., however, warned of their potentially damaging effect on the individuals concerned when their prison term ended and the women were separated. Finally, some women expressed great hostility toward lesbians, making it clear that, as with other social institutions, prisons are shaped by homophobia.

While most women would agree with J.C.'s statement that "because I am in prison, I am not able to have sex, I am lonely and angry" or J.'s claim that "I've never been so sexually frustrated in my life," others, like Y., saw prison as a unique time to explore aspects of sexuality and intimacy that were denied them on the outside. Y. had two children of her own, and outside the prison had a sometimes violent male partner. In prison, however, she had struck up an emotionally close friendship with a younger woman that eventually became sexual. As she puts it: "Me and J. have known each other for a year now. You'd think that we'd have started something already. I wonder how quick a man and a man would get together. If they were as close as we are, I'm sure they'd be fucking each other by now."

Gender norms permit women to have closer, more intimate friendships than men, without them being thought of as "lesbian." Indeed, under the "compulsory heterosexuality" identified by Adrienne Rich (1980), many safeguards exist in society to keep such relationships platonic. In prison, however, as Y. demonstrates, some of these barriers become destabilized:

> J. said to me that "If I was in prison for life, I think I'd be full-blown lesbian!" And I had to think about it, and you know I said to her, "You're right, you're probably right. You'd have to. You'd have to." You do get to like each other a lot, not physically, you know what I mean, but mentally, you like each other. Yeah, I've looked at her sometimes, and I've fantasized and she said she'd looked at me sometimes. You know, she said that if I was talking to my friend on the street and I said to her, "You know I've fantasized about you sometimes," I think she'd walk out on me and never be my friend again! That's where the closeness comes in.

This is not to say, however, that lesbian relationships in prison are immune from gender stereotypes. Indeed, women who seemed quite content to explore their own sexuality, like Y., were a lot less sanguine about similar behavior from men in prison. According to her, despite having a gay brother herself, "You'd more accept a woman being a lesbian than a man, you know, being in prison." Y. also described a lesbian relationship that turned violent as being riddled with gender stereotypes. Again, she said that

> they just deal with it like it was on the street. Physically, and mentally, they take it that their girlfriend is like a man, and they deal with it like a man. I mean on our landing one time, . . . she really thought that she was the man. She was beating up the girl in her room. I used to think to myself, "She really thinks that she's the man."

The existence first of prejudice against male homosexuality and second of violence within lesbian relations points once more to the insidious nature of heterosexism within society, and within prisons.

Conclusion: Subversive Identities

Inmates, like Judith Butler's more ambiguous figures (1995: 47), "are constituted through exclusion" since they are stigmatized as offenders, and separated from the rest of the world. One result of their situation, as I have shown throughout this chapter, is that in order to "get things done" they must somehow transcend the limitations inherent in their identities as prisoners to reconstruct themselves as agents. As I have suggested, often they do this by reaching across the divide between their current situation to their preconfinement sense of self, which included many other qualities and characteristics. In particular, they often lay claim to aspects of their embodied selves as mothers, members of ethnic groups, and sexual beings.

Race, gender, and sexuality all structure people's experiences of incarceration. The difficulty remains in how to integrate these issues into an analysis of imprisonment simultaneously, rather than one at a time. While certainly, under specific circumstances, individual aspects of identity may appear to be more relevant than others, an individual will of course usually experience her "self" coherently. She will be a woman and a lesbian, rather than sometimes one and sometimes the other. While arguably certain parameters of her identity may be disguised, others are always visible. With rare exceptions, she cannot divest herself of her race. Gender is also fairly hard to hide.

Taking identity as the site of criminological analysis in prison reveals the intersections that structure people's experiences and daily lives. It also enables a smaller-scale approach to questions of inequality and the negotiation of power. Perhaps most significantly, this strategy places the voices and experiences of individuals at the center of analysis. Sociologists must listen to prisoners to see what they have to say and to try to understand their perspectives.

Finally, by viewing prisoners as "concrete selves" rather than "generalized others," criminologists may become attuned to the variety of means at women's disposal to disrupt or resist the status quo. Such an approach allows for the incorporation of a range of human actions into the discussion of power. It also reveals the relationship between socioeconomic and cultural characteristics and the capacity for agency. In other words, it shifts an exploration of power from a purely instrumental capacity to "get things done" to the much more subtle and complex circumstances surrounding the decisions about what to do. This shift, from instrumental to agonistic, opens up new possibilities for interpreting prison life that can foster a new understanding of the complexity of power relations while demonstrating the shared humanity of those inside and beyond the prison walls.

Note

1. I have written elsewhere on this research. See, for example, Bosworth, 1996, 1999a, 1999b; and Bosworth and Carrabine, 2001.

8

Parallels in the Prison Experiences of Women and Men

Richard S. Jones and Thomas J. Schmid

A central argument in the recent social science literature on prisons has been that women's prison experiences must be understood as distinctive and fundamentally different from those of men who are serving time. Scholars supporting this argument have cited differing societal justifications for the incarceration of women and men, differing procedures and programs within correctional institutions, differing forms of inmate social organization, and the differing nature of relationships that female and male inmates maintain with the outside world (Bosworth, 1999b; Owen, 1998; Pollock-Byrne, 1990). While acknowledging the importance of these differences, we disagree with the conclusion that they necessitate separate theories or models of imprisonment for men and women. Our disagreement rests on our analysis of the parallels that exist between the prison experiences of women and those of the first-time, short-term male inmates we have studied.

We are not proposing that research on women's prisons should return to a reliance on the established models of men's imprisonment. Our specific argument here is that the prison experiences of both women and first-time men differ from those depicted in the literature on men's prisons, and that they appear to differ in many of the same ways. The traditional models derive primarily from research that has been conducted at men's institutions and guided by a handful of analytic issues, including deprivations faced by inmates, the nature of the inmate social organization and culture, prison socialization, external factors that affect inmates' adaptations, and the effects of imprisonment on inmates' lives. Like any analytic framework, this set of issues has limited as well as advanced sociological understanding. In particular, research on these issues has tended to depict inmates as the passive recipients of external forces generated in both the outside and the prison worlds. This depiction has increasingly been challenged by researchers working in alternative analytic frameworks, such as those examining the issue of legitimacy (Sparks, Bottoms, and Hay, 1996). In this chapter, we first present a phenomenological model of prison experience developed through our men's study. Then, after describing our research methods for both our women's and our men's studies, we examine three parallels between women's prison experiences and those of first-time male inmates.

A Phenomenological Model of Prison Experience

Our study of first-time male inmates addressed the fundamental question: How do new inmates *experience* prison? It soon became apparent that existing models of prison culture and socialization would be inadequate for our analysis. For example, the traditional concept of "prisonization" (Clemmer, 1958), and the deprivation and importation models that derive from it, begin with the premise that there is a monolithic "prison culture" into which inmates are gradually but inevitably socialized as they progress through their prison careers. Our analysis, however, sought to view inmates' lives experientially rather than as a matter of inevitable organizational stages. We did so by looking at how inmates conceptualized the prison, how they defined the problems presented by their imprisonment, how they responded to these problems, and how they viewed themselves within the prison world. We believe that a similar experiential focus, with emphases on problem solving and identity, has considerable value for the understanding of women's imprisonment.

Our model is based on the processes through which inmates who have no prior direct knowledge of prison come to know the prison world. Because the men we studied were first-time inmates who had been given relatively minor sentences (of two years or less), they were socially marginal vis-à-vis both the outside and the prison worlds. That is, when these men were sentenced to prison, they lost their status as free adults but had not yet achieved any meaningful status in prison. Although they do eventually participate in prison culture, their participation is inhibited by their continuing ties to, and identification with, the outside world. In this respect, their cultural situation is parallel to that of immigrants who expect to return to their country of origin within a few years' time (see Morawska, 1987; Shokeid, 1988) or who otherwise maintain a "sojourner orientation" (Gibson, 1988). Immigrant sojourners, however, can typically draw on shared symbols or institutions to fortify their transient adaptations to a new culture. New inmates, in contrast, have little in common with one another, and consequently have fewer collective resources to draw upon as they confront problems presented by their sudden immersion into a foreign culture (Schmid and Jones, 1999).

Building on this border-crossing analogy, our analysis centered on how inmates orient themselves to prison and how their orientations change as they progress through their sentences. New inmates, like recent immigrants, think about and try to prepare themselves for the world toward which they are heading. Our first question, therefore, involved an examination of the conceptualizations, or prison images, that inmates bring with them and the subsequent changes in imagery that take place as they acquire prison experience. We expect that their imagery will influence their actions, so we then asked: How do inmates adapt to the prison world, and how do their adaptation strategies change during their prison careers? Finally, because imprisonment constitutes an assault on inmates' identities, we asked: How does the prison experience induce changes in inmates' self-definitions? In contrast to the focus on internal and external determinants of prison adaptation found in much of the contemporary literature, our analysis examined inmates' experiential realities and their orientations to the practical problems of everyday prison life.

Our analysis led to a model of inmates who are actively engaged in social life and social action as interpretive processes. New inmates begin their interpretative work well before their arrival at the prison, by formulating an image of prison life and a rudimentary survival plan based on this imagery. As they enter prison, serve their time, and eventually exit the prison world, their imagery and the corresponding problems presented by their sentences (i.e., their prison orientations) change. And as their prison orientations change, so do their adaptation strategies and the "identity work" they perform in conjunction with these strategies. The key to understanding all of these changes is an appreciation of the continuous and simultaneous influence of both the outside world and the prison world throughout the inmates' prison experiences.

Table 8.1 presents an overview of the model. In this table we characterize inmates' experiences in terms of three broad interpretive phas-

Table 8.1   Orientation and Prison Imagery

Orientation	Preprison	Prison	Postprison
Inmate perspective	Outside looking in	Inside looking in	Inside looking out
Central concerns	Violence/uncertainty	Boredom	Uncertainty
Specific problems	Survival	Endurance	Reintegration
Orientation to space	Prison as separate world	Prison as familiar territory	Prison as separate world
Orientation to time	Sentence as lost time	Killing time/time as measure of success	Sentence as lost time/using time
Supportive others	Family and friends	Partners	"Real" family and friends
Perception of sentence	Justified and unfortunate	Arbitrary and unjust	Arbitrary and unjust (intensified)
Predominant emotion	Fear	Detachment	Apprehension (about outside)

es, representing their orientations vis-à-vis the prison and the outside worlds. Thus the *preprison orientation,* which inmates initiate before their arrival and modify based on early prison experiences, is essentially a perspective of an outsider looking into the prison. The subsequent *prison orientation* emerges after inmates have acquired months of actual prison experiences and insider understandings. It is an "insider looking in" orientation that focuses on inmates' day-to-day reality in the institution. As we discuss elsewhere (Schmid and Jones, 1990, 1993), inmates' outside orientations are held in abeyance during this interpretive phase, but nonetheless continue to affect their prison adaptations. The *postprison orientation* offers an "insider looking out" perspective. As they prepare for their exit from the prison and anticipate their return to the outside world, inmates gradually move away from their prison orientation toward a "postprison" orientation, in which their outsider perspective is again incorporated more directly into their views of the prison.

So how is this model relevant for the sociological analysis of women's imprisonment? The central theme of our model is that inmates' adaptations and ultimately their identities are simultaneously grounded in, and therefore shaped by, both the outside and the prison social worlds. Data from our men's study demonstrate that the concurrent influence of these social worlds involves something more than the "importation" of outside values or customs into the prison. Instead, these men experience prison as sojourners, in that they cross a cultural border between the outside world and the prison and then actively interpret and adapt to prison culture, but with the belief that their adaptations are temporary and that they will be returning to their lives in the outside world. The literature on women's prisons has established that correctional policies and programs clearly differ for women and men, and that "prison culture" is demonstrably different in women's and men's institutions. But the idea that the outside world has a continuing influence on inmates' prison experiences is also a prominent theme in this literature (Giallombardo, 1966; Heffernan, 1972; Owen, 1998; Bosworth, 1999b), and we believe that this similitude warrants empirical examination and theoretical development.

Methods

We examined parallels in women's and men's prison experiences using data from two of our studies on imprisonment. Our women's study, which employed a variety of research methods, began when one of us participated as a group leader in a parenting-skills course at Midwestern Correctional Institution for Women (MCIW). This class, which was attended by eighteen inmates, met two evenings a week for three months. Following this, permission was granted to conduct a formal study of the prison. Data collected include interviews with thirty-one inmates, and two-hour follow-up interviews with five key informants. Other sources of information include inmates' responses to the Twenty Statements Test (TST) (Meltzer, Petras, and Reynolds, 1975) and observations and informal conversations in various programs and locations within the prison over an eighteen-month period (Jones, 1993).

For the men's study, data were derived principally from ten months of participant observation at a maximum-security prison, also located in the upper midwestern United States. One of us was an inmate serving a felony sentence of one year and a day, while the other participated in the study as an outside researcher. Relying on traditional ethnographic methods, this approach offered us general observations of hundreds of prisoners, extensive fieldnotes based on repeated, often daily, contacts with about fifty inmates, and personal relationships established with a smaller number of inmates. We subsequently returned to the prison to conduct focused interviews with twenty additional prisoners, identified by prison officials as first-time inmates serving sentences of two years or less (Jones and Schmid, 2000: 183–197).

Experiential Parallels

We focus here on evidence that demonstrates an interplay of outside and prison worlds in three aspects of inmates' experiences: their prison imagery and problem definition, their adaptations to prison culture, and their identity work in prison.

Parallels in Imagery and Problem Definition

For first-time inmates, women or men, the interplay of outside and inside orientations begins before imprisonment, in the interpretive work they perform to prepare themselves for incarceration. Inmates construct an image of prison based on available cultural resources, most notably the often-stereotypical conceptions presented in fictional and journalistic accounts:

> Oh, you can watch it on TV . . . the news. They'll come out on the news and say there's a stabbing or a drug-related mishap in [the state] prison. . . . That's the only thing a person's got to go by, is what they watch on TV or what they hear.

> The gay women, and these great big, burly women. I got this from TV. You know how TV plays everything up and exaggerates.

The first of these interview excerpts is from our men's study; the second is from our women's study. Our data from both projects include numerous examples of inmates pointing to media bases for their early views of prison. At MCIW, in fact, we found that women often arrive with imagery based on stereotypes of men's prisons:

> I thought it was going to be like men's prisons, with bars and things like that. I was really scared of violence, of being confined, and what I would be up against with the other residents.

> I was scared because I didn't know what I was walking into—guns, bars, and violence.

These data illustrate how men's prison imagery dominates media depictions but also suggest how this imagery can serve as an interpretive frame for women.

In both studies, we found that inmates supplement media with various secondary sources, including stories from more experienced prisoners in county jails, information from others, and inmates' own prior experiences with the criminal justice system. In the following excerpt, a new male inmate describes his impression of maximum-security inmates, based on conversations with jail cellmates while he was awaiting transfer to prison:

> It made me fearful because of the type of people I was talking to. I felt, oh my god, is this the type of person, with this intellectual level, I am going to be dealing with for I don't know how long? I knew I was capable of probably handling it, mentally, but I know it's a great big mental adjustment because you don't know to what extent that people are going to fly off the lid, that they are mentally stable or how much importance that male ego or machoism or whatever—that's a real big thing to them.

A comparable "outsider looking in" orientation is evident in the expectations of women anticipating their sentences at MCIW:

> I was scared to death. I was told to watch out for the women, that I was going to get attacked in the showers, and to watch out for the rapes, cockroaches, and stuff like that. It kind of made me sick. You hear so much about gays that I was afraid that they would get you in the corner and rape you.

Similar expectations, crafted from similar cultural resources, are reported by Owen (1998) in her ethnography of the Central California Women's Facility. For men and women, the process of preparing for an initial prison sentence begins with the "cognitive work" of building a mental image of the prison they are about to enter.

As inmates assemble a picture of prison life and imaginatively project themselves into it, their imagery incorporates a mixture of public stereotypes and their own fears. The preprison imagery of male inmates is dominated by the themes of uncertainty and violence, including sexual violence, and the specific problems they focus on are those of physical survival. For women, initial images are also dominated by an "institutional uncertainty" (Galtung, 1961) about what will happen to them, including concerns about prison sexuality. Although fear of violence is not universally present in women's imagery, it is a theme that nonetheless appears regularly in our data:

> I was scared at first. I didn't know what to think about this place. You know . . . what kind of people were here or how they were going to act toward somebody. You know, because there was a riot up at [a maximum-security prison for men]. I thought, "God, what if that happens here and somebody ends up getting killed."

Whether or not women fear violence, they do express concern over the "kind of people" who are in prison and the problem of not being able to trust other inmates:

> Realizing the people that I was going to be in here with, you know, murderers and people like that—I've never been around violent people before. Being around people you can't trust—you know, they're young and temperamental; you never know what's going to happen. They are like a live fuse waiting to go off.

> Women are just different. For instance, men will fight at the drop of a hat, whereas a woman will try to turn and get others involved in it and say stuff behind people's back. They will not come out with it to your face. You know, women like to gossip a lot, and in doing so, they're out to see people hurt.

Distrust of other inmates, which is commonly noted in research on women's imprisonment (see Bosworth, 1999b; Owen, 1998; Greer, 2002), is equally prominent in the data from our men's study:

> I thought the inmates would be—like you wouldn't be able to talk to them. It was hard time they were doing here—and I thought you wouldn't be able to talk to them. If you said something to them, I thought they would try to hurt you.

> I thought they'd be more or less like, you know, the animals that you run into on the street—and ghetto types and that type of thing—rather rough, trying to beat you out of something continually.

For both women and first-time male inmates, then, surviving prison is fundamentally viewed as a problem of dealing with an untrustworthy inmate population.

As with the men we studied, women's earliest prison experiences tend, on balance, to reinforce their fears. All MCIW inmates begin their sentences at a separate reception center, which, with its bars, cells, and isolation procedures, approximates outsiders' imagery of what a prison should look like. And even though MCIW's campuslike architecture contrasts with this image, the majority of inmates (54 percent) report being very frightened at the time of their arrival. An even greater majority (72 percent) find institutional reception activities to be humiliating, as illustrated by the following statements:

> To have someone tell you to bend over and spread your cheeks is the most degrading thing that you could ever be asked to do. I mean, I've never been raped, but in my mind it is the same thing as rape. I'll never get used to it. You just come to accept it. For some women, they've been invaded all of their lives.

> It's horrible, degrading; it makes you feel like you are nothing, just trash. You're treated like garbage. I really hated it. It strips you of all your dignity.

> I felt bummed by being numbered. I don't like people considering me like a number instead of a human being. You're this certain number, and it makes me feel like nobody.

Compare these statements with those of first-time male inmates:

> They took me to the security center—took me downstairs. . . . Before they took me into there, the goon squad undressed me. They were nasty. . . . They told me to take my clothes off, and they looked up my ass with a proctoscope, thinking that I had drugs on me. They were a little bit disappointed; they didn't find anything. Went through me quite thoroughly, as a matter of fact.

> They brought me into a room and strip-searched me. One guard commented on how pretty I was, and suggested I grow a beard, while the other guard said I didn't have to worry because of my size. Needless to say, I didn't really need to hear that conversation.

In both prisons, in-processing procedures mark inmates' passage into the "other world" of the prison. And in both institutions, the emotional effect is the same: these activities dramatically heighten inmates' feelings of vulnerability and challenge their outside identities.

Our data suggest that men and women respond to their vulnerability in similar ways. All of the men and a majority of the women we talked with believe that they had to present themselves differently in prison, by "appearing tough" and by becoming more reserved in their interactions with others:

> When people see weakness they take advantage of that. I have to protect myself. I can't let anyone think I'm weak. I can't cry. Anger is violence and tears is fears.

> Kindness is a considerable weakness in here. As far as being friendly to any one person—it's a lot, lot harder to do in here than it is outside. You'll get taken advantage of. You have to work with what you have. . . . I kinda tried to present that I'm not to be led around by the nose. . . . I like to watch people. I'll watch people's eyes when they ain't watching me—but I don't look into people's eyes very much.

> I had to be more assertive, follow rules and keep calm. You don't have to be tough, but you get respect for standing up for yourself.

> Well, I learned that you can't act like—you can't get the attitude where you are better than they are. Even where you might be better than them, you can't strut around like you are. Basically, you can't stick out. You don't stare at people and things like that. I knew a lot of these things from talking to people, and I figured them out by myself. I sat down and figured out just what kind of attitude I'm going to have to take.

> You can't mouth them back [i.e., other inmates]. You don't dare say anything back to them.

In this sampling of interview excerpts, men's and women's statements are indistinguishable. (The first, third, and fifth quotes are from women, the second and fourth from men.) Although women ultimately adapt to prison in different ways, their initial responses to imprisonment—grounded in an outsider's experiential orientation and based on similar prison imagery constructed from similar cultural resources—are directly parallel to those of the male inmates we studied.

As the women at MCIW get further into their sentences, their prison images and adaptive responses become increasingly dissimilar from those of men. Even so, the process through which their imagery changes is fundamentally the same: they receive conflicting accounts from official and unofficial sources; they remain distrustful of fellow inmates generally but find ways of interacting with some of them; with the help of these inmates they actively interpret the conflicting information presented to them, refashioning their understanding of prison and their responses to it. As part of this interpretive process, inmates learn about and take into account the social organization and culture of the prison (or, more accurately, representations of this social organization and culture as presented to them by others). The outcomes of this interpretive process differ for women and men because, as is well established in the literature (see, for example, Owen, 1998; Pollock-Byrne, 1990, Mawby, 1982; Heffernan, 1972), the social organizations of men's and women's prisons are in fact quite dissimilar.

As inmates come to accept an "insider's" orientation toward prison, the problems presented by their imprisonment become more clearly defined. For men, problems of physical survival remain the primary focus for several months and then gradually become secondary to problems of enduring an unchanging daily routine. For women, the fear of violence recedes rapidly, as do many aspects of their institutional uncertainty, but not their distrust of other inmates. In general, women come to see the problems of imprisonment as isolation from their family and friends, a dispossession of outside family roles (see Ward and Kassebaum, 1965; McGowan and Blumenthal, 1976; Owen, 1998), and frustration with rules and procedures that treat them like children:

> For instance, the petty rules. I thought prison was going to be that you're locked up and it's enough to be locked up, and they put you in your cell and you do what you want in there. But they can put you in your cell here, and you still can't do what you want. They've got control of every little personal thing that you do, which is really hard to accept.

Parallels in Adaptation

All inmates, regardless of sex, length of sentence, or prior prison experience, must somehow accommodate themselves to the social organization and culture of the prison. This is true even for short-term inmates, particularly during the middle of their sentences, when they are temporally furthest from the outside world. Meisenhelder (1985) has argued that (long-term) imprisonment affects the experience of temporality by removing inmates from any meaningful connection with outside events, thereby promoting a "present time" orientation. But even short-term inmates are encouraged to adopt a present time orientation, by the "do your own time" norms that have been documented in both men's and women's' prisons (see Owen, 1998; Jones and Schmid, 2000) and by a reciprocal control of information that evolves between inmates and their visitors or correspondents. That is, after emotion-provoking contacts in the early weeks of their sentences, communication between inmates and outsiders becomes constricted over time, as inmates seek to reassure outsiders by withholding their fears or negative experiences and outsiders try to shield inmates from news that might upset them. We documented this process in our men's study (Jones and Schmid, 2000: 95–97) and we found it to be equally present in our data from the women at MCIW. In concert with their "present time" focus, inmates also find it necessary to situate themselves in, and accommodate themselves to, the social organization of the prison.

When we examine the interplay of outside and prison world orientations on inmates' overall adaptations to prison culture, then, the principal question of interest is: How do inmates manage an orientation toward the outside world during the middle of their sentences, when they are also likely to adopt an insider's perspective on prison life? Our data suggest that men and women establish different strategies as they accommodate themselves to differing forms of prison social organization, but that they do so in ways that are nonetheless experientially parallel, and in keeping with a sojourner's approach to prison culture.

The men we studied were able to retain some level of outside orientation because of the sociological ambivalence that remained present throughout their sentences (Schmid and Jones, 1993). Their ambivalence allowed them to negotiate a minimal level of participation in the prison world while at the same time inhibiting full participation. Specifically, these men were able to create a strategy that let them move about the prison, interacting with a variety of other inmates and participating in a variety of activities, while nonetheless maintaining existential distance from the prison world. This strategy reduced their institutional uncertainty because it enabled them to learn the social organization of the prison, including racial and other subdivisions, the distinction between inmates and more experienced "convicts," and the central ideas of the "inmate code." Elements of their strategy included consciously developed impression management skills, normative guidelines for exploring prison territory and selectively interacting with others, a tentative acceptance of experienced inmates' "do your own time" practices (including cognitive minimization of the importance of outside contacts and efforts to suppress thoughts about the outside), and participation in legal and illegal diversionary activities to combat boredom. Their most important adaptive tactic, however, because it was directly connected to all of their other tactics, was participation in a prison "partnership."

A partnership is a friendship with one other inmate, usually another first-time inmate. The relationship typically begins as one of a small number of tentative acquaintanceships, based on common backgrounds or interests, that develop during the initial weeks of an inmate's sentence. This relationship is strengthened through the inmates' mutual exploration of a prison world viewed as hostile, and is further reinforced by its acknowledgment by other inmates and staff.

The most important function of a partnership is to help both inmates "make sense" out of prison life. Partners explore institutional territory together, compare their prior expectations about prison, and exchange information and advice about prison norms, inmate groups, the prison economy and other aspects of the prison world. This mutual interpretation of prison culture directly addresses new inmates' overriding concerns during the early months of their sentences, in that it reduces their uncertainty about the prison and provides them with some protection from the inmate population they fear.

As inmates progress through their sentences, their partnerships contribute to their prison adaptations in additional ways. Above all else, an inmate's partner is someone with whom he can share his prison experience, on both a material level (e.g., by sharing food and other canteen items) and an emotional level (e.g., exchanging news from home, advice, and personal thoughts). Partnerships frequently take on an advocacy function, so that one partner will intercede with officials or other inmates when necessary. As partnerships strengthen over time, they also affect inmates' identity work, a point we return to below.

Previous studies on the culture of women's prisons have established that women experience many of the same deprivations of incarceration as do men, but that they develop substantially different social structures. In particular, women tend to organize into relatively enduring primary relationships, often involving both dyadic homosexual attachments and extensive "fictive families." The specific forms of these relationships vary considerably from study to study—and presumably from institution to institution (see Heffernan, 1972; LeShanna, 1969; Leger, 1987; MacKenzie, Robinson, and Campbell, 1989; Mawby, 1982; Moyer, 1980; Van Wormer, 1987). Similarly, the kinship terms used to describe familylike relationships also vary by institution and study (Selling, 1931; Foster, 1975; Ball, 1972; Brown, 1977). At MCIW, most women participate in one of three types of relationships: the "quasi-family," the "couple," or the "rap partner."

"Quasi-family" is a term we have used to describe a common form of primary relationship between an experienced inmate (a "mom") and anywhere from one to fifteen other inmates ("kids"). While many inmates believe these groupings are essentially like outside families, others believe the term is somewhat misleading, and that the "mom" role is really that of a counselor or adviser. There are usually two mothers in each housing unit; when one leaves, another woman typically takes on the position. There is little competition between the "moms," and "kids" will sometimes seek advice from more than one mom. The most frequently cited reasons for inmates performing the role of "mom" are the respect they receive from other inmates and the opportunity to express their nurturing feelings. Inmates who adopt the "kid" role are generally younger, are less secure at the institution, and often report that they do not have a strong relationship with outside family members. According to inmate estimates, approximately 50 percent of inmates participate in quasi-family relationships.

Both the prison literature and the popular media have emphasized the role of homosexuality in women's prison. Physical and romantic "couple" relationships do exist at MCIW, although inmate estimates of how many women participate in these relationships vary greatly. When the question was asked in terms of a sexual affair during incarceration, estimates ranged from 5 to 100 percent, with an average estimate of approximately 45 percent. The most revealing aspect of these data, however, is that inmates who had served less than three months gave the highest estimates (75 to 100 percent), suggesting that their estimates reflected their outsiders' acceptance of stereotypes, their lack of direct knowledge about the prison, and their own concerns about homosexuality in prison. When the question was phrased in terms of an enduring "couple" relationship, estimates were considerably lower, with 41 percent of the inmates estimating that 5 to 15 percent of the women at MCIW were involved in such relationships.

Inmates who acknowledged participation in couple relationships reported that they were open about their situation and emphasized that their relationships developed out of a voluntary courtship process rather than coercive pressure. Although some women had a difficult time understanding why anyone would become involved in a couple relationship, the majority saw these relationships as fulfilling the same basic needs as quasi-families: emotional involvement, sharing, and providing a sense of belonging and trust. Unlike quasi-families, couple relationships also provide some combination of love, sex, or "romance."

One reason for the widely varying estimates of the number of women involved in couple relationships is that it is difficult to distinguish between couples and another common form of relationship, "rap partners," who are most often defined simply as good friends. The two dyadic relationships are thought to address essentially the same needs, except that rap partners provide "companionship" rather than sexual gratification. As expressed by one inmate:

> I think there is a lot less sex going on around here than people think, because if you're in a friendship, some people think you are lovers. It's just having a good buddy. We have a lot of that and there is no sexual business going on. It's just straight up friends. This is the most common type of situation.

Rap partners at MCIW are thus participating in essentially the same kind of relationship as the partnerships of male inmates.

If we focus on the specific behaviors of the men and women we studied, we would conclude that they have adapted to prison in very different ways. If we examine their adaptations in experiential terms, however, it becomes apparent that their differing strategies have accomplished similar results. In both institutions, inmates enter prison with outsiders' stereotypical understandings of the prison world, with the view that their sentences are forcibly removing them from their outside network of family and friends, and with a fearful distrust of the inmate population. In both prisons, inmates form affective relationships that approximate the kind of relationships available to them on the outside and enable them to keep the "general inmate population" at arm's length. All of these relationship forms, moreover, are recognized within the larger prison social organization. Women's relationships are more centrally located, in that quasi-families, couples, and rap partners essentially constitute the prison organization at MCIW and, especially in quasi-families, involve a mixture of new and more experienced inmates. (Although partnership is an acknowledged component of the men's prison organization, the men we studied virtually always formed partnerships with other first-time inmates, an arrangement that reinforced their marginal position within the prison culture.) In both the women's and men's prisons, then, affective relationships help inmates to learn about prison organization and culture and to reach a limited accommodation with this social system, but also to see themselves as something other than full participants in it. Their affective relationships, in other words, allow them to act as cultural sojourners. Their affective relationships also support forms of identity work that help inmates to remain at least partially oriented toward the outside world throughout their sentences.

Parallels in Identity Work

At the same time that inmates are struggling to adapt to their changing conceptions of the prison, they are also grappling with questions of who they are, in relation to both the prison world and the outside world. Following Schutz's argument (1962) that a person's sense of self while working toward a goal is experienced as his or her total self, inmates' adaptive work and identity work can be seen as different components of a single interpretive process. In the prior section we examined how male and female inmates develop different adaptive strategies to accomplish similar experiential goals—negotiation of the prison world while maintaining some existential distance from it. In this section we examine how their differing forms of identity work accomplish similar results.

The primary difference between the identity work observed in our men's and women's studies follows the differences observed in their adaptations. First-time male inmates are more likely to remain at the fringes of the prison social organization, participating in it only minimally and primarily through their partnerships. Their identity work, consequently, is largely conducted apart from prison culture. Although it is certainly influenced by their partnerships, much of it takes place through private cognitive activity. Women inmates are able to form adaptive relationships that are more centrally connected to the prison social organization, and their identity work is conducted through these relationships.

First-time male inmates are generally aware that their identities are being challenged by their imprisonment, and this awareness affords them some protection against radical identity change. Their identity work begins in self-dialogues they initiate before their arrival at the institution and continue through the early weeks of their imprisonment. In addition to formulating their initial imagery and adaptive tactics, inmates use self-dialogues to contemplate what their prison sentences mean for their lives. With few exceptions, they report strong feelings of vulnerability, discontinuity, and differentiation from other inmates, emotions that reflect both the degradations of their early institutional experiences and their outsiders' perspective on the prison world. These emotions, in turn, constitute the essential motivation for initial adaptive strategies that emphasize self-insulation.

Inmates soon discover that they cannot remain socially insulated. Beyond their need for firsthand information about prison, their behavior is also influenced by the ambivalence that emanates from their marginality in the prison and outside worlds. Our analysis suggests that inmates are able to express both directions of their ambivalence—and thus remain existentially grounded in both worlds—by drawing a distinction between their "true" identities (i.e., their outside, preprison identities) and the "false" identities they create for the prison world. For most of a new inmate's sentence, his preprison identity remains a "subjective" or "personal" identity while his prison identity serves as his "objective" or "social" basis for interaction in prison (see Weigert, 1986; Goffman, 1963).

As we discuss elsewhere (see Schmid and Jones, 1991; Jones and Schmid, 2000), this conceptual bifurcation of an inmate's self is based on two conscious and interdependent identity-preservation tactics. First, after coming to believe that he cannot "be himself" in prison because he would be too vulnerable, he decides to "suspend" his preprison identity for the duration of his sentence. That is, he resolves not to be changed by his prison experience, protecting himself by choosing not to reveal himself to others. Implicit in this tactic is the belief that he will again "be his old self" after his release. Because this tactic leaves him with little basis for interaction within the prison, his second tactic is the creation of an identity that facilitates cautious interaction with others. This tactic consists of his increasingly sophisticated impression management skills, which are initially designed to hide his vulnerability, but which gradually evolve into an alternative identity felt to be more suitable to the prison world.

A consequence of these tactics is that much of the inmate's identity work is conducted through solitary introspection. There are some exceptions: his limited interactions with family and friends, especially at the beginning of his sentence, are likely to be based on his preprison identity. More significantly, he interacts with his partner in terms of his preprison identity as well as his prison identity. He views most of his daily contacts with inmates and staff as inauthentic, however, because they are grounded in the false front he has created for the prison world.

Like other cultural sojourners, these men seek to define themselves through their relationship to the world they have recently left behind, and to which they expect to return. Their efforts at self-definition follow a distinctive pattern. In self-dialogues before and just after their arrival at prison, inmates try to assess how they will be affected by their imprisonment and resolve not to be changed by the experience. In the middle of their sentences, they consciously attempt to suppress self-dialogues, in keeping with their present time orientation. During those infrequent times of introspective dialogues that nonetheless occur, inmates continue to think of themselves in terms of their outside identities, but may also experience doubts about their ability to revive their suspended identities. In the final months of their sentences, as inmates shift back to an outsider's perspective, their reemerging self-dialogues include efforts to reconcile their preprison and prison identities. As with their self-dialogues at the beginning of their sentences, their identity work at the end of their imprisonment is a private activity, disconnected from their daily prison activities.

Identity work by women, as documented in our study and as reported in the literature, differs considerably from the men's identity work we have just described. In experiential terms, however, there are two ways in which it is comparable. First, women inmates, particularly at the beginning of their sentences, perform many of the same identity-work activities. Second, women's identity work, like that of first-time male inmates, is simultaneously grounded in both the outside world and the prison world.

We established, in our earlier discussion of inmates' prison images, that women and men often begin their prison sentences in a phenomenological orientation characterized by intense emotions and feelings of vulnerability, a distrust of other inmates, and a belief that it is impossible to "be yourself" in prison. For women as well as men, this orientation is associated with self-reflection and impression management.

As part of our research at MCIW, we asked inmates to complete the Twenty Statements Test, which calls for respondents to give multiple written answers to the self-defining question "Who am I?" (Meltzer, Petras, and Reynolds, 1975). We found that few women were able to provide more than four or five responses, an inhibition that is undoubtedly related to their isolation from the social contexts of their outside identities. The responses they did provide, however, are revealing. The most frequent category of responses, using Zurcher's coding scheme (1977), is the "reflective" mode. Within this category inmates defined themselves in ways that counter public stereotypes of prisoners or criminals—that is, as loving, caring, sensitive, loyal, strong, and intelligent. These responses suggest that inmates are actively engaged in identity work to resist the definitions of their selves implicit in their imprisonment. Our interview data and those of other researchers (see Greer, 2002; Bosworth, 1999b; Owen, 1998; McCorkel, 1998) further document self-reflective activities that are generally parallel to those of first-time inmates in our men's study.

Earlier, we cited data that both men and women respond to their intense emotions at the beginning of their sentences with conscious efforts to hide their vulnerability, by acting reserved or "tough." Similar evidence of impression management is reported by Bosworth (1999b), who notes that women make use of such "masking" for a variety of reasons, including both self-protection and a consideration for others. Greer (2002) has examined the emotional management strategies used by women to project the impression that they are in control of their emotions. In these studies, as in our men's study, inmates' impression management activities are grounded directly in their distrust of other inmates and their beliefs that they cannot "be themselves" in prison.

The women at MCIW also engage in identity work that is quite different from that of inmates in our men's project. One of the most consistent themes in the literature is that women's self-definitions are anchored primarily in their outside, conventional identities rather than in identities associated with their participation in the prison world or in criminal social worlds (Ward and Kassebaum, 1965; Giallombardo, 1966; Heffernan, 1972; Owen, 1998; Bosworth, 1999b). Our MCIW data support the finding that women's identities remain embedded in the outside world but further suggest that their outside identities become conjoined with their prison identities.

When we look closer at the TST data, the single most frequent response given by inmates is the self-definition of "mother." As noted earlier, 80 percent of the women we interviewed were mothers. For these women, the conventional identity of "mother" tends to structure the entire prison experience, including the problems presented by imprisonment. The problem most frequently cited by inmates in general is separation from family and friends. The primary problem confronting the inmate-mother is more specific: it is determining what to do with her children during her incarceration. Most of the inmate-mothers at MCIW reported that they could not count on the father to take care of their children; instead, they relied on parents, siblings, in-laws, cousins, or friends. One-third of these women further reported that their children had to be separated, because they were unable to find someone who could accommodate all of their children.

Our data show that inmates' concerns about their relationship with their children are justified. For example, over 50 percent of these women received no visits from their children during their incarceration. One mother, who had been in prison for over four years, had only one visit from her children during this time. Most mothers, especially those with infants, worried that their children might become too attached to their temporary caretakers. As described by one of the women we interviewed:

> I'm real concerned about my daughter, because she was only four months old when I was arrested. And, I found out from my son that she calls my sister Mom and my sister's kids her brother and sister. I'm not really worried about my son, because he was five when I was arrested and he is ready for me to come home right now. So, I told him, you have pictures of me and you show them to her and you tell her that this is her Mom and that I love her very much, and give her a kiss and a hug. He really liked that idea, so I am hoping that he can kind of teach her who I am. But I don't know.

Those who are fortunate to have visits or telephone calls with their children find these contacts to be highly emotional and sometimes painful experiences.

> After a visit is the saddest time in prison, very sad. Anticipating the visit is the highest time, and after the visit is the lowest.

> It makes you feel good, very close and accepting. But after we hang up, I get an attitude, and that shows me that I miss them and my freedom.

> I talked with her on the phone. I wanted to cry, it really hurt, but it felt so good to hear her little voice. She cried as soon as she heard my voice, so I won't call her anymore because of what it puts her through.

Although such contacts may reassure inmate-mothers about their children's welfare, they also emphasize the separation of mothers from their children.

Both the centrality of the mother identity and the problems that imprisonment presents to inmate-mothers are well documented (see Sobel, 1982; Lundberg, Sheekley, and Voelker, 1975; Owen, 1998). An accompanying theme in much of this research, however, is a disjunction that exists between inmates' self-definitions or self-presentations and their actual parenting behaviors. There are indications of this among the women at MCIW, in that only 68 percent of the inmate-mothers were living with their children prior to their incarceration. What accounts for this disparity between expressed identity and behavior? Bosworth (1999b) provides an intriguing answer to this question in her analysis of identity—including idealized identities of femininity and motherhood—as a form of resistance to the restrictions of imprisonment. Our research supports this hypothesis, and further suggests that inmates' identity work relies heavily on the idea of "motherhood" not only in terms of its outside meanings but in terms of its meaning within the prison world as well.

Inmates at MCIW make frequent use of mother-and-child concepts as part of their prison imagery and adaptation strategies. The most notable are found in the quasi-family relationships that we have already described. Our data suggest that the mother identity in these quasi-families, as viewed by both "moms" and "kids," constitutes an idealized version of the motherhood role. The following descriptions of the "mom" role are all from "kids" in a quasi-family:

> They are usually older and have longer sentences, and they have more of the real-life experiences. They kind of keep you in line and out of trouble. And if you don't stay out of trouble, then you have them breathing down your neck.

> They are active in things around here. They help the younger girls adjust, they give advice, and they are someone that you can be open with since there is such a lack of trust around here. They are the most respected of inmates.

> She shows concern for me, gives me time, and if it's my birthday, she remembers it. I go to her for advice when I need it. And she sticks by me. Sometimes, though, they will just out and out tell you you're messing up. Like I was floating down the hallway one day and she told me she wanted [me] to meet her in the shower so we

can talk. When I got there, she told me to sober up and turned on the shower, and then she told me how that wasn't good for me and stuff.

The "moms" see their role in much the same way:

> It's being patient with them. Offering advice and constructive criticism. We help them sort through their problems. It's a thing called trust, a feeling that you have found someone in here that you can really trust.

> [An inmate "kid"] tells me her problems and I give her good, sound advice. I listen to what she has to say, even when things bother her, upset and hurt her. And if she is doing something that is not right, then I tell her so.

Throughout our interviews, inmates consistently used the same words to describe the "moms": they are women who are kind, patient, wise, and concerned; they are women who provide both advice and comfort; they are women who will work to keep their "kids" out of trouble.

Holstein and Gubrium (1994) have analyzed the concept of family as a "descriptive practice" rather than as an objective social institution. From their perspective, family rhetoric is viewed as a discursive process through which domestic social relationships are interpreted, represented, and organized. The concept of family is invoked, in a wide variety of organizational and social settings, to declare interpersonal attachments that are based on nurturing and concern, whether or not they are also grounded in biological kinship. Clearly, the quasi-families at MCIW exemplify this rhetorical usage, organizing relationships in a manner that helps women adapt to the uncertainty and mistrust they experience as part of their imprisonment. But inmates' rhetorical use of mother-and-child concepts has another important outcome—it continuously reinforces an idealized exemplification of what it means to have a mother or to be a mother:

> There are some people in here who are really into motherhood. . . . When I first came in, there were several who wanted to mother me. Some people can take it and some can't. You can walk around these grounds on any given day and here somebody say, "Mom, mom, look what I did today." It's something you can understand. . . . The people that are portraying the mother need to be able to give that nurturing feeling.

> She is open and patient. She is the kind of mom that every girl would like their mom to be like.
>
> They give you that motherly touch, that motherly feeling. They give you a lot of advice. They voice their opinion and they try to comfort you. It's the way that they like to do their time. They are some of the most respected [women] in here.

Both inmates and staff acknowledge the respect that is granted to "moms" in prison; it is a natural extension of the respect that should be given to any mother, inside or outside prison.

If we look at the specific women who perform the mother role at MCIW, a number of patterns emerge. As suggested by the inmates we have quoted, mothers tend to be older and therefore have more "life experience." They also have more experience in the particular social organization at MCIW: in our sample, the "moms" were more likely to be serving sentences of ten to twenty-five years while nearly all of the "kids" were serving sentences of five years or less. At the same time, none of the "moms" had served prior prison sentences while 25 percent of the "kids" had been previously incarcerated. The "moms" also have an experiential basis for their advice: they were far less likely to receive prison disciplines (two or less per year) than were inmate "kids" (four or more per year, with most receiving one or two per month). Significantly, all of the "moms" had retained custody of their natural children, while this was true for only 36 percent of the "kids."

Imprisonment severely challenges inmates' outside identities. Bosworth's analysis (1999b) begins with the recognition that these challenges typically include both the disruption of women's outside roles as wives, girlfriends, or mothers and an array of institutional expectations for inmates to engage in traditional and passive feminine behaviors. Her analysis illustrates how inmates resist these expectations, not by rejecting them outright but rather by redefining or reshaping them in ways that assert positive, active identities. The idealized mother role that inmates reinforce through their participation in the quasi-families at MCIW can be viewed in these terms. "Motherhood" in these families is a kind and nurturing identity but also a strong and assertive one that commands great respect from others. Motherhood in the outside world is also a core identity for the majority of inmates at MCIW. Giving respect to motherhood within the prison world ennobles the idea of motherhood generally, regardless of how individual inmates have performed this role in their own lives.

Women inmates engage in various forms of identity work throughout their sentences, including several forms that are also practiced by men: self-dialogues, impression management, and management of emotional experience and displays. Women also engage in distinctive forms of identity work. It is theoretically important that much of their identity work in prison takes place through the affective relationships in which they participate, as part of their adaptation to prison culture. (Although we have focused here specifically on the mother role within quasi-families, our data suggest that similar identity work is conducted through the component roles of the couple and rap partner relationships.) These relationships permit a more integrative form of identity work than is practiced by first-time male inmates. It is of equal theoretical importance, however, that both groups of inmates remain oriented to the outside throughout their sentences, and that they consequently address issues of their outside identities as well as their prison identities.

Discussion

The analytic issues that guided research into men's prisons, and the resulting deprivation and importation models of imprisonment, also influenced early research on women's prisons. This work has led to the understanding that women face many of the same deprivations as men, but that they develop a substantially different form of social organization and culture, characterized by a lower allegiance to the idea of an "inmate code" and a tendency to organize into relatively enduring primary relationships. As researchers have sought to examine other aspects of women's imprisonment, however, conceptual reliance on the men's prison literature has been increasingly criticized, and researchers have argued that women's prison experiences must be understood as fundamentally different from those of men. We believe that the limitations of the men's prison literature lie more in the underlying issues that have been addressed than in the selection of men's prisons as research sites. Foremost among these limitations is a representation of prison experience in terms of competing (i.e., deprivation versus importation) deterministic models of behavior.

It is the determinism of these traditional models that is being challenged by research on both men's and women's prisons. Our study of first-time male inmates, conducted within a phenomenological perspective, presents a model of prison experiences in which inmates are actively constructing and modifying their imagery of the prison world, defining the problems presented by their imprisonment, developing adaptive strategies to address these problems, and engaging in identity work to mitigate the effects of their imprisonment on their self-definitions. Because the inmates we studied remained at least partially oriented to the outside world throughout these activities, the underlying metaphor we used is that of cultural sojourners, who cross a cultural border when they enter the prison, actively interpret and adapt to a new culture while they are inside, but view these adaptations as temporary adjustments until they can return to the outside world.

Differences between women's and men's prison experiences should continue to receive close empirical examination. Imprisonment will be best understood, however, by investigating similarities as well as differences in inmate experiences, from a variety of conceptual frameworks. In the analysis presented here, we have identified several parallels—and noted specific differences—in the ways that women and first-time male inmates deal with their imprisonment. Whether pursuing similar or dissimilar lines of action, however, the women and men we studied were unquestionably involved in active interpretations of their worlds rather than passive responses to their prison environments.

Parallels in the prison experiences of the women and men we studied are especially pronounced at the beginning of inmates' sentences, when they are constructing their initial cognitive images of the prison, defining the problems presented to them, and devising initial means of confronting these problems. We found women's and men's images to be strikingly similar, and crafted from the same (outsider's) cultural resources, including media depictions of men's prisons. Both groups begin their sentences with a high degree of uncertainty about the prison world, a generalized mistrust of other inmates, a fear of violence or sexual predation, and feelings of personal vulnerability. Women and men modify their prison images and problem definitions at different rates and in different forms, but the process by which they make these changes remains parallel: despite their distrust of the inmate population they nonetheless find ways to interact with specific other inmates and to make use of these interactions to interpret the prison world. In this manner they gradually acquire a more realistic (insider's) understanding of prison organization and culture, and reduce their institutional uncertainty.

Two reasons often given for the argument that women's and men's prison experiences must be understood separately are that women remain more closely connected to their outside roles and that the social organization and culture of men's and women's prisons are dissimilar. Both of these assertions are well supported by empirical evidence. Despite these differences, however, our research reveals two fundamental parallels. First, both groups remain at least partially oriented to the outside world throughout their imprisonment, even during the middle of their sentences, when they also tentatively adopt present time, "do your own time" norms. This is a point of considerable theoretical and practical importance. Delineating how inmates manage the conflicting demands of outside and prison worlds is essential to understanding the processes and effects of imprisonment. Second, both women and men accommodate themselves to prison culture by establishing affective relationships within the prison world. These relationships (partnerships for men; quasi-families, couples, or rap partners for women) approximate the kind of relationships available to them on the outside, enable them to negotiate their way through prison culture, and allow them to see themselves as less than full participants in the prison world.

We found additional parallels, and differences, when we examined inmates' identity work. At the beginning of their sentences, when they view the prison as outsiders, women and men engage in similar identity management activities. In particular, in response to their emotional and physical vulnerability and their sense that they cannot "be themselves" in prison, both men and women attempt to present themselves differently to others. Over time, as they define the problems of their imprisonment differently, and as they accommodate themselves to very different inmate social systems, their identity work, like their adaptive behaviors, becomes less similar. First-time male inmates distinguish between their authentic outside identities and their artificial prison identities and eventually seek to resolve the differences between these identities through a renewed self-dialogue at the end of their sentences. The women at MCIW, in contrast, are able to make use of their affective relationships in prison to reinforce central outside identities, such as motherhood. While behaviorally different, however, this identity work is experientially parallel in its simultaneous orientation to both the outside world and the prison world.

Our men's study resulted in a model of the prison experience in which first-time inmates approach their sentences as a border crossing into a separate and terrifying world and cautiously negotiate their way through this world as cultural sojourners. Our women's study has identified a number of ways in which women similarly work to connect their outside and prison world orientations. This analytic framework does not apply equally to all women or men in prison and it clearly requires further empirical investigation. Nonetheless, we believe that the experiential parallels we have identified begin to establish a conceptual bridge between the research literatures on women's and men's prisons, and consequently extend sociological understanding of imprisonment.

9

Ultramasculine Stereotypes and Violence in the Control of Women Inmates

Faith E. Lutze

A patriarchal system of power has been used as a framework to explain violence as a tool to control women. In patriarchal systems men are socialized to dominate women socially, legally, and politically (Belknap, 2001; Kilmartin, 2000). Male power defines individual interaction (private and public), the law, and the formation of policy and institutions. When women challenge male power it is met with resistance at the individual and institutional levels. Although there are multiple venues that explain the dynamics of how males maintain control and resist challenges to their power (see Bowker, 1998; Kirk and Okazawa-Rey, 2001), perhaps nowhere are there better examples than those that take place in the criminal justice system in general and more specifically in prisons.

The last several decades have brought about a plethora of research on how patriarchal systems have created disparity for women as workers, victims, and offenders in the criminal justice system (see Belknap, 2001; Muraskin, 2000b; Price and Sokoloff, 1995; Van Wormer and Bartollas, 2000). For women and girls who are victims, research has shown a reluctance of the criminal justice system to intervene on their behalf when they are beaten by their spouse, raped by family members or acquaintances, or harassed and stalked by men who expect uninhibited access to them (Chesney-Lind and Shelden, 1998; Koss et al., 1994). For female offenders, research has shown that they are often arrested and severely sanctioned for crimes related to their sexuality (e.g., prostitution), violation of their roles as wife and mother (e.g., killing an abusive spouse, adultery, infanticide, drug use), or when committing more traditional crimes related to supporting their family (e.g., shoplifting, theft, embezzlement) (for a review, see Belknap, 2001; Butler, 1997; Chesney-Lind and Shelden, 1998).

Many scholars have highlighted the irony of a system that fails to use its power to protect women from male abuse yet is quick to use its power to sanction women who act in their own defense (Browne, 1987; Chesney-Lind and Shelden, 1998). This chapter builds upon prior research by making the connection between the pattern of behavior used by individual men to establish control of women through domestic violence and its translation into how prisons maintain control of women— a relationship that guards male privilege and maintains social order. The dynamic of male power that will be explored here relates the institutionalization of ultramasculine sex-role stereotypes to domestic violence and women's experiences in prison.

Masculinity and Individual Violence

Gender socialization is considered to be one of the primary influences of behavior. Men and women are socialized from birth into gender-specific roles based on social definitions of masculinity and femininity (Kilmartin, 2000; Kirk and Okazawa-Rey, 2001). Sex roles for men and women determine the parameters of what is appropriate behavior and what is acceptable interaction between men and women. The socialization into sex roles takes place within a patriarchal system that places men in positions of social, legal, economic, religious, and political power and women in positions of subservience to men (Belknap, 2001; Dougherty, 1998; Kilmartin, 2000). As a result, masculinity is generally defined in terms considered to be positive and powerful, such as strong, independent, achieving, hardworking, dominant, heterosexual, tough, aggressive, unemotional, physical, competitive, and forceful (Kilmartin, 2000: 6). Femininity tends to be described in opposition to masculinity and the attributes are perceived as being weaker or lesser than those of men (see Kilmartin, 2000; Kirk and Okazawa-Rey, 2001). Women are expected to be weak, dependent, passive, emotional, noncompetitive, heterosexual, and subservient. Women's gender role then is defined in direct relationship to that of men (Kirk and Okazawa-Rey, 2001).

Sex-role stereotypes for men, within a patriarchal system of power, when taken to their extreme, result in ultramasculine interpretations of social order. *Ultramasculinity* refers to the acceptance of, or overreliance upon, extreme sex-role stereotypes of what it is to be a "real man." Thus men may only be strong, aggressive, independent, emotionless, and heterosexual. To be anything else, or to show feminine attributes, is to be lesser than a man, to be weak, and to be vulnerable to attack and the potential of becoming an acceptable victim by other males (for similar discussions, see Kilmartin, 2000; Messerschmidt, 1993; Lutze and Murphy, 1999; Sim, 1994).

Adherence to an ultramasculine framework can have negative consequences for both men and women. For instance, men are much more likely to commit violent crime and to be the victims of violent crime than women (Belknap, 2001; Chesney-Lind and Shelden, 1998). The use of violence by men against other men has been correlated with some men's belief that violence is an acceptable means to protect one's image, to engender respect from others, and to maintain dominance (Kilmartin, 2000; Toch, 1998).[1] Some have argued that because men are publicly limited in the extent of emotions that they may show (i.e., boys don't cry), anger becomes one of the few acceptable feelings that men can openly express and the use of aggression becomes an acceptable means to solve disputes (i.e., boys will be boys) (see Lutze and Murphy, 1999; Toch, 1998). This limited array of responses often places men in an all-or-nothing situation in which violence is the only acceptable means to respond. To walk away shows weakness and to remain means to have to protect one's manhood. Thus men are more likely to be subjected to social interactions in which violence is a predictable and likely outcome.

Gender socialization in a patriarchal system has also been used to explain violence toward women. Part of masculine identity is to be superior to women (Kilmartin, 2000; Schwartz and DeKeseredy, 1997). Superiority lends itself to the right of male privilege that provides support for men to discipline women. Men's prerogative to discipline women is reflected in the types of violence that women experience. Although women are much less likely to be the victim of violent crime than are men, the pattern of women's violent victimization is different than that of men. Women who are raped, stalked, assaulted, harassed, or murdered are significantly more likely to be victimized by a male intimate or acquaintance than are males (Koss et al., 1994; LaViolette and Barnett, 2000). Thus, instead of thinking about these crimes as isolated incidents, they should be considered as existing on a continuum of behaviors in which the underlying connection "is the abuse, intimidation, coercion, intrusion, threat and force men use to control women" (Kelly, 1988: 76).

Along this continuum of violence toward women, domestic violence is an interesting framework to use to make the connection between male violence in society and institutional violence in prison because it encompasses the full context of ultramasculine behavior. The legal emphasis of domestic violence has traditionally focused on the actual (physical) assault, but the social definition considers a broader pattern of behavior that establishes control in general and utilizes physical violence when other methods of control begin to fail or need reinforcement (Koss et al., 1994; LaViolette and Barnett, 2000). The social definition of domestic violence includes intimidation, isolation from others, male privilege, exploitation of children, economic control, threats of violence, and physical violence that may include hitting, kicking, choking, and rape (Koss et al., 1994; LaViolette and Barnett, 2000; Van Wormor and Bartollas, 2000).

I argue that all of these methods used to establish control in domestically violent relationships emerge in similar ways to control women in prison. Just as ultramasculinity helps to define individual-level violence toward women, it works within a patriarchal structure to similarly institutionalize the control of women within the prison.

Masculinity and Institutional Violence

Although the primary purpose of this chapter is to consider women's prison and how masculinity influences the control of women inmates, it is important to first make the connection between masculinity in male prisons and its translation into women's prisons. Traditionally prisons have been designed by men for the control of other men, and the acceptance of ultramasculine stereotypes permeates male prisons in ways that narrowly define what is acceptable in the treatment of men (see Lutze and Murphy, 1999; Toch, 1998). Therefore to punish men is to strip them of their manhood—to dominate them, by stripping them of their independence, their ability to achieve legitimate success, their ability to work, their ability to compete, and their heterosexuality. To be a male inmate is to have to maintain one's manhood in the face of institutionalized masculinity by maintaining some level of independence and dominance (if necessary through defiance) by being tougher, stronger, and more aggressive than one's captors and other inmates, and by defending one's heterosexuality (for male inmates' accounts of prison life, see Abbott, 1981; Gordon and Inmates of the Washington Corrections System, 2000; Hassine, 1996; Johnson and Toch, 2000).

Therefore, male prisons are in a constant state of men attempting to emasculate other men and men resisting that emasculation. The institutional climate in male prisons is one that supports the establishment and reinforcement of a masculine identity that legitimizes an inmate's use of violence and aggression (see Lockwood, 1982; Sim, 1994; Toch, 1998; Wright, 1991). Trapped in this narrow definition of masculinity, prison policies are developed to control the levels of aggression used to emasculate others, whether perpetrated by guards or inmates.[2]

The ultramasculine environment that exists in men's prisons and the policies developed to control it are often extrapolated to women's prisons. This process of extrapolation creates an odd contradiction that women should be treated like men but act according to their appropriate sex role as women. Consequently, a similar cycle of control emerges in women's prisons, where the process of male aggression remains intact but women are to acquiesce to its threat (whereas men are to defend against it). Thus to control women in prison is not to strip them of their womanhood, but to restore them to it—to ensure that they remain weak, dependent, passive, emotionally insecure, noncompetitive (with males), heterosexual, and subservient. The means utilized to accomplish this is to strip women of their personal relationships, their support networks, their children, their emotional capacity to cope maturely with their situation, and their ability to control their bodies and their sexuality. Basically, the institution replicates the same systematic pattern of behavior used by individual men in free society to dominate individual women through domestic violence.

Women's Experience in Prison and Its Relationship to Domestic Violence: Combining Individual and Institutional Control

The dominant political philosophy of how offenders should be treated, the numerous prison policies regarding women inmates, and women's experiences of incarceration provide evidence of the parallels between ultramasculinity, domestically violent relationships, and the treatment of women in prison. Women's prisons replicate the control of women by individual men in abusive relationships through institutional responses related to (1) the general climate of control, (2) isolation from external support networks and threats to children, (3) discipline and violence, (4) prison adjustment, and (5) treatment responses.

The General Climate of Control: Male Privilege

Male privilege is the power granted to men in a patriarchal society to assume control of political, economic, legal, and social realms within their individual social status (e.g., race, class, religion, etc.).[3] Within abusive relationships this means that men assume the privilege to define the parameters of the relationship with the expectation of dominance in decisionmaking within the relationship.

The privilege of possessing the power to define how others will be treated institutionalizes the gendered perspectives of white, upper-class men along ultramasculine stereotypes of how other men and women should be treated (see Smart, 1995). Male privilege has most recently been illustrated during a period of political conservatism that has resulted in a "get tough" approach to how the criminal justice system should be governed. Conservative policies have targeted violent, drug-using, male offenders (Clear, 1994; Girshick, 1999). The movement to control these men through harsher penalties and the traditional convenience of transferring male institutional responses to women have widened the net to include increasing numbers of women, especially poor and minority, in prison (see Austin and Irwin, 2001).

Danner (2000: 217) captures the sentiment of the connection between violence against individual women and institutionalized male privilege when she states:

> Women need far less protection from strangers than from supposed protectors, especially intimate partners, relatives, and acquaintances. But the debates surrounding the crime bills and recent research demonstrate that women are also at risk from the lawmakers and even some law enforcers, most of whom are men, nearly all of them white, and with respect to politicians, legislators, and judges, members of the elite social classes.

Chesney-Lind and Shelden (1998: 74) also argue:

> The official actions of the juvenile justice system should be understood as major forces in girls' oppression; these actions have historically served to reinforce the obedience of all young women to demands of patriarchal authority, no matter how abusive and arbitrary.

Other scholars have discovered this same pattern of neglect and sanctioning related to battered women and victims of rape, sexual harassment, and stalking (see Browne, 1987; Koss et al., 1994).

Male privilege also allows men to define male behavior as the norm. In such a gendered system, then, attempts at establishing equality bring about what Bloom and Chesney-Lind (2000) refer to as "vengeful equity." As Girshick points out (1999: 24):

> The "neutral" standard turns out to be a male standard, and one that is not neutral at all. . . . Attempts to equal treatment cannot yield fair treatment because women and men are different in their societal resources, degree of economic marginalization, family circumstances, rates of victimization, and gender norms and expectations. When held to a male standard, women will always lose.

Thus equity for women has translated from probation and treatment in the community to increasingly being placed in "no frills," stark prison environments for longer periods of time and equal access to harsher sanctions such as boot camp prisons and chain gangs (Bloom and Chesney-Lind, 2000; for related discussions, see also Lutze and Brody, 1999; Marcus-Mendoza, Klein-Saffran, and Lutze, 1998). Male privilege also determines where women offenders should be kept and whom they should interact with during their incarceration. This has led to isolation and limited interaction with their family.

Isolation from External Support and Threats to Children

In domestically violent relationships the perpetrator often isolates the victim from support networks such as family and friends so that he may establish complete control of his partner without outside interference (LaViolette and Barnett, 2000). In addition to isolation, the perpetrator of domestic violence will also threaten the victim with separation from, or harm to, the children if she attempts to leave or to challenge his abusive behavior. Interestingly, women's prisons similarly achieve control by locating prisons in rural areas or single locations within a state far from the home of the offender, where family, friends, children, and legal support reside (Belknap, 2001; Rafter, 1985).

An inmate's family, friends, and children can provide an important network of support during what is a very stressful time for most offenders. People who are normally relied upon during difficult times are no longer readily accessible. Metzger (2000a: 138–139), an inmate doing time in Delaware, expresses the feelings of separation from her network:

> Never is there a lack of companionship or of people who care at home. I can always find someone who shares a common interest, someone who will talk when I need counsel, listen when I need to be heard, or hug me whether I need it or not. Prison is coldness. . . . I find myself thrust into a city of strangers with whom I have nothing in common except my incarceration. . . . It's a chilling feeling to realize that no one's life here would be significantly changed if I were to die tomorrow. Loneliness breeds and thrives in the belly of the monster known as prison. It strikes constantly and insidiously and it never goes away.

Another inmate serving time in California relates:

> I've been in prison since I was seventeen, I have been abandoned by my family members, and anyone else who knew me out there. Being in prison forces you to use everything that you have just to survive. From day to day, whatever, you know it's very difficult. It's difficult to show compassion, or to have it when you haven't been extended it. (Owen 1998: 190)

In addition to the loss of familial support networks, the rural location of women's prisons often hampers access to legal support. Belknap (2001: 65) argues that distance provides greater control over women because of limited access to the legal process, which results in limited contact with attorneys due to the inconvenience of travel (time and money) and less access to law libraries and to jailhouse lawyers. Limited access to the legal process further weakens women's ability to even attempt to maintain control over their reproductive freedom and custody of and contact with their children.

Incarcerated women have had limits placed on their reproductive freedom. Many pregnant inmates have either been coerced into abortions or forced to give birth and then give up the child to adoption or foster care (Belknap, 2001; Henriques and Gilbert, 2000). Keeping and maintaining custody of children is in a constant state of jeopardy. It is common for prisons to limit the number and length of physical and phone contacts with children (Belknap, 2001; McClellan, 1994). In some states, a failure to maintain contact with children in foster care may lead to termination of the parent's rights (Belknap, 2001). Prison policies and limited access to legal assistance place women and their children in constant jeopardy of permanent separation. An inmate in Girshick's study (1999: 115) reports:

> I can see my kids two hours a week. I have a daughter that's eight months old and [since being imprisoned] I've seen her less than twenty-four hours of her life. My other two kids I've seen less than forty-eight hours of their lives [since I've been imprisoned]. In Raleigh, I got to see my kids maybe once a month, sometimes just once every other month because the drive was so hard, and when the baby was first born, she got so sick when they would drive, they couldn't bring her up.

In spite of research that shows that maintaining ties with children has positive outcomes—for the prison in reducing disciplinary problems, for the inmate in increasing the odds that she will not recidivate, and for the children through better adjustment to the trauma of separation and the reduced risk of going to prison like their mother—little has been done to support this primary relationship. Belknap (2001: 179) concludes: "[I]t is ironic that prisons have unabashedly programmed female offenders into their 'proper' gender roles as wives and mothers but simultaneously make few or no provisions for them to maintain contact with even their youngest children."

Thus, like an abuser who maintains control of his spouse through isolation and the constant threat to her relationship with her children, the prison accomplishes similar control by placing women's prisons far from home and isolating women from their support networks. Limited access to the legal process enhances the power and control of the prison and legitimizes the threat necessary to keep women inmates silent and "in their place." The power and threat are further legitimized through staff who often dislike working with women offenders, who infantilize inmates through disciplinary procedures, and who subject them to the constant threat of violence through the perpetration of sexual and physical abuse.

Correctional Misogyny: Discipline and Victimization

In a domestically violent relationship the perpetrator establishes control through the constant threat of violence if his partner does not submit to his wishes. Women in abusive relationships quickly learn to focus their thoughts and behavior on the needs of the abuser so that he will not become violently upset (Browne, 1987; LaViolette and Barnett, 2000; Koss et al., 1994). This means that she adapts every aspect of her behavior to meeting his needs instead of her own. This empowers the abuser to make the rules and to change the rules of their relationship at any time. This behavior is often based on misogynous attitudes, serves to make her completely dependent on him, and establishes his right to discipline her when necessary to ensure continued compliance.

Research on women's prisons provides ample evidence of the same methods as those used to establish control in abusive relationships. It is common knowledge among those who work in or study prisons that most correctional officers prefer to work with male inmates rather than female inmates (Pollock, 1984; Rasche, 2000). Women are perceived by correctional officers as being more demanding, argumentative, less likely to follow the rules, harder to handle, openly emotional, and wanting more personal attention (Owen, 1998; Pollock, 1984; Rasche, 2000). As Rasche (2000: 243) points out, "In short, correctional officers did not think there was anything they could do about the greater difficulty posed by female inmates because it was a product of nature. Women inmates were just being women." This gendered perspective of women as inherently more "bitchy," "nagging," or "needy" than men is reinforced and institutionalized through what inmates refer to as "petty rules."

Research shows that many rules that are not necessary for prison security are strictly enforced in women's prisons. These rules limit the decisions that female inmates can make (McClellan, 1994). Additionally, women are often subjected to security procedures that physically violate their person, and they are subjected to unofficial acts of physical violence including rape (Henriques and Gilbert, 2000).

Each of these attributes of the prison environment—reducing women to a childlike status, dislike of working with women, and the constant threat of personal invasion—work together to establish a climate of fear and control.

An environment that is defined by ultramasculinity ensures that female inmates conform to their gender role. As Van Wormer and Bartollas (2000: 62) point out:

> The formal structure of the women's prison in many ways belies the informal treatment women receive within the prison walls. At the

personal level, women are treated not as tough men, but as children; they are infantilized. Harsh punishments are meted out for cursing, disrespect, and other minor violations. Called "girls" by staff or "ladies" as at New Bedford, but never "women," female prisoners are encouraged to display "good" passive behavior by prison officials.

Infantilization is further supported by policies that sanction women for talking while waiting in line, displaying too many family photographs, failing to eat all of the food on their plates, forbidding women to speak their primary language (English only), and sending women to "their room" for these petty infractions (Belknap, 2001: 63, 190; McClellan, 1994: 85; Owen, 1998).

Thus, like in an abusive relationship, female inmates must pay close attention to what most of us would consider insignificant behavior in order to avoid direct conflict with the guards so that disciplinary action will not be taken. Disciplinary action in a domestically violent relationship may mean withholding something of value, verbal abuse and the threat of violence, or physical violence. Similarly, in prison the methods of control, both informal and formal, often violate the mental and physical integrity of the person through withholding something of importance to the inmate or acting aggressively toward her.

Informally, correctional officers may subject women inmates to mental abuse through the use of derogatory, often sexualized name-calling, increased surveillance, inconsistent rule enforcement, and delays in requests for services or access to various parts of the institution related to work, education, and programs (Van Wormer and Bartollas, 2000). For example, an inmate in Owen's study (1998: 71) reports:

> They tell me that I am a fuck-up and I tell them, "No, I am not a fuck-up, but I don't conform." Now I am conforming to the life that I want to lead in here. They want me to go by a narrow set of rules that they change daily. Okay, okay, I can follow this rule today, but why should I follow the rule because you will change it?

Another inmate in Owen's study (1998: 162) reports that officers will

> get real petty, call us bitches and things you wouldn't believe. Some of the young officers are into their power, they stay in the bubble. You know there are some officers that are personal with you, say,

"Hi, how are you this morning, here's your breakfast," but not everybody.

Although all officers do not participate, this mental abuse is common and serves to continuously undermine attempts to achieve or maintain independence.

Formal disciplinary action may take the form of confining an inmate to her cell, sending her to the "hole," where she is deprived of what few comforts or routines she has established, taking away visitation with children and family, and taking away the "good time" that she has accumulated (see McClellan, 1994). In addition, formal sanctions under the guise of security may be used to invade her "personal" space by searching her cell for contraband and destroying her property. Metzger (2000a: 140) relates:

> At home a person can be reasonably secure in the fact that his or her dwelling place will not be entered by unwanted outsiders wearing the guise of authority. This is not so for those of us in prison. At any time a staff member may enter a prisoner's room or cell and deface or confiscate personal property. This is done often, and it leaves the prisoner feeling helpless and enraged. One of the pleasures of home is receiving mail that has been unopened, unread by others, and with contents intact. Prisoners have no such pleasure.

Pat searches and strip searches are also powerful methods of control (Henriques and Gilbert, 2000). For a woman who is not "playing by the rules," pat searches can be used at any time and resistance to them can result in a full strip search. Therefore, she must submit or risk greater violation of her person. Van Wormer and Bartollas (2000: 69–70) recognize that

> The prisoner must surrender again and again to degrading rituals in which the state has taken ownership of her body/self. Prisoners who do not submit readily to body-part searchers, which may be performed by male guards, typically are forced to strip for more thorough searches. This is how power is negotiated, how the new prisoner is moved into the status of "nonperson" as a passive recipient of whatever the guards choose to mete out.

In addition to strip searching there is the constant possibility of having to, or being expected to, exchange sex for basic human needs (Watterson, 1996). This sexual extortion by correction officers helps to ensure that women continue to see themselves as a commodity to be used by men. Interestingly, sexual extortion is often viewed as consensual because the woman "willingly" engages in the sexual exchange to gain access to material goods and privileges (see Belknap, 2001; Henriques and Gilbert, 2000). It is ironic how the prison does not let women make the most basic decisions regarding their existence, reduces them to a childlike status (a status in free society that prohibits children under the age of sixteen from legally consenting to sex), and yet ignores this power imbalance and suggests that women are equals in bartering sex for basic needs when faced with sexual propositions by powerful corrections officers. In addition, even if the offender views this sexual exchange as one based on romantic love or heterosexual access within the prison (for a review, see Belknap, 2001; Butler, 1997; Watterson, 1996), the administration does not condone her ability to choose homosexual relationships with other inmates for the same purpose. In an ultramasculine environment, a male definition of sexuality defines what is appropriate access (male aggressor) and sexual behavior (heterosexual only).

In addition to sexual extortion, historical as well as recent research shows that women are also subject to the constant threat of rape by corrections officers (see Belknap, 2001; Butler, 1997; Christianson, 1998; Henriquez and Gilbert, 2000; Rafter, 1985; Watterson, 1996). Although sexual assault is not formally condoned, its relative frequency and silent acceptance allow it to be used as an effective means of control. Women in prison who are raped by male corrections officers (and, at times, female officers) are often coerced into silence through threats of further violence, threats of losing children and existing support networks, and the often too real perception that no one will believe them because they are inmates (see Henriquez and Gilbert, 2000).

The dynamics of control outlined earlier—male privilege, isolation, misogyny, infantilization—all coalesce to minimize the victim's ability to respond to and cope with her situation while at the same time ensuring the individual officer's power and the institution's ability to maintain control of the entire inmate population. This constant threat of violence, combined with many women's prior experiences of abuse, makes for a very complex institutional climate to which inmates must adjust.

Coping and Adjustment:
Learned Hopefulness and Learned Helplessness

Women in domestically violent relationships have been found to adjust their behavior based on experiences of learned hopefulness and learned helplessness. Learned hopefulness is a "a battered woman's ongoing belief that her partner will change his abusive behavior or that he will change his personality" (Barnett and LaViolette, 1993: 16). They hope that the violence will end and the lovable qualities of their spouse will return. This hope often provides the foundation for a woman's decision to remain with her partner and the acceptance of an apology with the promise that the violence will never happen again. Periods of nonviolence give hope that it will not happen again. Learned helplessness results when repeated personal attempts at acquiescence fail, when attempts at getting external assistance from family, friends, clergy, social services, and police fall short, and when the fear and stress of victimization continue (for a general discussion, see Barnett and LaViolette, 1993).

Women in prison also experience learned hopefulness and helplessness. Hope for women in prison is the belief that if they acquiesce to the demands of their captors, they will continue to progress toward release and not lose credits for "good time," not lose contact with family, and maintain or achieve access to better housing units, programs, and job assignments. For women with life sentences, similar things are important to their existence, and hope may be further magnified by pending appeals or commutation of their sentence. Metzger (2000b: 219) captures the potential irony of such hope:

> The manipulation game is an insidious game. Its perpetrators are those in power; maybe even your own family and friends play their parts. The object of the game is to dangle the carrot, that hope of freedom, endlessly, endlessly, until with each passing year it seems more and more foolish to risk blowing the time you have accumulated, the time you have wasted. Hope is a beautiful thing if you are one of the few lucky ones in this game of political roulette and you make it out. But if hope turns out to be fruitless, then it becomes destructive—a tool used by the vicious to control the helpless. Tell me—who will listen, and what do we do if they won't?

Helplessness is further exacerbated by prison policies that hinder women's ability to reach out to others for support. In addition to isolation from the outside, women are dissuaded from forming personal relationships with other inmates. In some institutions, any public display of affection is interpreted as a potential homosexual liaison and forced separation is imminent (Belknap, 2001). Women quickly learn that their personal methods of coping with the prison environment through friendship or intimacy with other inmates will be quickly responded to through formal sanctions, while attempts to use formal mechanisms to report abuse perpetrated by corrections officers will be met with resistance and disbelief (Henriques and Gilbert, 2000). Therefore, like men, women are expected to "do their own time" (see Girshick, 1999; Johnson, 2002), even though it is well known that women tend to need to connect with others to deal with stressful situations (Covington, 1998; Swift, 1998).

This pattern is a familiar one for women who have experienced abuse in prior relationships. Depending upon the study, 40 to 90 percent of women report having experienced some form of sexual, domestic, or emotional abuse prior to prison (see Belknap, 2001; Bloom and Chesney-Lind, 2000; Girshick, 1999; Owen, 1998; Sargent, Marcus-Mendoza, and Ho Yu, 1993). Oddly enough, these women may already have a method to cope with, and survive, the dynamic of power used in prison to achieve control.[4] Basically they are already capable of coping with "more of the same" regardless of whether their approach to survival is considered emotionally or physically healthy.

For some women, prison, in spite of its shortcomings, may be a safer environment than the one from which they were removed. For instance, inmates in Girshick's study (1999: 100; see also Owen, 1998) report:

> Coming to prison was the best thing that ever happened to me.... Because I was getting out of control. Alcohol. I was an alcoholic, still am.... I might even be dead.

> I don't know if I could have ever gotten clean enough [without prison]. But living the way I was living, with the drugs, and living with a drug dealer, I don't know if that would have ever happened for me.

Nonetheless, prison needs to be more than a place to escape the immediate violence of the street. It needs to respond to women's past experiences in a way that increases the opportunity for success in the future. Zaplin (1998b: 68; see also Covington, 1998: 128) argues that

While, in the short term, institutionalization temporarily does take them out of the violence and abuse at home and on the street, without programs that adequately address their rehabilitative needs, institutionalization does not modify their unhealthy behavior patterns such as drug use, or have long-term positive impact on recidivism rates. In point of fact, institutionalization that does not contribute to the positive alteration of the behavioral repertoires of female offenders often exacerbates their situations especially if they experience violence and abuse within the institutions themselves.

Treatment Programs: Conscience and Convenience

Traditionally women have had less access to prison programs than men (Morash, Haarr, and Rucker, 1994; Muraskin, 2000a) and most current programs have been designed by men for men and extrapolated to women's prisons (Covington, 1998). Not surprisingly, the programs that were designed specifically for women often prepared them to reenter society as better wives, mothers, and domestic servants instead of self-reliant, economically independent citizens (see Belknap, 2001; Girshick, 1999; Morash, Haarr, and Rucker, 1994; Rafter, 1985). Although this is still the case in many prison systems (Morash, Haarr, and Rucker, 1994), some women's prisons are attempting to provide treatment and vocational training that empower women to deal more effectively with past and future experiences (see Hannah-Moffat, 1995; Zaplin, 1998a).

For programs to be effective for women within a prison environment they must foster mutuality, empathy, and "power-with-others" instead of "power-over-others" (Covington, 1998). Most prison environments do not appear to possess these attributes. Therefore, programs that attempt to empower women inmates are often in direct conflict with the prison regime in which women must live (see Hannah-Moffat, 1995; Zaplin, 1998a). Zaplin (1998b: 69) states that

> even if multifaceted, rehabilitative programs are developed, their efficacy will likely be undermined by the social structure of the institutional environment as it exists today. Thus, for most female offenders, punishments rendered in institutional environments are not conducive to addressing their rehabilitative needs even in the best of circumstances.

Thus, changing the ultramasculine nature of women's prisons is necessary in order for programs and women to be successful. As long as we subscribe to the acceptance of ultramasculine environments in prison it will be difficult to move beyond the status quo of how offenders are treated. The shortcomings of ultramasculine environments in male prisons show the same effect as in women's prisons (Lutze and Murphy, 1999: 727):

> Male inmates and staff members may find it difficult to provide higher levels of support and emotional feedback in programs designed to accomplish rehabilitation because more personal, more caring forms of support are not perceived as acceptable masculine forms of communication. It may be that the prison environment is not "safe" enough to enable an inmate to depart from traditional male paradigms of communication.

Lutze and Murphy (1999) discovered that those male inmates who defined their environment as more ultramasculine were significantly more likely to feel isolated, helpless, and stressed.

The existence of an ultramasculine prison environment in women's prison promotes the same negative outcome. A "nonmutual, nonempathetic, disempowering, and unsafe setting make change and healing extremely difficult" (Covington, 1998: 128). The psychological and physical isolation that women in prison experience is bound to promote failure. This same state of being that is fostered in prison is highly correlated with the experiences women have in abusive relationships prior to prison, with drug use as a means to cope and feelings of helplessness (Covington, 1998). Thus the prison environment is promoting the very circumstances that enhance the likelihood of recidivism.

Prisons should be focused on enhancing the qualities that promote escape from abusive relationships. Research shows that women who successfully leave violent relationships tend to be employed, have higher levels of education, and have healthy connections with others outside of the battering relationship (Swift, 1998). Covington (1998) argues that women's programs should be designed to address the realities of women's lives and should be based on women's growth and development. Therefore, one would expect women's correctional environments to be as free as possible while still recognizing the need for public safety, to be culturally sensitive, and to provide educational and vocational opportunities, well-trained and diverse staff, and positive role models Covington, 1998: 120 [cites Bloom 1997]).

In spite of current attempts in some women's prisons to develop "women-centered" approaches, some argue that it may be impossible to create a prison environment that successfully employs the empowerment of women inmates within a male-defined criminal justice system that magnifies the structural inequalities of the general society (see Hannah-Moffat, 1995; Kendall, 1998; Zaplin, 1998a). Additional criticism suggests that attempting to create women-centered prisons in a misogynous system may hinder the creation of more successful community-based approaches (see Hannah-Moffat, 1995).

Although the futility of focusing on creating women-centered prisons has credibility given the expansive literature on the causes of gender inequality in society, the U.S. prison system is reluctant to change, and in reality some women offenders, especially the violent, need to be incarcerated, whether for the protection of others, punishment, or rehabilitation. Therefore, we must still consider whether it is possible to concurrently control and sanction negative behavior *and* empower the individual within a coercive environment (see Hannah-Moffat, 1995; Marcus-Mendoza, Klein-Saffran, and Lutze, 1998). Given that our current prison system is permeated with ultramasculine perspectives and practices (for both men and women), the task of balancing the use of appropriate power with the provision of an environment supportive of rehabilitation will be difficult (for related discussions, see Lutze, 1998; Lutze and Brody, 1999; Lutze and Murphy, 1999).

Current research suggests that we already know what to do to achieve women-centered prison environments that focus on the empowerment of women offenders (see Covington, 1998; Chesney-Lind and Shelden, 1998; Hannah-Moffat, 1995; Marcus-Mendoza, Klein-Saffran, and Lutze, 1998; Zaplin, 1998b). The problem in achieving change, however, centers around the difficulty of program implementation by those who are reluctant to give up existing political structures and who possess differing visions of gender equality. As Hannah-Moffat (1995: 149) states:

> The selective integration of some feminist ideas and not others contributes to the production of a feminized social control talk dressed up in therapeutic and feminist language. In some ways, these "women-centered reforms" only replace the discredited regimes with a less overt but nonetheless oppressive exercise of power.

Consequently, feminist perspectives included during program development are often lost, or selectively utilized, during the political process of implementation (see Hannah-Moffat, 1995).

This creates the materialization of "feminist-oriented" policy that relies upon what is easy to implement within the current power structure and ignores the elements that may be more complex or require structural changes in the existing system. Rothman (1980: 10), in his historical review of progressive-era prison reforms, argues that reformers believed that they could guard and help, protect and rehabilitate, maintain custody and deliver treatment through the same person in the same institution. He concludes (1980: 10): "In the end, when conscience and convenience met, convenience won. When treatment and coercion met, coercion won." One could easily add that when it comes to the treatment of women offenders, when ultramasculine prison environments and women-centered prisons meet, ultramasculinity will ultimately win.

Conclusion

Masculine sex-role stereotypes permeate women's prisons in ways that replicate the control utilized in abusive relationships. Women-centered treatment programs implemented against this narrowly defined ultramasculine backdrop are doomed to fail because the prison environment ensures dominance and control instead of empowerment. Failure for the institution and the offenders who pass through it will persist as long as coerced conformity to the institution drives offender care rather than supportive, safe environments that meet the rehabilitative needs of offenders (see Lutze, 2002).

Coerced conformity to institutions grounded in ultramasculine sex roles will continue to be detrimental to inmates, especially women. Although ultramasculine prison environments may also be harmful to men, at least men are socialized to defend against such attacks on their person and position within society. For many men, the institution's attempt to emasculate them is "temporary," for they will return to their "privileged" position as men upon their release.[5] For women, however, acquiescence to the coercive nature of the prison environment and the continuation of powerlessness within the family and their extended social networks is likely to extend indefinitely into their future.

Coerced conformity also allows institutions to relieve themselves of the responsibility for failing to reduce recidivism. A social-political climate that values accountability and places unrelenting responsibility for criminal behavior on offenders has been translated by prison administrators (often driven by state legislatures) to emphasize control and conformity to institutional rules rather than taking institutional responsibility for treatment milieus known to be successful. This approach places accountability for failure on the most powerless within the system. As Lutze (2002: 75) points out, "It is easier to shift full responsibility for criminal behavior to the offender and demand that they fix their problems, even though they may be powerless to do so, than it is to implement prison programs that teach them how to deal positively with their problems long term."

Holding institutions responsible for addressing the complex social and cognitive-behavioral needs of offenders is critical. The default approach of subjecting men and women to more of the same by institutionalizing ultramasculine sex-role stereotypes is unacceptable and absurd. Accepting overly simplistic approaches to corrections that replicate and contribute to the abuse of women is barbaric and should not continue in the face of decades of social change focused on gender equality, scholarly research that presents viable alternatives to traditional approaches to incarceration, and the evidence presented by the life experiences of women (and men) who survive a system that not only fails them but often contributes to their demise.

Notes

I dedicate this chapter to Nina, Marvel, and Phyllis. To Nina, who for more than fifty years has managed to survive physical and emotional abuse and still maintain her spirit and capacity to unconditionally love her family and friends. To Marvel and Phyllis, who for more than fifty years have been Nina's friends and who could not be driven away at any cost. To all three for refusing to "act their age" and for their willingness to bring a thirty-something into their circle of friendship.

1. It is important to note that adherence to masculine sex roles may vary over the life-span and in accordance to ethnic and cultural background (see Kilmartin, 2000). For example, older men may be less likely to strictly adhere to masculine expectations because they have already established a position that they are comfortable with and are not directly threatened by, or competing with, other men.

2. Individual accounts given by male inmates lend support for the level of violence used to establish dominance and survival in men's maximum-security institutions and the complexity of the institutional response that both supports

and attempts to control violence between men (correctional officers and inmates) and among men (inmate to inmate) in prison (see Abbott, 1981; Hassine, 1996; Gordon and Inmates of the Washington Corrections System, 2000; Johnson and Toch, 2000).

3. It is recognized that all men do not possess equal status and power within any particular society due to the historical effects of racism, classism, and heterosexism (see Kilmartin, 2000, for a review). Thus men may differ in the amount of power that they possess over other men and women, but all men within their socioeconomic position possess power over women through their status as men.

4. In a study of male offenders, Zamble and Porporino (1988) discovered that many of the offenders in their sample possessed poor coping strategies before prison, adapted those strategies to the prison environment, and then returned to the same poor coping strategies once released. Although I have not reviewed any specific studies to longitudinally address the coping strategies of women in prison, given what we know about women's experiences before, during, and after prison it is not unreasonable to believe that many women experience a similar process.

5. I am not arguing that the effects of incarceration on many men cannot be long-term or that their privileged position is not compromised by the identity of being an ex-convict, but that even with an experience of incarceration that is similar to that of women, they are more likely to be accepted into gender-privileged roles upon release.

10

Conclusion: Moving Forward

Jim Thomas

> How did I bring you here? Was it out of habit that you began where I must leave or did you, and why did you, reach here by way of what went before? I would understand both. Of course, there is no real end here, nor any real beginning, just a going on. (O'Neill, 1972: 264)

We have returned to the first act in our drama of gendered prison culture, to the point of moving forward. We have argued that sex-role stereotypes in prison not only provide a gendered mechanism of control, but also contribute to a debilitating prison culture that risks inhibiting prisoners' social development while simultaneously attempting to facilitate it. Because of the absurdity that women's prisons have been structured around the ultramasculine model deemed appropriate for men, males and females do not experience prisons in the same way. Therefore, not all constraints and punishments targeted for one are equally effective or appropriate for the other, especially if one carceral goal is to provide prisoners with experiences beneficial for social harmony and personal growth.

Although much remains unsaid, undone, and unaddressed, if successful, we have raised issues that will provoke methodological, conceptual, theoretical, and policy dialogue about prisons, gender, and social control. The contributors to this volume examined the gendered existence of control in women's prisons as a lens through which to view broader gendered reality. Although not all contributors have used the same terms or have written within the same perspective, they collectively have illustrated shared themes on which to pursue analysis of gender as a subtle yet powerful means of control.

Theoretical Musings

There is no shortage of theoretical and conceptual tools to help us understand prison culture and how prisoners experience it. Nor is there a shortage of theories of gender and power. However, relatively few prison studies attempt to systematically develop the theoretical implications of gendered control in prisons. Although theoretical synthesis lies outside the scope of this volume, the empirical works here nevertheless suggest several broader theoretical approaches.

We organized these studies within an existential framework as a way to view prison culture from an absurdist paradigm of power, freedom, control, and broader social domination. The intent was to encourage a reflexive way of looking at and thinking about prisoner culture by shifting our gaze to the lived conditions and experiences of prisoners as shaped by gender. This also provided a way to combine issues of social action, social constraint, and resistance in oppressive environments that suggest linkages to other theoretical approaches as well. For example, Foucault's studies of gender-as-power center on the modes of objectification by which people turn themselves into subjects, especially of sexuality (1982: 208). Power, for Foucault, is more than a relationship between people. It is also a way in which certain actions modify other actions and people (219). Prison power functions not so much to create prisoner automatons, but to discipline individuals to cultural conformity:

> The chief function of the disciplinary power is to "train," rather than to select and to levy; or, no doubt, to train in order to levy and select all the more. It does not link forces together in order to reduce them; it seeks to bind them together in such a way as to multiply and use them. Instead of bending all its subjects into a single uniform mass, it separates, analyzes, differentiates, carries its procedures of decomposition to the point of necessary and sufficient single units. It "trains" the moving, confused, useless multitudes of bodies and forces into a multiplicity of individual elements—small, separate cells, organic autonomies, genetic identities and continuities, combinary segments. Discipline "makes" individuals; it is the specific technique of a power that regards individuals both as objects and as instruments of its exercise. (1979: 170)

Foucault's emphasis on gender-based modes of objectification illustrates the process by which people turn themselves into controlled subjects as part of the ideologically formatted process of identity creation and maintenance (1982: 208). In prisons, for example, discipline is imposed by the techniques of the "total institution" (Goffman, 1961), which routinize every aspect of daily existence; identify, categorize, and record the prisoners' physical, emotional, medical, biographical, and psychological characteristics; and constantly monitor the prisoners' activity. In this way, gender becomes a self-sustaining control mechanism.

Gender for What?

There is another, less visible, and somewhat pernicious mechanism of discipline and control enforced by the overt asymmetrical power imbalances between and among the keepers and the kept on both sides of prison walls, one that we have not explored here: the heterosexual ideology that underlies gendered power. Therefore, following Ingraham's (1994) provocative question, we might ask: Gender for what? Heterosexual expectations and gender identity provide the obvious framework for how we interact with each other and form the subtle, deep structures of power, social control, and domination. One way this occurs is through the reinforcement of "heterogendering," which refers to the ways in which the processes and images of heterosexuality become institutionalized in ways that reinforce prisoners' identities such that they partially become their own control agents. The presumed naturalness of heterosexuality creates a set of fundamental images and courses of action that reinforce existing forms of social domination, especially in prisons. Because of its presumed invariance and immutability, heterogendering becomes an integral part of prisoners' identity. As an internalized and valued attribute, it thus becomes transformed into an ideological control mechanism, as Lutze and Murphy (1999) illustrated in their study of male boot camps. Heterogendered social existence and the ultramasculine cultural forms required to create and sustain it in both men's and women's prisons reflect a complex process of competing forces that contribute to the dysfunctional, deleterious prison environment.

This produces an ironic consequence in which ultramasculine traits of aggression, coercion, violence, and other predatory forms of power contribute to the survival and adaptation to prison life, reinforcing the gender-based victimization women experienced on the streets. For example, as on the streets, degradation games, verbal confrontations, and physical assaults commonly center on feminizing the target through sex-related slurs and challenges to sexuality. Whether male or female, calling a prisoner a "bitch" in the shower generally reflects a challenge to "honor" that must be rectified, usually with violence; the epithet of "punk" reflects sexual degradation in both men's and women's prisons; and even such a seemingly simple (and silly) guard command as "okay girls, let's riot" as a signal for men to begin marching back to their cellhouse from dinner typifies the way that heterogendered statuses pervade the language and imagery of prison culture.

Drawing from Foucault (1979: 23), heterogendering can be seen as a control technique that possesses its own specificity in conjunction with other ways of exercising power in prisons. Knowledge, in this case "ideological knowledge" of appropriate sexual and gender norms, constitutes a form of power over the body that translates into a mechanism of institutionalized yet subtle domination. This leads to Bem's insightful theoretical prescription: "[I]n order to interrupt the social reproduction of male power, we need to dismantle not only androcentrism and biological essentialism but also gender polarization and compulsory heterosexuality" (1998: ix).

Reenter Pirandello

Pirandello (1922, 1998) suggests how framing conventional research within an absurdist existential perspective draws attention to the uneasy tensions between freedom and constraint, hope, despair, and action. We have attempted to balance these tensions by suggesting ways to rethink gender as a subtle yet powerful tool of social control. The chapters in this volume imply that, by thinking about and then acting upon our social world, we are able to change our subjective interpretations and objective conditions. This offers hope for overcoming the ideational and structural obstacles that restrict perception and discussion of control by exploring the alternative meanings underlying the gendered nature of women's (and men's) prison experiences. The contributors challenge us to reflect on conceptual and existential alternatives by offering interpretative frameworks for examining the cultural experiences of both men and women.

Our narratives of prison life become an allegory for other forms of social existence in which the potential to act is obstructed and social actors remain powerless relative to their potential to engage and transcend their circumstances. As does Pirandello, the contributors here tweak the audience by blurring the boundaries between reality and the surrealism that underlies it. Who is the author who turns us into gendered subjects? Or do we, the subjects, author ourselves? Like Pirandello, the contributors here illustrate the terror, kindness, despair, loneliness, brutality, resistance, confusion, ambiguity, and even acceptance of everyday life. They emphasize the difficulty of sorting out necessary gender games from those that are unnecessary. They illustrate how the products of our research productions, like characters in the dramas in which we live and about whom we write, may take on an independence of their own. Each allows us to confront the dilemma of Smith's "everyday world as problematic" (1987) and the authorship of our existence, even in highly constrained cultures.

Sadly, texts contain silences, and silences can convey subtextual messages as meaningful as those overtly spoken. Although the contributors here are emphatic in their commitment both to prison and to social reform, they have offered relatively few explicit suggestions for action. This was, in part, the result of a conscious decision to avoid prescriptive platitudes for action, which are more appropriate for a separate volume. But it was also in part the result of frustration, even despair, in our uphill struggles to reform prisons over the years. Watterson nicely describes this dilemma:

> More than twenty-three years ago I was talking with a group of women in the kitchen of Ohio's state prison for women at Marysville, when a prisoner started shouting from across the room, "Why are you talking to her? What good's it gonna do? She ain't gonna do nothing!" She leaned on her mop, angry and unconvinced when the women I was talking to hollered back that I was writing a book that would "tell it like it is."
> "Well, even if she does write it like it is, people ain't gonna do nothing about it," she said. "They'll just say, 'Ain't that a shame,' and nothing will change. Twenty years from now it'll still be the same. We'll still be here. And it'll be just the same." (1996: xiii)

Most of the contributors to this volume have experienced similar conversations in prisons. As a consequence, while we wish to share our insights as prison researchers dedicated to reforming the prison system and reducing injustice, we have no illusions about the difficulties of reform.

Connell (1987: 17) observed that "personal life and collective social arrangements are linked in a fundamental and constitutive way."

His point was that theoretical integration of each is necessary in the process of understanding our collective and individual social existence and transforming that understanding into practice. The contributors here reinforce this by arguing that we cannot understand the gendered influences of prison control and punishment without placing them in the context of patriarchy and ultramasculinity both in male prisons and in the broader culture:

In other words, we need to sever all the culturally constructed connections that currently exist in our society and between what sex a person is and virtually every other aspect of human existence, including modes of dress, social roles, and even ways of expressing emotion and experiencing sexual desire (Bem, 1998: ix).

What Next?

At a recent convention of the American Correctional Association, a featured speaker described the benefits of a particular prison program on prisoners. The audience was impressed. At the conclusion of her presentation, a member of the audience asked, "But, did you talk to any prisoners?" The speaker acknowledged that she had not. Despite the well-meaning intentions of the speaker, the prisoners became invisible and the meaning of the program for them dissolved in an acidic vat of official discourse and administrative statistics. This is one example of how practitioners, the public, and even scholars tend to view prisons and prisoners' culture and experiences within it from the perceptions and perspective of others. The prisoners were silenced, perpetuating the symbolic violence created by a distorted lens.

In the past twenty years, prisoner demographics have changed, prison culture has changed, gender roles have changed, and prison policies have changed. What are the processes underlying these changes and what impact have the changes had on prisoners? Have gender games in prison been modified as a result of changes in gender culture in the outside world? How can an understanding of gendered prison culture contribute to reforms not only in prison, but in postrelease adjustment processes as well?

One answer supplied by the contributors here: Talk to prisoners! By bridging the gap between insiders and outsiders, and by refocusing our theoretical lenses, we can heed Bosworth's call to unite theory, data, and practice (1999b: 68–69), thus presenting a richer depiction of what occurs behind prison walls as well as on the other side. Especially by understanding prisoners' narratives as part of the wider social context of the matrix of domination of gender, class, and race, the interlocking processes that shape the prison experience as part of a larger totality of individual and social existence become clearer. Giving prisoners the opportunity to tell their stories allows for more than a simple reproduction of their narratives. It also allows the researcher to generate dialogue and engage in critique not only of the narratives, but also of the broader gender and other ideological frames—including our own—in which they are embedded.

In the outside world, the "lens of gender" creates a male-centered set of images in which men's experiences are taken as axiomatic and superimposed on women as an organizing principle that forges a cultural connection between sex and other aspects of human existence (Bem, 1992: 2). As in the outside world, this translates into prison policies in which special needs of men are considered axiomatic, and women's special needs are either treated as special cases or left unmet (Bem, 1992: 183). As a consequence, treating male and female prisoners identically has not resolved gender disparity, and in some ways has increased it. This requires a closer look at how women's unique preprison, prison, and postprison experiences should become part of policy formation.

But this raises a another point. If gender matters, where lies the line between recognizing gender differences in prison policies without reproducing prison experiences based on a gender hierarchy in which male needs are the paradigm for prison administration? The question is a bit misleading, because while redirecting attention to the inappropriateness of the crime-control male model as the standard for women, it ironically redirects attention away from challenging this model as inappropriate for men as well. Confronting patriarchy, of course, is part of the solution, as we recall Sabo, Kupers, and London's depiction (2001) of how deeply prisons embody the extreme hierarchical, predatory, and oppressive cultural games by which men create and preserve power over both women and other males. This returns us to the need to examine the subtle power of all heterogendered institutions as a dominant factor in the process of gender oppression in general and dysfunctional gender control in prisons in particular. To repeat the appeal by Sabo, Kupers, and London, expanding studies of men in prison can supplement feminist theory by including a critical analysis of males and masculinity in perpetuating gender domination of women in prison.

Of course, altering the fundamental structural and institutional arrangements that create and support patriarchy and other forms of unnecessary social domination requires radical social change of the kind that occurs slowly. Hence, working for long-term changes, even if successful, will have little immediate impact on prison culture, prisoners, or prison policy. A more modest solution lies in radical challenges to the excesses of the intensely punitive model that characterizes corrections in the United States (Beckett and Sasson, 2000; Welch, 1999). Translating prisoners' narratives into calls for specific prison programs and policies, or broader legislative and related changes, requires working with outside groups. This we can do on a daily basis through activism, teaching, speaking, and working in small ways to create incremental changes.

This, however, resurrects the old debate among political activists: Is it better to engage in incremental reform, as liberals prefer, or is it better to invest energies in challenging the fundamental social conditions that breed injustice? The contributions here suggest that both are possible. At the incremental level, working with individual prisoners or prisoner and family groups, challenging prison policies, and involvement with prison reform agencies are a few ways to bring about minimalist reform. The contributors here strongly advocate the view that prison reformers can focus on programs that help the individual while also contributing to altering the prisoner culture and environment. They acknowledge the dialectical relationship between the unique deprivational environmental of prisons and the broader sociocultural framework imported into the institution in shaping prisoner culture and behavior. They also recognize that we cannot alter the fundamental gendered nature of control in prisons while ignoring the gendered social imbalances in the broader society. This means that prison programs that emphasize vocational or therapeutic training, or even life skills, are in themselves unlikely to change the gendered prison culture. But the contributors also recognize that reducing the dysfunctional constraints of the prison environment by implementing prison programs that stress individual self-help, independence, and life skills could be effective in the short term by facilitating adaptation to prison culture and postrelease adjustment. This requires raising broader issues by aligning with outside special interest groups, engaging in public dialogue and critique, and challenging gender imbalances at every opportunity. While these alone won't lead to dramatic shifts in the patriarchal power structure, they nonetheless can incrementally help individual offenders while simultaneously providing small tiles in the broader mosaic on which more fundamental changes are eventually built.

Many of us have been challenged by ideological purists who dismiss such incremental reform as a dangerous strategy that ultimately reproduces those very social constraints that we oppose. In the purists' view, only radical social changes can alter gender oppression and prison policy. Anything else, they argue, is liberal reformism that does nothing but reproduce social oppression while creating the illusion that "something is being done." We are left with the question, then, of whether what we do is futile not only because of the difficulties of social change, but also because it subverts our own goals by reproducing oppression.

Faced with similar debates in the 1960s, Gorz distinguished between "reformist reforms" and "nonreformist reforms." Reformist reforms, he argued, are those that subordinate their objectives to the interests of the dominant power. "Reformism rejects those objectives and demands—however deep the need for them—which are incompatible with the preservation of the system" (1968: 7). A nonreformist reform, by contrast, is a reform that challenges fundamental beliefs, institutions, and structures, and is "conceived not in terms of what is possible within the framework of a given system and administration, but in view of what should be made possible in terms of human needs and demands" (7).

The contributors to this volume are guided not by "what is," but by "what could be." Our goal, seemingly simple, has been to continue to move forward in our research with women in prison and to share our insights in a public forum in which discussion and the sharing of ideas ignite new possibilities for change through nonreformist reforms. The intent is to move beyond being mere witnesses who give testimony, to being active participants in the process of social change. We invite our readers to do the same in connecting prison existence for men and women with the broader gendered processes that shape it, in order to take the next step of contributing to changes to our shared Pirandellian prisons.

References

Abbott, Jack. 1981. *In the Belly of the Beast: Letters from Prison.* New York: Vintage.
ACA (American Correctional Association). 1990. *The Female Offender: What Does the Future Hold?* Laurel, MD: ACA.
Acoca, Leslie. 1998. "Defusing the Time Bomb: Understanding and Meeting the Growing Health Care Needs of Incarcerated Women in America." *Crime and Delinquency* 44(1): 49–69.
Agozino, Biko. 1997. *Black Women and the Criminal Justice System: Towards the Decolonisation of Victimisation.* Aldershot: Ashgate.
AIM (Aid to Inmate Mothers), Inc. 2001. "Facts About Mothers in Prison." Available at www.inmatemoms.org/facts.htm.
Alarid, Leanne Fiftal. 1996. "Women Offenders' Perceptions of Confinement: Behavior Code Acceptance, Hustling, and Group Relations in Jail and Prison." Ph.D. diss., Sam Houston State University, Huntsville, TX.
Albor, Teresa. 1995. "The Women Get Chains." *The Nation,* February 20, pp. 234–237.
Alexander, Ruth M. 1995. *The "Girl Problem": Female Sexual Delinquency in New York, 1900–1930.* Ithaca, NY: Cornell University Press.
AMA (American Medical Association). 1992. *Diagnostic and Treatment Guidelines on Domestic Violence.* Washington, DC: AMA.
Amnesty International. 1999. "United States of America: Not Part of My Sentence—Violations of the Human Rights of Women in Custody." Available at www.web.amnesty.org.
———. 2000. "United States of America." Available at www.web.amnesty.org.
Andrews, Matthew Page. 1933. *The Founding of Maryland.* New York: Appleton-Century.
APA (American Psychological Association). 1996. *Violence and the Family: Report of the American Psychological Association.* Presidential Task Force on Violence and the Family. Washington, DC: APA.

Arata, Catalina M. 2000. "From Child Victim to Adult Victim: A Model for Predicting Sexual Revictimization." *Child Maltreatment* 5(1): 28–38.
Arnold, Regina. 1990. "Processes of Victimization and Criminalization of Black Women." *Social Justice* 17:153–166.
Auherhahn, Kathleen, and Elizabeth Dermody Leonard. 2000. "Docile Bodies? Chemical Restraints and the Female Inmate." *Journal of Criminal Law and Criminology* 90(2): 599–634.
Austin, James, and John Irwin. 2001. *It's About Time: America's Imprisonment Binge*. 3rd ed. Belmont, CA: Wadsworth.
Ball, D. W. 1972. "The 'Family' as a Sociological Problem: Conceptualization of the Taken-for-Granted as a Prologue to Social Problem Analysis." *Social Problems* 19:297–307.
Barak, Gregg, Jeanne M. Flavin, and Paul S. Leighton. 2001. *Class, Race, Gender, and Crime: Social Realities of Justice in America*. Los Angeles: Roxbury.
Barnett, Ola, and Alyce LaViolette. 1993. *It Could Happen to Anyone: Why Battered Women Stay*. 1st ed. Thousand Oaks, CA: Sage.
Barry, Ellen. 1989. "Pregnant Prisoners." *Harvard Women's Law Journal* 12:189–205.
Baunach, Phyllis J. 1985. *Mothers in Prison*. New Brunswick, NJ: Transaction.
Beattie, L. Elisabeth, and Mary Angela Shaughnessy. 2000. *Sisters in Pain: Battered Women Fight Back*. Lexington: University Press of Kentucky.
Beck, Allen. 1991. *Profile of Jail Inmates, 1989*. Washington, DC: U.S. Department of Justice, April.
———. 2000. *Prisoners in 1999*. Washington, DC: U.S. Department of Justice.
Beck, Allen J., and Paige M. Harrison. 2001. *Prisoners in 2000*. Washington, DC: Bureau of Justice Statistics.
Beck, Allen J., and Jennifer C. Karberg. 2001. *Bureau of Justice Statistics Bulletin: Prisoners at Midyear 2000*. Washington, DC: U.S. Department of Justice.
Beck, Allen J., Jennifer C. Karberg, and Paige M. Harrison. 2002. *Bureau of Justice Statistics Bulletin: Prison and Jail Inmates at Midyear 2001*. Washington, DC: U.S. Department of Justice.
Beck, Allen J., and Christopher J. Mumola. 1999. *Prisoners in 1998*. Washington, DC: U.S. Government Printing Office, p. 9.
Beckett, Katherine, and Theodore Sasson. 2000. *The Politics of Injustice: Crime and Punishment in America*. London: Pine Forge Press.
Belknap, Joanne. 1996. "Access to Programs and Health Care for Incarcerated Women." *Federal Probation* 60(4): 34–39.
———. 2001. *The Invisible Woman: Gender, Crime, and Justice*. 2nd ed. Belmont, CA: Wadsworth.
Bem, Sandra Lipsitz. 1992. *The Lenses of Gender: Transforming the Debate on Sexual Inequality*. New Haven: Yale University Press.
———. 1998. *An Unconventional Family*. New Haven: Yale University Press.
Benhabib, Seyla. 1995. "Feminism and Postmodernism: An Uneasy Alliance." In Seyla Benhabib, Judith Butler, Drucilla Cornell, and Nancy Fraser, *Feminist Contentions: A Philosophical Exchange*, pp. 17–34. New York: Routledge.

Benhabib, Seyla, Judith Butler, Drucilla Cornell, and Nancy Fraser. 1995. *Feminist Contentions: A Philosophical Exchange*. New York: Routledge.

Berger, Peter L., and Thomas Luckmann. 1967. *The Social Construction of Reality: A Treatise in the Sociology of Knowledge*. Garden City, NY: Doubleday-Anchor.

Bill, Louise. 1998. "The Victimization and Revictimization of Female Offenders." *Corrections Today*, December, pp. 106–112.

BJS (Bureau of Justice Statistics). 1994. *Criminal Victimization 1994*. Washington, DC: U.S. Department of Justice.

———. 1995. *Violence Against Women: Estimates from the Redesigned Survey*. Washington, DC: U.S. Department of Justice, August.

———. 1999. *Women Offenders*. Washington, DC: U.S. Department of Justice, Office of Justice Programs, December.

———. 2001. *Medical Problems of Inmates, 1997*. Washington, DC: U.S. Department of Justice.

Bledsoe, Albert Taylor. 1857. *An Essay on Liberty and Slavery*. Philadelphia: Lippincott.

Bloom, Barbara. 1993. "Incarcerated Mothers and Their Children: Maintaining Family Ties." In *Female Offenders: Meeting the Needs of a Neglected Population*, pp. 60–68. Laurel, MD: American Correctional Association.

Bloom, Barbara, and Meda Chesney-Lind. 2000. "Women in Prison: Vengeful Equity." In R. Muraskin, ed., *It's a Crime: Women and Justice*, 2nd ed., pp. 183–204. Upper Saddle River, NJ: Prentice Hall.

Bloom, Barbara, and David Steinhart. 1993. *Why Punish the Children?* San Francisco: National Council on Crime and Delinquency.

Bloomfield, Maxwell. 1976. *American Lawyers in a Changing Society, 1776–1876*. Cambridge: Harvard University Press.

Blume, E. Sue. 1990. *Secret Survivors: Uncovering Incest and Its Aftereffects in Women*. New York: Wiley.

Bordt, Rebecca L., and Michael C. Musheno. 1988. "Bureaucratic Co-optation of Informal Dispute Processing: Social Control as an Effect of Inmate Grievance Policy." *Journal of Research in Crime and Delinquency* 25(1): 7–26.

Bosworth, Mary. 1996. "Resistance and Compliance in Women's Prisons: Towards a Critique of Legitimacy." *Critical Criminology: An International Journal* 7(2): 5–19.

———. 1999a. "Agency and Choice in Women's Prisons: Towards a Constitutive Penology." In S. Henry and D. Milovanovic, eds., *Constitutive Criminology at Work: Agency and Resistance in the Constitution of Crime and Punishment*, pp. 205–226. Albany: State University of New York Press.

———. 1999b. *Engendering Resistance: Agency and Power in Women's Prisons*. Aldershot: Ashgate.

Bosworth, Mary, and Eamonn Carrabine. 2001. "Reassessing Resistance: Race, Gender, and Sexuality." *Punishment and Society* 3(4): 501–515.

Boudin, Kathy. 1998. "Lessons from a Mother's Program in Prison: A Psychosocial Approach Supports Women and Their Children." *Women & Therapy* 21(1):103–125.

Boudouris, James. 1996. *Parents in Prison: Addressing the Needs of Families.* Lanham, MD: American Correctional Association.

Bourdieau, Pierre. 1986. "The Forms of Capital." In J. G. Richardson, ed., *Handbook of Theory and Research for the Sociology of Education,* pp. 241–258. New York: Greenwood Press.

———. 1991. *Language and Symbolic Power.* Cambridge: Harvard University Press.

———. 2001. *Masculine Domination.* Stanford, CA: Stanford University Press.

Bourdieu, Pierre, and Jean-Claude Passeron. 1979. *The Inheritors: French Students and Their Relation to Culture.* Chicago: University of Chicago Press.

Bourdieu, Pierre, and Loïc J. D. Wacquant. 1992. *An Invitation to Reflexive Sociology.* Chicago: University of Chicago Press.

Bowker, Lee. 1981. "Gender Differences in Prisoner Subcultures." In L. H. Bowker, ed., *Women and Crime in America,* pp. 409–419. New York: Macmillan.

———, ed. 1998. *Masculinities and Violence.* Thousand Oaks, CA: Sage.

Braidotti, Rosi. 1994. *Nomadic Subjects: Embodiment and Sexual Difference in Contemporary Feminist Theory.* New York: Columbia University Press.

Brenzel, Barbara M. 1983. *Daughters of the State: A Social Portrait of the First Reform School for Girls in North America, 1856–1905.* Cambridge: MIT Press.

Brown, J. D. 1977. "A Field Study of Two Subsystems in a Women's Prison." Unpublished Ph.D. diss., Rutgers University.

Browne, Angela. 1987. *When Battered Women Kill.* New York: Free Press.

Browne, Angela, Brenda Miller, and Eugene Maguin. 1999. "Prevalence and Severity of Lifetime Physical and Sexual Abuse Among Incarcerated Women." *International Journal of Law and Psychiatry* 22(3–4): 301–322.

Burkhart, Kathryn. 1973. *Women in Prison.* New York: Doubleday.

Butler, Anne. 1997. *Gendered Justice in the American West: Women Prisoners in Men's Penitentiaries.* Urbana: University of Illinois Press.

Butler, Judith. 1987. "Variations on Sex and Gender: Beauvoir, Wittig, and Foucault." In Seyla Benhabib and Drucilla Cornell, eds., *Feminism as Critique: Essays on the Politics of Gender in Late-Capitalist Societies,* pp. 128–142. Cambridge: Polity Press.

———. 1990. *Gender Trouble: Feminism and the Subversion of Identity.* New York: Routledge.

———. 1995. "Contingent Foundations." In S. Benhabib, J. Butler, D. Cornell, and N. Fraser, eds., *Feminist Contentions: A Philosophical Exchange,* pp. 35–57. New York: Routledge.

Caiazza, Amy B., ed. 2000. *The Status of Women in Arizona.* Washington, DC: Institute for Women's Policy Research.

Cambanis, Thanassis. 2002. "Ex-Prisoner Says She Was Strip-Searched in View of Men." *Boston Globe* (online). Available at www.boston.com/dailyglobe2/...rip_searched_in_view_of_men+shtml.

Camp, Christy Marie. 2000a. "Doing Life with the Possibility of Life." September. Available at www.lairdcarlson.com/celldoor/00203/camp00203doinglife.htm.

———. 2000b. "Sleep with One Eye Open." March. Available at www.lairdcarlson.com/celldoor/00201/camp00201sleep.htm.

———. 2000c. "Another Day in Paradise . . ." November. Available at www.lairdcarlson.com/celldoor/00302/camp00302paradise.htm.

Carlen, Pat. 1983. *Women's Imprisonment: A Study in Social Control.* London: Routledge and Kegan Paul.

———. 1985. "Law, Psychiatry, and Women's Imprisonment: A Sociological View." *British Journal of Psychiatry* 146 (June): 618–621.

———. 1994. "Why Study Women's Imprisonment? Or Anyone Else's?" *British Journal of Criminology* 34(Special Issue): 131–139.

Chandler, Edna W. 1973. *Women in Prison.* Indianapolis: Bobbs Merrill.

Chesler, Phyllis. 1991. *Mothers on Trial: The Battle for Children and Custody.* San Diego, CA: Harcourt Brace Jovanovich.

Chesney-Lind, Meda. 1989. "Girls' Crime and Woman's Place: Toward a Feminist Model of Female Delinquency." *Crime and Delinquency* 35(1): 5–29.

———. 1991. "Patriarchy, Prisons, and Jail: A Critical Look at Trends in Women's Incarceration." *Prison Journal* 51(1): 51–67.

———. 1995. "Rethinking Women's Imprisonment: A Critical Examination of Trends in Female Incarceration." In B. Price and N. Sokoloff, eds., *The Criminal Justice System and Women: Offenders, Victims, and Workers*, pp. 105–117. New York: McGraw-Hill.

———. 1997. *The Female Offender: Girls, Women, and Crime.* Thousand Oaks, CA: Sage.

Chesney-Lind, Meda, and Joycelyn M. Pollock-Byrne. 1995. "Women's Prisons: Equality with a Vengeance." In Joycelyn M. Pollock-Byrne and Alida V. Merlo, eds., *Women, Law, and Social Control*, pp. 155–175. Boston: Allyn and Bacon.

Chesney-Lind, Meda, and Noelie Rodriguez. 1983. "Women Under Lock and Key: A View from the Inside." *Prison Journal* 63(2): 47–65.

Chesney-Lind, Meda, and R. Shelden. 1998. *Girls, Delinquency, and Juvenile Justice.* 2nd ed. Pacific Grove, CA: Brooks/Cole.

Christianson, Scott. 1998. *With Liberty for Some: Five Hundred Years of Imprisonment in America.* Boston: Northeastern University Press.

Chu, James A. 1992. "The Revictimization of Adult Women with Histories of Childhood Abuse." *Journal of Psychotherapy Practice and Research* 1: 259–269.

Clark, Judy. 1995. "The Impact of the Prison Environment on Mothers." *Prison Journal* 75(3) (September): 306–329.

Clear, Todd. 1994. *Harm in American Penology: Offenders, Victims, and Their Communities.* Albany: State University of New York Press.

———. 1996. "Backfire: When Incarceration Increases Crime." Paper presented at a conference organized by Vera Institute of Justice, January. Published in the *Journal of the Oklahoma Criminal Justice Research Consortium* 3. Available at www.doc.state.ok.us/docs/ocjrc/ocjrc96/toc.htm.

Clemmer, Donald. 1958. *The Prison Community.* New York: Holt, Rinehart, and Winston.

Collins, Patricia Hill. 1990. *Black Feminist Thought: Knowledge, Consciousness, and the Politics of Empowerment.* Boston: Unwin Hyman.
Conly, Catherine. 1998. *The Women's Prison Association: Supporting Women Offenders and Their Families.* Washington, DC: National Institute of Justice.
Connell, R. W. 1987. *Gender and Power: Society, the Person, and Sexual Politics.* Stanford, CA: Stanford University Press.
Connelly, Mark Thomas. 1980. *The Response to Prostitution in the Progressive Era.* Chapel Hill: University of North Carolina Press.
Correctional Service of Canada. 2001a. "Creating Choices: The Report of the Task Force on Federally Sentenced Women." Available at www.csc-scc.gc.ca/text/prgrm/fsw/choices/toce.shtml.
———. 2001b. "Mothers in Prison: Perspectives on the Mother's Role During Incarceration and upon Reintegration." Available at www.csc-scc.gc.ca/text/rsrch/regional/outline-r68.html.
Cott, Nancy F. 1987. *The Grounding of Modern Feminism.* New Haven: Yale University Press.
Covington, Stephanie. 1998. "The Relational Theory of Women's Psychological Development: Implications for the Criminal Justice System." In R. Zaplin, ed., *Female Offenders: Critical Perspectives and Effective Interventions,* pp. 113–131. Gaithersburg, MD: Aspen.
Culverson, Donald R. 1998. "The Welfare Queen and Willie Horton." In C. R. Mann and M. S. Zatz, eds., *Images of Color, Images of Crime,* pp. 97–107. Los Angeles: Roxbury.
Daane, Diane. 2002. "Pregnant Prisoners: Health, Security, and Special Needs Issues." In Susan F. Sharp, ed., *The Incarcerated Woman: Rehabilitative Programming in Women's Prisons,* pp. 61–72. Upper Saddle River, NJ: Prentice Hall.
Dalley, Lanete P. 2002. "Policy Implications Relating to Inmate Mothers and Their Children: Will the Past Be the Prologue?" *Prison Journal* 82 (June): 234–268.
Daly, Kathleen, and Meda Chesney-Lind. 1988. "Feminism and Criminology." *Justice Quarterly* 5(4): 497–538.
Danner, Mona. 2000. "Three Strikes and It's Women Who Are Out: The Hidden Consequences for Women of Criminal Justice Policy Reforms." In R. Muraskin, ed., *It's a Crime: Women and Justice,* 2nd ed., pp. 215–224. Upper Saddle River, NJ: Prentice Hall.
Davis, Angela Y. 1998. "Public Imprisonment and Private Violence: Reflections on the Hidden Punishment of Women." *New England Journal on Criminal and Civil Confinement* 24(2): 339–351.
de Beaumont, Gustave, and Alexis de Tocqueville. 1833. *On the Penitentiary System in the United States.* Translated by Francis Lieber. Philadelphia: Carey, Lee, and Blanchard.
de Beauvoir, Simone. 1953. *The Second Sex.* London: Pan Books.
Dearing, Susan. 2002. "The War on Drugs and Women Prisoners." In Leanne Fiftal Alarid and Paul Cromwell, eds., *Correctional Perspectives: Views from Academics, Practitioners, and Prisoners,* pp. 40–47. Los Angeles: Roxbury.

Deveaux, Monique. 1996. "Feminism and Empowerment: A Critical Reading of Foucault." In Susan J. Hekman, ed., *Feminist Interpretations of Michel Foucault,* pp. 211–238. University Park: Pennsylvania State University Press.

Diamond, Irene, and Lee Quinby, eds. 1988. *Feminism and Foucault: Reflections on Resistance.* Boston: Northeastern Press.

Diaz-Cotto, Juanita. 1996. *Gender, Ethnicity, and the State: Latina and Latino Prison Politics.* Albany: State University of New York Press.

———. 2000. "Race, Ethnicity, and Gender in Studies of Incarceration." In Joy James, ed., *States of Confinement: Policing, Detention, and Prisons,* pp. 123–131. New York: St. Martin's Press.

Dix, Dorothea. 1967 (1845). *Remarks on Prisons and Prison Discipline in the United States.* Introduction by Leonard D. Savitz. 2nd ed. Montclair, NJ: Patterson Smith.

Dobash, Russell, R. Emerson Dobash, and Sue Gutteridge. 1986. *The Imprisonment of Women.* New York: Blackwell.

Dougherty, Joyce. 1998. "Power-Belief Theory: Female Criminality and the Dynamics of Oppression." In R. Zaplin, ed., *Female Offenders: Critical Perspectives and Effective Interventions,* pp. 133–159. Gaithersburg, MD: Aspen.

Dowden, Craig, and D. A. Andrews. 1999. "What Works for Female Offenders: A Meta-Analytic Review." *Crime and Delinquency* 45(4): 438–452.

Drummond, Tamerlin. 2001. "Mothers in Prison." Available at www.time.com/time/magazine/printout/0,8816,58996,00.html.

Durham, Alexis M. 1994. *Crisis and Reform: Current Issues in American Punishment.* Boston: Little, Brown.

Dutton, Mary Ann. 1992. "Assessment and Treatment of Post-Traumatic Stress Disorder Among Battered Women." In D. W. Foy, ed., *Treating PTSD: Cognitive-Behavioral Strategies,* pp. 69–98. New York: Guilford Press.

Dutton, Mary Ann, Laura C. Hohnecker, Paulin M. Halle, and Kimberly J. Burghardt. 1994. "Traumatic Responses Among Battered Women Who Kill." *Journal of Traumatic Stress* 7(4): 549–564.

Dutton, Mary Ann, Sean G. Perrin, Kelly R. Chrestman, and Paulin M. Halle. 1990. "MMPI Trauma Profiles for Battered Women." Paper presented at the annual convention of the American Psychological Association, Boston, August.

Ekstrand, Laurie, Danny Burton, and Eric Erdman. 1999. *Women in Prison: Issues and Challenges Confronting U.S. Correctional Systems.* Washington, DC: General Accounting Office.

Enos, Sandra. 2001. *Mothering from the Inside: Parenting in a Women's Prison.* Albany: State University of New York Press.

Erez, Edna. 1992. "Dangerous Men, Evil Women: Gender and Parole Decision-Making." *Justice Quarterly* 9 (March): 105–126.

Esslin, Martin. 1961. *The Theatre of the Absurd.* New York: Anchor Books.

Faith, Karlene. 1993. *Unruly Women: The Politics of Confinement and Resistance.* Vancouver: Press Gang.

FBI (Federal Bureau of Investigation). 1997. *Uniform Crime Reports for the United States, 1997.* Washington, DC: FBI, U.S. Department of Justice.

Federal Bureau of Prisons. 1932. *Federal Offenders 1930–31.* Washington, DC: Federal Bureau of Prisons.
———. 1935. *Federal Offenders 1933–34.* Leavenworth, KS: Federal Prison Industries.
———. 1938. *Federal Offenders 1936–37.* Leavenworth, KS: Federal Prison Industries.
Feinman, Clarice. 1986. *Women in the Criminal Justice System.* 2nd ed. New York: Praeger.
Ferrari, Fran, Andrew Spivak, Leslie Robinson, and Bill Chown. 2001. "Comparing Rankings of the U.S. States for Child-Raising Quality and Incarceration Rate." Available at www.doc.state.ok.us/docs/childrearing.htm.
Ferraro, Kathleen J., and Angela M. Moe. 2003. "Malign Neglect or Benign Respect: Women's Health Care in a Carceral Setting." *Women and Criminal Justice* 14(4): 9–40.
Ferraro, Kathleen J., and Angela M. Wan. 2003. "Mothering, Crime, and Incarceration." *Journal of Contemporary Ethnography* 32(1): 9–40.
Finkelhor, David, and Angela Browne. 1985. "The Traumatic Impact of Child Sexual Abuse: A Conceptualization." *American Journal of Orthopsychiatry Quarterly* 55(4) (October): 530–541.
Finkelhor, David, Gerald Hotaling, I. A. Lewis, and Christine Smith. 1990. "Sexual Abuse in a National Survey on Adult Men and Women." *Child Abuse and Neglect* 14:19–28.
Flavin, Jeanne. 2001. "Feminism for the Mainstream Criminologist: An Invitation." *Journal of Criminal Justice* 29:1–15.
Flexner, Eleanor. 1996. *Century of Struggle: The Women's Rights Movement in the United States.* Cambridge: Harvard University Press.
Flynn, Elizabeth Gurley. 1963. *The Alderson Story: My Life as a Political Prisoner.* New York: International Publishers.
Fogel, Catherine I. 1993. "Hard Time: The Stressful Nature of Incarceration for Women." *Issues in Mental Health Nursing* 14:367–377.
Fonow, Margaret M., and Jacqueline A. Cook, eds. 1991. *Beyond Methodology: Feminist Scholarship as Lived Research.* Bloomington: Indiana University Press.
Foster, T. W. 1975. "Make-Believe Families: A Response of Women and Girls to the Deprivations of Imprisonment." *International Journal of Criminology and Penology* 3:71–78.
Foucault, Michel. 1977. *Discipline and Punish: The Birth of the Prison.* New York: Vintage.
———. 1978. *The History of Sexuality: An Introduction.* New York: Pantheon Books.
———. 1979. *Discipline and Punish: The Birth of the Prison.* New York: Vintage.
———. 1982. "Afterward: The Subject and Power." In H. L. Dreyfus and P. Rabinow, eds., *Michel Foucault: Beyond Structuralism and Hermeneutics,* pp. 208–226. Chicago: University of Chicago Press.
Fraser, Nancy. 1989. *Unruly Practices: Power, Discourse, and Gender in Contemporary Social Theory.* Minneapolis: University of Minnesota Press.

Freedman, Estelle. 1981. *Their Sister's Keepers: Women's Prison Reform in America, 1830–1930.* Ann Arbor: University of Michigan Press.

———. 1996a. *Maternal Justice: Miriam Van Waters and the Female Reform Tradition.* Chicago: University of Chicago Press.

———. 1996b. "The Prison Lesbian: Race, Class, and the Construction of the Aggressive Female Homosexual, 1915–1965." *Feminist Studies* 22(2): 397–423.

Fuss, Diana. 1989. *Essentially Speaking: Feminism, Nature, and Difference.* London: Routledge.

Gabel, Katherine, and Denise Johnston. 1995. *Children of Incarcerated Parents.* New York: Lexington Books.

Galtung, J. 1961. "Prison: The Organization of Dilemma." In D. R. Cressey, ed., *The Prison,* pp. 109–127. New York: Holt, Rinehart, and Winston.

Gat, Irit. 2000. "Incarcerated Mothers: Effects of the Mother/Offspring Life Development Program." Poster Presentation, American Psychological Association Meetings, Psychologists in Public Service Session, August.

Gaudin, James M., Jr., and Richard Sutphen. 1993. "Foster Care vs. Extended Family Care for Children of Incarcerated Mothers." *Journal of Offender Rehabilitation* 19(3/4): 129–147.

Gelsthorpe, Lorraine, and Allison Morris, eds. 1990. *Feminist Perspectives in Criminology.* Philadelphia: Open University Press.

Giallombardo, Rose. 1966. *Society of Women: A Study of a Women's Prison.* New York: Wiley.

Gibson, M. A. 1988. *Accommodation Without Assimilation: Sikh Immigrants in an American High School.* Ithaca, NY: Cornell University Press.

Giddens, Anthony. 1991. *Modernity and Self-Identity: Self and Society in the Late Modern Age.* Cambridge: Polity Press.

Gilfus, Mary E. 1988. "Seasoned by Violence/Tempered by Love: A Qualitative Study of Women and Crime." Ph.D. diss., Florence Heller Graduate School for Advanced Studies in Social Welfare, Brandeis University, Waltham, MA.

———. 1992. "From Victims to Survivors to Offenders: Women's Routes of Entry and Immersion into Street Crime." *Women and Criminal Justice* 4(1): 63–89.

Gilliard, Darrell K. 1999. *Prison and Jail Inmates at Midyear 1998.* Washington, DC: U.S. Department of Justice.

Gilroy, Paul. 1987. *"There Ain't No Black in the Union Jack": The Cultural Politics of Race and Nation.* London: Routledge.

———. 1993. *The Black Atlantic: Modernity and Double Consciousness.* Cambridge: Harvard University Press.

Girshick, Lori B. 1999. *No Safe Haven: Stories of Women in Prison.* Boston: Northeastern University Press.

Goffman, Erving. 1961. *Asylums: Essays on the Social Situation of Mental Patients and Other Inmates.* Garden City, NY: Anchor Books.

———. 1963. *Stigma: Notes on the Management of Spoiled Identity.* Englewood Cliffs, NJ: Prentice Hall.

———. 1977. "The Arrangement Between the Sexes." *Theory and Society* 4(3): 301–331.

Goodenough, Ward H. 1981. *Culture, Language, and Society.* Menlo Park, CA: Benjamin/Cummings.
Goodstein, Lynne, Doris Layton MacKenzie, and R. Lance Shotland. 1984. "Personal Control and Inmate Adjustment to Prison." *Criminology* 22 (August): 343–369.
Gordon, Robert, and Inmates of the Washington Corrections System. 2000. *The Funhouse Mirror: Reflections on Prison.* Pullman: Washington State University Press.
Gorz, Andre. 1968. *Strategy for Labor: A Radical Proposal.* Boston: Beacon Press.
Gray, Tara, G. Larry Mays, and Mary K. Stohr. 1995. "Inmate Needs and Programming in Exclusively Women's Jails." *Prison Journal* 75(2) (June): 186–202.
Greenfeld, Lawrence A., and Tracy L. Snell. 1999a. *Bureau of Justice Statistics Bulletin: Women Offenders.* Washington, DC: U.S. Department of Justice.
———. 1999b. *Women Offenders.* Special Report no. NCJ 175688. Washington, DC: Bureau of Justice Statistics.
Greer, Kimberly. 2002. "Walking an Emotional Tightrope: Managing Emotions in a Women's Prison." *Symbolic Interaction* 25(1): 117–139.
Hagan, John. 1996. "The Next Generation: Children of Prisoners." Paper presented at a conference organized by Vera Institute of Justice, January. Published in the *Journal of the Oklahoma Criminal Justice Research Consortium* 3. Available at www.doc.state.ok.us/docs/ocjrc/ocjrc96/toc.htm.
Hairston, Creasie Finney. 1991a. "Family Ties During Imprisonment: Important to Whom and for What?" *Journal of Sociology & Social Welfare* 18(1): 87–104.
———. 1991b. "Mothers in Jail: Parent-Child Separation and Jail Visitation." *Affilia* 6(2): 9–27.
Hairston, Creasie Finney, and Patricia Lockett. 1985. "Parents in Prison: A Child Abuse and Neglect Prevention Strategy." *Child Abuse & Neglect* 9(4): 471–477.
———. 1987. "Parents in Prison: New Directions for Social Services." *Social Work* 32: 162–164.
Hannah-Moffat, Kate. 1995. "Feminine Fortresses: Women-Centered Prison?" *Prison Journal* 75(2): 135–164.
———. 1999. "Moral Agent or Actuarial Subject: Risk and Canadian Women's Imprisonment." *Theoretical Criminology* 3(1): 71–94.
———. 2000. "Re-forming the Prison: Rethinking Our Ideals." In K. Hannah-Moffat and M. Shaw, eds., *An Ideal Prison? Critical Essays on Women's Imprisonment in Canada,* pp. 30–40. Halifax, Nova Scotia: Fernwood.
———. 2001. *Punishment in Disguise: Penal Governance and Federal Imprisonment of Women in Canada.* Toronto: Toronto University Press.
Harlow, Caroline Wolf. 1998. *Profile of Jail Inmates, 1996.* Special Report no. NCJ 164620. Washington, DC: Bureau of Justice Statistics.
———. 1999. *Prior Abuse Reported by Inmates and Probations: Selected Findings.* Special Report no. NCJ 172879. Washington, DC: Bureau of Justice Statistics.

Harris, Jean Wahl. 1993. "Comparison of Stressors Among Female vs. Male Inmates." *Journal of Offender Rehabilitation* 19(1–2): 43–56.
Harris, Mary B. 1936. *I Knew Them in Prison*. New York: Viking.
Hart, Cynthia B. 1995. "Gender Differences in Social Support Among Inmates." *Women and Criminal Justice* 6(2): 67–88.
Hassine, Victor. 1996. *Life Without Parole: Living in Prison Today*. Los Angeles: Roxbury.
Hayner, Norman S., and Ellis Ash. 1939. "The Prisoner Community as a Social Group." *American Sociological Review* 4 (June): 362–369.
Haywood, Thomas W., Howard M. Kravitz, Laurie B. Goldman, and A. Freeman. 2000. "Characteristics of Women in Jail and Treatment Orientations: A Review." *Behavior Modification* 24(3): 307–324.
Heffernan, Esther. 1972. *Making It in Prison: The Square, the Cool, and the Life*. New York: Wiley-Interscience.
———. 1994. "Banners, Brothels, and a 'Ladies Seminary.'" In John W. Roberts, ed., *Escaping Prison Myths: Selected Topics in the History of Federal Corrections*, pp. 37–79. Washington, DC: American University Press.
Heney, Jan. 1996. "Dying on the Inside: Suicide and Suicidal Feelings Among Federally Incarcerated Women." Ph.D. diss., Carleton University, Ottawa, Canada.
Heney, Jan, and Connie M. Kristiansen. 1998. "An Analysis of the Impact of Prison on Women Survivors of Childhood Sexual Abuse." In J. Harden and M. Hill, eds., *Breaking the Rules: Women in Prison and Feminist Therapy*, pp. 29–44. Binghamton, NY: Haworth Press.
Henriques, Zelma. 1996. "Imprisoned Mothers and Their Children: Separation-Reunion Syndrome Dual Impact." *Women and Criminal Justice* 8(1): 77–95.
Henriques, Zelma, and Evelyn Gilbert. 2000. "Sexual Abuse and Sexual Assault of Women in Prison." In R. Muraskin, ed., *It's a Crime: Women and Justice*, 2nd ed., pp. 253–268. Upper Saddle River, NJ: Prentice Hall.
Holstein, J. A., and J. F. Gubrium. 1994. "Constructing Family: Descriptive Practice and Domestic Order." In T. Sarbin and J. Kitsuse, eds., *Constructing the Social*, pp. 233–251. London: Sage.
Holt, K. E. 1982. "Nine Months to Live: The Law and the Pregnant Inmate." *Journal of Family Law* 20(3): 523–542.
hooks, bell. 1981. *Ain't I a Woman: Black Women and Feminism*. Boston: South End Press.
Huggins, Denise. 2000. "A Study of Family Units Formed in Female Correctional Facilities in the State of Texas." Paper presented at the annual meeting of the American Society of Criminology, San Francisco, November.
Human Rights Watch. 1996. *All Too Familiar: Sexual Abuse of Women in U.S. State Prisons*. Available at www.hrw.org/hrw/summaries.
Humphries, Drew, John Dawson, Valerie Cronin, Phyllis Keating, Chris Wisniewski, and Jennine Eichfeld. 1995. "Mothers and Children, Drugs and Crack: Reactions to Maternal Drug Dependency." In Clarice Feinman,

ed., *The Criminalization of a Woman's Body*, pp. 203–211. New York: Harrington Press.
IDOC (Illinois Department of Corrections), Dwight Correctional Center. 2002. Personal Communications. August.
IDOC–Rules (Illinois Department of Corrections–Rules). n.d. *Title 20: Corrections, Criminal Justice, and Law Enforcement.* Chapter I: Department of Corrections; Subchapter e: Operations: Personal Property—Part 535.
Ingraham, Chrys. 1994. "The Heterosexual Imaginary: Feminist Sociology and Theories of Gender." *Sociological Theory* 12(2) (July): 203–219.
Irwin, John, and Donald R. Cressey. 1962. "Thieves, Convicts, and the Inmate Culture." *Social Problems* 10 (Fall): 142–155.
Jacobs, James B. 1977. *Stateville: The Penitentiary in Mass Society.* Chicago: University of Chicago Press.
Janusz, L. 1991. "Separate but Unequal: Women Behind Bars in Massachusetts." *Odyssey*, pp. 6–17.
Johnson, Robert. 2002. *Hard Time: Understanding and Reforming the Prison.* 3rd ed. Belmont, CA: Wadsworth.
Johnson, Robert, and Hans Toch. 2000. *Crime and Punishment: Inside Views.* Los Angeles: Roxbury.
Jones, Richard S. 1993. "Coping with Separation: Adaptive Responses of Women Prisoners." *Women and Criminal Justice* 5: 71–97.
Jones, Richard. S., and Thomas J. Schmid. 2000. *Doing Time: Prison Experience and Identity Among First-Time Inmates.* Stamford, CT: JAI.
JusticeWorks Community. 2001. "Mothers in Prison, Children in Crisis Campaign." Available at www.justiceworks.org/html/mothers.html-ssi.
Kelly, Liz. 1988. *Surviving Sexual Violence.* Minneapolis: University of Minnesota Press.
Kendall, Kathleen. 1993. *Literature Review of Therapeutic Services for Women in Prison.* Ottawa: Correctional Service of Canada.
———. 1994. "Therapy Behind Prison Walls." *Prison Service Journal* 96 (November): 2–11.
———. 1998. "Evaluation of Programs for Female Offenders." In R. Zaplin, ed., *Female Offenders: Critical Perspectives and Effective Interventions,* pp. 361–379. Gaithersburg, MD: Aspen.
———. 2000a. "Anger Management with Women in Coercive Environments." In E. Horn and S. Warner, eds., *Positive Directions for Women in Secure Environments,* pp. 35–41. Leicester: British Psychological Society.
———. 2000b. "Psy-ence Fiction." Paper presented at the annual meeting of the American Society of Criminology, San Francisco, November.
———. 2000c. "Psy-ence Fiction: Inventing the Mentally-Disordered Female Prisoner." In K. Hannah-Moffat and M. Shaw, eds., *An Ideal Prison? Critical Essays on Women's Imprisonment in Canada,* pp. 82–93. Halifax, Nova Scotia: Fernwood.
Kent, James. 1832. *Commentaries on the American Laws.* 2nd ed. 4 vols. New York: O. Halsted.
Kilmartin, Christopher. 2000. *The Masculine Self.* 2nd ed. Boston: McGraw-

Hill.
Kilpatrick, D. G., C. N. Edmunds, and A. K. Seymour. 1992. *Rape in America: A Report to the Nation.* Arlington, VA: National Victim Center.
Kirk, Gwyn, and Margo Okazawa-Rey. 2001. *Women's Lives: Multicultural Perspectives.* 2nd ed. Mountain View, CA: Mayfield Press.
Kitzinger, Sheila. 2001. "Mothers and Babies in Prison." Available at www.sheilakitzinger.com/prisons.htm.
Kline, Sue. 1993. "A Profile of Female Offenders in State and Federal Prisons." In *Female Offenders: Meeting the Needs of a Neglected Population,* pp. 1–6. Laurel, MD: American Correctional Association.
Klungness, Elizabeth J. 1993. *Prisoners in Petticoats: The Yuma Territorial Prison and Its Women.* Yuma, AZ: Yuma County Historical Society.
Koban, Linda A. 1983. "Parents in Prison: A Comparative Analysis of the Effects of Incarceration on the Families of Men and Women." *Research in Law, Deviance, & Social Control* 5:171–183.
Kondo, Dorinne K. 1990. *Crafting Selves: Power, Gender, and Discourses of Identity in a Japanese Workplace.* Chicago: University of Chicago Press.
Koons, Barbara A., John D. Burrow, and Merry Morash. 1997. "Expert and Offender Perceptions of Program Elements Linked to Successful Outcomes for Incarcerated Women." *Crime and Delinquency* 43(4): 512–532.
Koss, Mary, and Thomas E. Dinero. 1989. "Discriminant Analysis of Risk Factors for Sexual Victimization Among a National Sample of College Women." *Journal of Consulting and Clinical Psychology* 57:242–250.
Koss, Mary, Lisa Goodman, Angela Browne, Louise Fitzgerald, Gwendolyn Keita, and Nancy Russo. 1994. *No Safe Haven: Violence Against Women at Home, Work, and the Community.* Washington, DC: American Psychological Association.
Krais, Beate. 1993. "Gender and Symbolic Violence: Female Oppression in the Light of Pierre Bourdieu's Theory of Social Practice." In C. Calhoun, E. LiPuma, and Moishe Postone, eds., *Bourdieu: Critical Perspectives,* pp. 156–177. Chicago: University of Chicago Press.
Kruttschnitt, Candace. 1981. "Social Status and Sentences of Female Offenders." *Law & Society Review* 15(2): 247–266.
Kruttschnitt, Candace, Rosemary Gartner, and Amy Miller. 2000. "Doing Her Own Time? Women's Responses to Prison in the Context of the Old and the New Penology." *Criminology* 38(3): 301–337.
Kurshan, Nancy. 2001. "Women and Imprisonment in the U.S." Available at www.prisonactivist.org/women/women-and-imprisonment.html.
Lake, Elise S. 1993. "An Exploration of the Violent Victim Experiences of Female Offenders." *Violence and Victims* 8(1): 41–51.
Landes, A. B., S. Squyres, and J. Quiram. 1997. *Violent Relationships, Battering, and Abuse Among Adults.* Wylie, TX: Information Plus.
LaViolette, Alyce, and Ola Barnett. 2000. *It Could Happen to Anyone: Why Battered Women Stay.* 2nd ed. Thousand Oaks, CA: Sage.

Leger, R. G. 1987. "Lesbianism Among Women Prisoners: Participants and Non-Participants." *Criminal Justice and Behavior* 14:448–467.

Lekkerkerker, Eugenia C. 1931. *Reformatories for Women in the United States.* Batavia, Holland: J. B. Wolters Uitgevers-Maatschappij.

Leonard, Elizabeth Dermody. 2000. "Convicted Survivors: Comparing and Describing California's Battered Women Inmates." Paper presented at the annual meeting of the American Society of Criminology, San Francisco, November.

———. 2001. "Convicted Survivors: Comparing and Describing California's Battered Women Inmates." *Prison Journal* 81(1): 73–86.

Lerner, Gerda. 1993. *The Creation of Feminist Consciousness from the Middle Ages to 1870.* New York: Oxford University Press.

LeShanna, L. 1969. "Family Participation: Functional Responses of Incarcerated Females." Unpublished master's thesis, Bowling Green University, Bowling Green, OH.

Leventhal, Rachel. 2000. "Lost in the Shuffle." *Doubletake* (Winter): 42–59.

Lichtenstein, Alex. 1996. *"Twice the Work of Free Labor": The Political Economy of Convict Labor in the New South.* London: Verso.

Liebling, Alison. 1994. "Suicides Amongst Women Prisoners." *Howard Journal* 33(1): 1–9.

Lockwood, Daniel. 1982. "Reducing Prison Sexual Violence." In R. Johnson and H. Toch, eds., *The Pains of Imprisonment,* pp. 257–265. Newbury Park, CA: Sage.

Lord, Elaine. 1995. "A Prison Superintendent's Perspective on Women in Prison." *Prison Journal* 75(2): 257–269.

Lovell, Terry. 2000. "Thinking Feminism with and Against Bourdieu." *Feminist Theory* 1(1): 11–32.

Lundberg, D. A., A. Sheekley, and T. Voelker. 1975. "An Exploration of the Feelings and Attitudes of Women Separated from Their Children Due to Incarceration." Unpublished master's thesis, Portland State University.

Lutze, Faith E. 1998. "Are Shock Incarceration Programs More Rehabilitative Than Traditional Prison? A Survey of Inmates." *Justice Quarterly* 15(2): 547–563.

———. 2002. "Conscience and Convenience in Boot Camp Prison: An Opportunity for Success." *Journal of Forensic Psychology Practice* 2(4): 71–81.

Lutze, Faith, and David Brody. 1999. "The Eighth Amendment and Boot Camp: Mental Abuse as Cruel and Unusual Punishment." *Crime and Delinquency* 45(2): 242–255.

Lutze, Faith., and David Murphy. 1999. "Ultramasculine Prison Environments and Inmate Adjustment: It's Time to Move Beyond the 'Boys Will Be Boys' Paradigm." *Justice Quarterly* 16(4): 709–733.

Lynch, Michael, Raymond Michalowski, and W. Byron Groves. 2000. *The New Primer in Radical Criminology: Critical Perspectives on Crime, Power, and Identity.* 3rd ed. Monsey, NY: Criminal Justice Press.

MacKenzie, Doris Layton, James W. Robinson, and Carol S. Campbell. 1989. "Long-Term Incarceration of Female Offenders: Prison Adjustment and Coping." *Criminal Justice and Behavior* 16:223–238.

———. 1995. "Long-Term Incarceration of Female Offenders: Prison Adjustment and Coping." In Timothy J. Flanagan, ed., *Long-Term Imprisonment: Policy, Science, and Correctional Practice*, pp. 128–137. Thousand Oaks, CA: Sage.

MacPherson, Sir William. 1999. *The Stephen Lawrence Inquiry.* Volumes 1 and 2. London: HMSO.

Mann, Coramae Richey. 1984. *Female Crime and Delinquency.* Tuscaloosa: University of Alabama Press.

Mannheim, Karl. 1936. *Ideology and Utopia.* New York: Harcourt, Brace, and World.

Marcus-Mendoza, Susan, Jody Klein-Saffran, and Faith Lutze. 1998. "A Feminist Examination of Boot Camp Prison Programs for Women." *Women and Therapy* 21(1): 173–185.

Markovic, Vesna. 1995. "Pregnant Women in Prison: A Correctional Dilemma." *Keeper's Voice* 16(3). Available from the Office of International Criminal Justice, www.oicj.acsp.uic.edu/spearmint/public/pubc/kv/kv160333.cfrn.

Martineau, Harriet. 1838. *Retrospect of Western Travel.* Vol. 1. London: Saunders and Otley.

Mauer, Marc, Cathy Potler, and Richard Wolf. 1999. *Gender and Justice: Women, Drugs, and Sentencing Policy.* Washington, DC: Sentencing Project.

Mawby, R. I. 1982. "Women in Prison: A British Study." *Crime and Delinquency* 28(1): 24–39.

McCarthy, Belinda R. 1980. "Inmate Mothers: The Problems of Separation and Reintegration." *Journal of Offender Counseling, Services, and Rehabilitation* 4:199–212.

McClellan, Dorothy S. 1994. "Disparity in the Discipline of Male and Female Inmates in Texas Prisons." *Women and Criminal Justice* 5(2): 71–97.

McClellan, Dorothy S., David Farabee, and Ben M. Crouch. 1997. "Early Victimization, Drug Use, and Criminality: A Comparison of Male and Female Prisoners." *Criminal Justice and Behavior* 24(4) (December): 455–476.

McCorkel, Jill A. 1998. "Going to the Crackhouse: Critical Space as a Form of Resistance in Total Institutions and Everyday Life." *Symbolic Interaction* 21(3): 227–252.

McGee, Zina. 2000. "The Pains of Imprisonment: Long-Term Incarceration Effects on Women in Prison." In R. Muraskin, ed., *It's a Crime: Women and Justice,* 2nd ed., pp. 205–213. Upper Saddle River, NJ: Prentice Hall.

McGinn, Elinor Myers. 1993. *At Hard Labor: Inmate Labor at the Colorado State Penitentiary.* New York: Peter Lang.

McGowan, B. G., and K. L. Blumenthal. 1976. "Children of Women Prisoners: A Forgotten Minority." In L. Crites, ed., *The Female Offender,* pp. 86–103. Lexington, MA: D. C. Heath.

McQuaide, Sharon, and John H. Ehrenreich. 1998. "Women in Prison: Approaches to Understanding the Lives of a Forgotten Population." *Affilia: Journal of Women & Social Work* 13(2) (Summer): 233–247.

Meisenhelder, T. 1985. "An Essay on Time and the Phenomenology of Imprisonment." *Deviant Behavior* 6:39–56.
Melish, Joanne Pope. 1998. *Disowning Slavery: Gradual Emancipation and "Race" in New England, 1780–1860.* Ithaca, NY: Cornell University Press.
Meltzer, B., J. Petras, and L. T. Reynolds. 1975. *Symbolic Interactionism: Genesis, Varieties, and Criticism.* London: Routledge & Kegan Paul.
Messerschmidt, J. 1993. *Masculinities and Crime: Critique and Reconceptualization of Theory.* Lanham, MD: Rowman and Littlefield.
Metzger, Diane. 2000a. "Life in a Microwave." In R. Johnson and H. Toch, eds., *Crime and Punishment: Inside Views,* pp. 138–140. Los Angeles: Roxbury.
———. 2000b. "The Manipulation Game." In R. Johnson and H. Toch, eds., *Crime and Punishment: Inside Views,* pp. 216–219. Los Angeles: Roxbury.
Miller, Jody. 2001. *One of the Guys: Girls, Gangs, and Gender.* New York: Oxford University Press.
Miller, Theresa A. 2000. "Sex and Surveillance: Gender, Privacy, and the Sexualization of Power in Prison." *George Mason University Civil Rights Law Journal* 10(2) (Summer): 291–356.
Mills, R., and H. Barrett. 1990. "Meeting the Special Challenge of Providing Health Care to Women Inmates in the '90s." *American Jails* 4 (September–October): 55–57.
Milovanovic, Dragan, and Jim Thomas. 1989. "Overcoming the Absurd: Prisoner Litigation as Primitive Rebellion." *Social Problems* 36 (February): 48–60.
Moore, Joan. 1996. "Bearing the Burden: How Incarceration Weakens Inner City Communities." Paper presented at a conference organized by the Vera Justice Institute, January. Published in the *Journal of the Oklahoma Criminal Justice Research Consortium* 3. Available at www.doc.state.ok.us/docs/ocjrc/ocjrc96/toc.htm.
Morash, Merry, Timothy S. Bynum, and Barbara A. Koons. 1998. *Women Offenders: Programming Needs and Promising Approaches.* Washington, DC: U.S. Department of Justice.
Morash, Merry, Robin Haarr, and Lila Rucker. 1994. "A Comparison of Programming for Women and Men in U.S. Prisons in the 1980s." *Crime and Delinquency* 40(2): 197–221.
Morash, Merry, and Lila Rucker. 1990. "A Critical Look at the Idea of Boot Camp as a Correctional Reform." *Crime and Delinquency* 36 (April): 204–222.
Morawska, E. 1987. "Sociological Ambivalence: The Case of East European Peasant-Immigrant Workers in America, 1890s–1930s." *Qualitative Sociology* 10(3): 225–250.
Morris, Allison, and Chris Wilkinson. 1995. "Responding to Female Prisoners' Needs." *Prison Journal* 75, pt. 3 (September): 295–305.
Moses, Marilyn. 1995. *Keeping Incarcerated Mothers and Their Daughters Together: Girl Scouts Beyond Bars.* Washington, DC: National Institute of Justice.

Moyer, Imogene L. 1980. "Leadership in a Women's Prison." *Journal of Criminal Justice* 8:233–241.

Mumola, Christopher. 2000. *Bureau of Justice Statistics Bulletin: Incarcerated Women and Their Children.* Washington, DC: U.S. Department of Justice.

Muraskin, Roslyn. 1993. "Disparate Treatment in Correctional Facilities." In Roslyn Muraskin and Ted Alleman, eds., *It's a Crime: Women and Justice,* pp. 211–225. Englewood Cliffs, NJ: Prentice Hall.

———. 2000a. "Disparate Treatment in Correctional Facilities." In R. Muraskin, ed., *It's a Crime: Women and Justice,* 2nd ed., pp. 225–236. Upper Saddle River, NJ: Prentice Hall.

———, ed. 2000b. *It's a Crime: Women and Justice.* 2nd ed. Upper Saddle River, NJ: Prentice Hall.

Nightline. 1999. *Women in Prison* series. October–November.

O'Brien, Patricia. 2001. *Making It in the Free World.* Albany: State University of New York Press.

O'Keefe. Maura. 1998. "Posttraumatic Stress Disorder Among Incarcerated Battered Women: A Comparison of Battered Women Who Killed Their Abusers and Those Incarcerated for Other Offenses." *Journal of Traumatic Stress* 11(1): 71–85.

Oklahoma Department of Corrections. 1998. *Oklahoma Department of Corrections 1998 Annual Report.* Oklahoma City: Oklahoma Department of Corrections.

———. 1999. *Female Offender Task Force Work Summary.* Oklahoma City: Oklahoma Department of Corrections.

———. 2000. *Female Offender Task Force 2000 Work Summary.* Oklahoma City: Oklahoma Department of Corrections.

O'Neill, John. 1972. *Sociology as a Skin Trade: Essays Toward a Reflexive Sociology.* London: Heinemann.

Oshinsky, David M. 1996. *"Worse Than Slavery": Parchman Farm and the Ordeal of Jim Crow Justice.* New York: Free Press.

Owen, Barbara. 1988. *The Reproduction of Social Control: A Study of Prison Workers at San Quentin.* New York: Praeger.

———. 1998. *"In the Mix": Struggle and Survival in a Women's Prison.* Albany: State University of New York Press.

Owen, Barbara, Barbara Bloom, and T. Farmon. 2000. "Operational and Management Issues in Women's Prisons." Paper presented at the annual meeting of the American Society of Criminology, San Francisco, November.

Parkinson, Diana. 2001. "Doulas for Women Prisoners." Available at www.sheilakitzinger.com/prisons.htm.htm.

Pirandello, Luigi. 1922. *Three Plays: Six Characters in Search of an Author.* New York: E. P. Dutton.

———. 1998. *Pirandello: Plays.* Evanston, IL: Northwestern University Press.

Pisciotta, Alexander W. 1994. *Benevolent Repression: Social Control and the American Reformatory-Prison Movement.* New York: New York University Press.

Polan, Diane. 1982. "Toward a Theory of Law and Patriarchy." In David Kairys, ed., *The Politics of Law: A Progressive Critique*, pp. 294–303. New York: Pantheon Books.

Pollack, Shoshana. 2000. "In Search of Autonomy: Imprisoned Women's Negotiation of Gender and Sexual Identity Within Relationship." Paper presented at the annual meeting of the American Society of Criminology, San Francisco.

Pollock, Joycelyn. 1984. "Women Will Be Women: Correctional Officers' Perceptions of the Emotionality of Women Inmates." *Prison Journal* 64 (Spring/Summer): 84–92.

———. 1986. *Sex and Supervision: Guarding Male and Female Inmates.* New York: Greenwood Press.

———. 1990. *Prisons: Today and Tomorrow.* Gaithersburg, MD: Aspen.

———. 1998. *Counseling Women in Prison.* Thousand Oaks, CA: Sage.

Pollock-Byrne, Joycelyn M. 1990. *Women, Prison, and Crime.* Belmont, CA: Wadsworth.

———. 2002. *Women, Prison, and Crime.* 2nd ed. Belmont, CA: Wadsworth.

Prendergast, Michael L., Jean Wellisch, and Gregory P. Falkin. 1995. "Assessment of and Services for Substance-Abusing Women Offenders in Community and Correctional Settings." *Prison Journal* 75(2): 240–256.

Price, Barbara, and Natalie Sokoloff. 1995. *The Criminal Justice System and Women: Offenders, Victims, and Workers.* New York: McGraw-Hill.

Propper, Alice M. 1982. "Make Believe Families and Homosexuality Among Imprisoned Girls." *Criminology* 20(1): 127–139.

Rafter, Nicole Hahn. 1983. "Chastising the Unchaste: Social Control Functions of a Woman's Reformatory, 1894–1931." In Stanley Cohen and Andrew Scull, eds., *Social Control and the State*, pp. 288–311. Oxford: Basil Blackwell.

———. 1985. *Partial Justice: Women in State Prisons, 1800–1935.* Boston: Northeastern University Press.

———. 1990. *Partial Justice: Women, Prisons, and Social Control.* 2nd ed. New Brunswick, NJ: Transaction.

Rand, Michael. 1998. *Criminal Victimization 1997: Changes 1996–1997, with Trends 1993–1997.* Washington, DC: Bureau of Justice Statistics National Crime Victimization Survey, Office of Justice Programs, U.S. Department of Justice.

Rasche, Christine. 2000. "The Dislike of Female Offenders Among Correctional Officers: Need for Specialized Training." In R. Muraskin, ed., *It's a Crime: Women and Justice*, 2nd ed., pp. 237–252. Upper Saddle River, NJ: Prentice Hall.

Reed, Diane F., and Edward L. Reed. 1997. "Children of Incarcerated Parents." *Social Justice* 24(3): 152–169.

Reiman, Jeffrey. 1998. *The Rich Get Richer and the Poor Get Prison.* Boston: Allyn and Bacon.

Reinharz, Shulamit. 1992. *Feminist Methods in Social Research.* New York: Oxford University Press.

Resick, Patricia A. 1993. "The Psychological Impact of Rape." *Journal of Interpersonal Violence* 8(2) (June): 223–255.

Rice, A., L. Smith, and F. Janzen. 1999. "Women Inmates, Drug Abuse, and the Salt Lake County Jail." *American Jails* 13 (July–August): 43–47.

Rich, Adrienne. 1980. "Compulsory Heterosexuality and Lesbian Existence." *Signs* 5(4): 631–690.

Richie, Beth E. 1996. *Compelled to Crime: The Gender Entrapment of Battered Black Women.* New York: Routledge.

———. 2001. "Challenges Incarcerated Women Face as They Return to Their Communities: Findings from Life History Interviews." *Crime and Delinquency* 47(3): 368–389.

Root, Maria P. P. 1992. "Reconstructing the Impact of Trauma on Personality." In L. S. Brown and M. Ballou, eds., *Personality and Psychopathology: Feminist Reappraisal,* pp. 229–263. New York: Guilford Press.

Rose, Nikolas. 1989. *Governing the Self: The Shaping of the Private Self.* London: Routledge.

———. 1996. *Inventing Our Selves: Psychology, Power, and Personhood.* New York: Cambridge University Press.

Ross, Frederick A. 1857. *Slavery Ordained by God.* Philadelphia: J. P. Lippincott.

Ross, Luana. 1998. *Inventing the Savage: The Social Construction of Native American Criminality.* Austin: University of Texas Press.

Ross, Phyllis Harrison, and James E. Lawrence. 1998. "Health Care for Women Offenders." *Corrections Today* 60(7): 122–129.

Rothman, David. 1971. *The Discovery of the Asylum: Social Order and Disorder in the New Republic.* Boston: Little, Brown.

———. 1980. *Conscience and Convenience: The Asylum and Its Alternatives in Progressive America.* Boston: Little, Brown.

Sabo, Don, Terry A. Kupers, and Willie London. 2001. *Prison Masculinities.* Philadelphia: Temple University Press.

Sargent, Elizabeth, Susan Marcus-Mendoza, and Chong Ho Yu. 1993. "Abuse and the Woman Prisoner: A Forgotten Population." In Beverly R. Fletcher, Lynda Dixon Shaver, and Dreama G. Moon, eds., *Women Prisoners: A Forgotten Population,* pp. 55–64. Westport, CT: Praeger.

Saunders, Daniel G. 1994. "Posttraumatic Stress Symptom Profiles of Battered Women: A Comparison of Survivors in Two Settings." *Violence and Victims* 9(1): 31–44.

Sawicki, Jana. 1996. "Feminism, Foucault, and 'Subjects' of Power and Freedom." In Susan J. Hekman, ed., *Feminist Interpretations of Michel Foucault,* pp. 159–178. University Park: Pennsylvania State University Press.

Schaefer, Michael A. 1994. "A Comparison of Female Inmates with and Without Histories of Prostitution on Selected Psychosocial Variables." Ph.D. diss., Graduate School of Counseling Psychology, University of Southern California.

Schafer, N. E., and A. B. Dellinger. 1999. "Jailed Parents: An Assessment." *Women and Criminal Justice* 10(4): 73–91.

Schlossman, Steven L. 1977. *Love and the American Delinquent.* Chicago: University of Chicago Press.

Schmid, T. J., and R. S. Jones. 1990. "Experiential Orientations to the Prison

Experience: The Case of First-Time, Short-Term Inmates." *Perspectives on Social Problems* 2:189–210.

———. 1991. "Suspended Identity Dialectic: Identity Transformation in a Maximum Security Prison." *Symbolic Interaction* 14 (Winter): 415–432.

———. 1993. "Ambivalent Actions: Prison Adaptation Strategies of First-Time, Short-Term Inmates." *Journal of Contemporary Ethnography* 21(4): 439–463.

———. 1999. "Personal Adaptations to Cultural Change: International Students' Responses to Cultural and Interactional Challenges." *Perspectives on Social Problems* 11:317–342.

Schor, Naomi, and Elizabeth Weed, eds. 1994. *The Essential Difference*. Bloomington: Indiana University Press.

Schrag, Clarence. 1954. "Leadership Among Prison Inmates." *American Sociological Review* 19 (February): 37–42.

Schutz, A. 1962. *Collected Papers II: The Problem of Social Reality*. The Hague: Martinus Nijhoff.

Schwalbe, Michael, Sandra Godwin, Daphne Holden, Douglas Schrock, Shealy Thompson, and Michele Wolkomir. 2000. "Generic Processes in the Reproduction of Inequality: An Interactionist Analysis." *Social Forces* 79(2): 419–452.

Schwartz, Martin, and Walter DeKeseredy. 1997. *Sexual Assault on the College Campus: The Role of Male Peer Support*. Thousand Oaks, CA: Sage.

Seabury, Samuel, Rev. 1861. *American Slavery Distinguished from the Slavery of English Theorists and Justified by the Law of Nature*. 2nd ed. New York: Mason and Brothers.

Selling, L. 1931. "The Pseudo-Family." *American Journal of Sociology* 37 (September): 247–253.

Sharp, Susan F., Adrienne Braley, and Susan Marcus-Mendoza. 2000. "Focal Concerns, Race and Sentencing of Female Drug Offenders." *Free Inquiry in Creative Sociology* 28:3–16.

Sharp, Susan F., and Susan Marcus-Mendoza. 2000. "Female Inmates in Oklahoma: Issues in Sentencing, Transfers, and Parenting." Paper presented at the American Society of Criminology Meetings, November.

———. 2001. "It's a Family Affair: Incarcerated Women and Their Families." *Women and Criminal Justice* 12(4): 21–49.

Sharp, Susan F., Susan T. Marcus-Mendoza, Robert G. Bentley, Debra B. Simpson, and Sharon R. Love. 1998. "Gender Differences in the Impact of Incarceration on the Children and Families of Drug Offenders." *Journal of the Oklahoma Criminal Justice Research Consortium* 4 (August): 1–14.

———. 1999. "Gender Differences in the Impact of Incarceration on the Children and Families of Drug Offenders." In Marilyn Corsianos and Kelly Train, eds., *Interrogating Social Justice*, pp. 217–246. Toronto: Canadian Scholars' Press.

Sharswood, George, ed. 1859. *Commentaries on the Laws of England in Four Books by William Blackstone, with Notes Selected from the Editions of Archbold, Christian, Coleridge, Chitty, Stewart, Kerr and Others and a*

Life of the Author by George Sharswood, Chief Justice of the Supreme Court of Pennsylvania. Philadelphia: Childs & Peterson.

Shaw, Margaret. 1992. "Issues of Power and Control: Women in Prison and Their Defenders." *British Journal of Criminology* 32(4): 438–453.

Shaw, Nancy, Irene Browne, and Peter Meyer. 1981. "Sexism and Medical Care in a Jail Setting." *Women and Health* 6(1–2): 5–24.

Shelden, Randall G. 2001. *Controlling the Dangerous Classes: A Critical Introduction to the History of Criminal Justice.* Boston: Allyn and Bacon.

Shokeid, M. 1988. *Children of Circumstances: Israeli Emigrants in New York.* Ithaca, NY: Cornell University Press.

Siegal, Nina. 1997. "Mother's Day in Prison: Why 10,000 Californians Need Family-Oriented Alternatives to Incarceration." Available at www.sfbg.com/\news/31/32/features/ prison.html.

Sim, Joe. 1990. *Medical Power in Prisons: The Prison Medical Service in England, 1774–1989.* Philadelphia: Open University Press.

———. 1994. "Tougher Than the Rest? Men in Prison." In T. Newburn and E. Stanko, eds., *Just Boys Doing Business: Men, Masculinities, and Crime,* pp. 100–152. New York: Routledge.

Singer, Mark I., and Janet Bussey. 1995. "The Psychosocial Issues of Women Serving Time in Jail." *Social Work* 40(1) (January): 103–114.

Smart, Carol. 1995. *Law, Crime, and Sexuality: Essays in Feminism.* Thousand Oaks, CA: Sage.

Smith, Dorothy E. 1987. *The Everyday World as Problematic: A Feminist Sociology.* Boston: Northeastern University Press.

Sobel, Suzanne B. 1982. "Difficulties Experienced by Women in Prison." *Psychology of Women Quarterly* 7:107–118.

Sparks, R., A. Bottoms, and W. Hay. 1996. *Prisons and the Problem of Order.* Oxford: Clarendon Press.

Spivak, Gayatri, with Elizabeth Rooney. 1994. "In a Word." In N. Schor and E. Weed, eds., *The Essential Difference,* pp. 151–184. Bloomington: Indiana University Press.

Stanley, Amy Dru. 1998. *From Bondage to Contract: Wage Labor, Marriage, and the Market in the Age of Slave Emancipation.* Cambridge: Cambridge University Press.

Stanton, Elizabeth Cady. 1881. *History of Woman Suffrage.* Edited by Elizabeth Cady Stanton, Susan B. Anthony, and Matilda Joslyn Gage. New York: Fowler & Wells.

Steffensmeier, Darrell, Jeffery Ulmer, and John Kramer. 1998. "The Interaction of Race, Gender, and Age in Criminal Sentencing: The Punishment Cost of Being Young, Black, and Male." *Criminology* 36:763–798.

Stephens, Richard. 2002. *Convict Criminology.* Belmont, CA: Wadsworth.

Stewart, Abigail J. 1994. "Toward a Feminist Strategy for Studying Women's Lives." In C. E. Franz and A. J. Stewart, eds., *Women Creating Lives: Identities, Resilience, and Resistance,* pp. 11–35. Boulder: Westview Press.

Swift, Carolyn. 1998. "Surviving Violence: Women's Strength Through

Connection." In R. Zaplin, ed., *Female Offenders: Critical Perspectives and Effective Interventions*, pp. 245–263. Gaithersburg, MD: Aspen.

Sykes, Gresham M. 1958. *The Society of Captives: A Study of Maximum Security Prisons*. Princeton: Princeton University Press.

Taub, Nadine, and Elizabeth M. Schneider. 1982. "Perspectives on Women's Subordination and the Role of Law." In David Kairys, ed., *The Politics of Law: A Progressive Critique*, pp. 117–139. New York: Pantheon Books.

Teplin, Linda A., Karen M. Abram, and Gary M. McClelland. 1996. "Prevalence of Psychiatric Disorders Among Incarcerated Women." *Archives of General Psychiatry* 53 (June): 505–512.

———. 1997. "Mentally Disordered Women in Jail: Who Receives Services?" *American Journal of Public Health* 87(4): 604–609.

Thomas, Charles W., and David M. Petersen. 1977. *Prison Organization and Inmate Subcultures*. Indianapolis: Bobbs-Merrill.

Thomas, Jim. 1984. "Some Aspects of Negotiated Order, Mesostructure, and Loose Coupling in Maximum Security Prisons." *Symbolic Interaction* 7 (Fall): 213–231.

———. 2002. "Some Thoughts on Bosworth's *Engendering Resistance:* Challenging Symbolic Violence in Prisoner Culture Research." *Violence Against Women* 8 (March): 403–412.

Thomas, Jim, and James B. Marquart. 1988. "Dirty Knowledge and Clean Conscience: The Dilemmas of Ethnographic Research." In D. Maines and C. Couch, eds., *Information, Communication, and Social Structure*, pp. 81–96. Springfield, IL: Charles C. Thomas.

Tjaden, Patricia, and Nancy Thoennes. 2000. *Extent, Nature, and Consequences of Intimate Partner Violence: Findings from the National Violence Against Women Survey*. Special Report no. NCJ 181867. Washington, DC: U.S. Department of Justice.

Toch, Hans. 1977. *Living in Prison: The Ecology of Survival*. New York: Free Press.

———. 1998. "Hypermasculinity and Prison Violence." In L. Bowker, ed., *Masculinities and Violence*, pp. 168–178. Thousand Oaks, CA: Sage.

Trevino, A. Javier. 1996. *The Sociology of Law: Classic and Contemporary Perspectives*. New York: St. Martin's Press.

Tsenin, Kay. 2000. "One Judicial Perspective on the Sex Trade." In *Research on Women and Girls in the Justice System*, pp. 15–25. Washington, DC: National Institute of Justice.

Turk, Austin. 1976. "Law as a Weapon in Social Conflict." *Social Problems* 23 (February): 276–291.

U.S. General Accounting Office. 1999. *Misconduct by Correctional Staff: Report to the Honorable Eleanor Homes Norton*. Washington, DC: U.S. General Accounting Office.

Useem, Bert, and Peter Kimball. 1989. *States of Siege: U.S. Prison Riots, 1971–1986*. New York: Oxford University Press.

Van Maanen, John. 1988. *Tales from the Field*. Chicago: University of Chicago Press.

Van Wormer, Katherine S. 1987. "Female Prison Families: How Are They Dysfunctional?" *International Journal of Comparative and Applied Criminal Justice* 11:263–271.

Van Wormer, Katherine S., and C. Bartollas. 2000. *Women and the Criminal Justice System*. Boston: Allen and Bacon.

Vera Justice Institute. 1996. Conference organized by Vera Justice Institute. January.

Walker, Lenore E. A. 1993. "The Battered Woman Syndrome Is a Psychological Consequence of Abuse." In R. J. Gelles and D. R. Loseke, eds., *Current Controversies on Family Violence*, pp. 133–153. Newbury Park, CA: Sage.

Wan, Angela M., and Kathleen J. Ferraro. 2000. "Jail Culture: Women's Stories of Survival and Resistance." Paper presented at the annual meeting of the American Society of Criminology, San Francisco, November.

Ward, David, and Gene Kassebaum. 1965. *Women's Prison: Sex and Social Structure*. Chicago: Aldine.

Watterson, Kathryn. 1996. *Women in Prison: Inside the Concrete Womb*. Rev. ed. Boston: Northeastern University Press.

Watts, Harold, and Demetra Smith Nightingale. 1996. "Adding It Up: The Economic Impact of Incarceration on Individuals, Families, and Communities." Paper presented at a conference organized by Vera Justice Institute, January. Published in the *Journal of the Oklahoma Criminal Justice Research Consortium* 3. Available at www.doc.state.ok.us/docs/ocjrc/ocjrc96/toc.htm.

Weber, Max. 1965. *The Theory of Social and Economic Organization*. New York: Free Press.

Weigert, A. J. 1986. "The Social Production of Identity: Metatheoretical Foundations." *Sociological Quarterly* 27(2): 165–183.

Welch, Michael. 1996. *Corrections: A Critical Approach*. New York: McGraw-Hill.

———. 1999. *Punishment in America: Social Control and the Ironies of Imprisonment*. Sage: London.

Wertheimer, Barbara Mayer. 1977. *We Were There: The Story of Working Women in America*. New York: Pantheon Books.

Wheeler, Patricia A., Rebecca Trammell, Jim Thomas, and Jennifer Findlay. 1989. "Persephone Chained: Parity or Equality in Women's Prisons?" *Prison Journal* 69 (Spring/Summer): 88–102.

Wheeler, Stanton. 1961. "Socialization in Correctional Communities." *American Sociological Review* 26 (October): 697–712.

Widom, Cathy S. 1992. *The Cycle of Violence*. National Institute of Justice Research in Brief. Washington, DC: U.S. Department of Justice, September.

———. 1995. *Victims of Childhood Sexual Abuse: Later Criminal Consequences*. National Institute of Justice Research in Brief. Washington, DC: U.S. Department of Justice, March.

Wittig, Monique. 1981. "One Is Not Born a Woman." *Feminist Issues* 1 (Fall): 47–54.

Wonders, Nancy. 1996. "Determinate Sentencing: A Feminist and Postmodern Story." *Justice Quarterly* 13 (December): 611–648.
Wright, Kevin. 1991. "The Violent and Victimized in the Male Prison." *Journal of Offender Rehabilitation* 16(3–4):1–25.
Young, Iris M. 1990. *Justice and the Politics of Difference.* Princeton: Princeton University Press.
———. 1997. *Intersecting Voices: Dilemmas of Gender, Political Philosophy, and Policy.* Princeton: Princeton University Press.
Young, Vernetta. 1986. "Gender Expectations and Their Impact on Black Female Offenders and Victims." *Justice Quarterly* 3 (September): 305–328.
Zaitzow, Barbara H. 1996. "Hurts So Bad: The Impact of Abuse History on Crime Commission by Women Offenders." Paper presented at the American Society of Criminology Meetings, Chicago.
———. 2001. "Whose Problem Is It Anyway? Women Prisoners and HIV/AIDS." *International Journal of Offender Therapy and Comparative Criminology* 45(6) (December): 673–690.
Zamble, Edward, and Frank Porporino. 1988. *Coping, Behavior, and Adaption in Prison Inmates.* New York: Springer-Verlag.
Zaplin, Ruth. 1998a. *Female Offenders: Critical Perspectives and Effective Interventions.* Gaithersburg, MD: Aspen.
———. 1998b. "Female Offenders: A Systems Perspective." In R. Zaplin, ed., *Female Offenders: Critical Perspectives and Effective Interventions,* pp. 65–79. Gaithersburg, MD: Aspen.
Zaplin, Ruth, and Joyce Dougherty. 1998. "Programs That Work: Mothers." In R. Zaplin, ed., *Female Offenders: Critical Perspectives and Effective Interventions,* pp. 331–347. Gaithersburg, MD: Aspen.
Zupan, Linda L. 1992. "Men Guarding Women: An Analysis of the Employment of Male Correction Officers in Prisons for Women." *Journal of Criminal Justice* 20(4): 297–309.
Zurcher, L. A. 1977. *The Mutable Self.* Beverly Hills: Sage.

The Contributors

Mary Bosworth is assistant professor of sociology at Wesleyan University. She is the author of *Engendering Resistance* and *The U.S. Federal Prison System*. Her research interests include race, gender, and punishment in England, the United States, and France. She is currently working on a historical comparative analysis of race and imprisonment in each of those countries.

M. Elaine Eriksen is a graduate student in sociology at the University of Oklahoma, specializing in criminology. Her research interests center on the criminal justice system's response to women and drug use as well as the effects of incarceration on the children of female drug users.

Kathleen J. Ferraro is director of the women's studies program and associate professor at Arizona State University. She is a scholar activist focusing on women, violence, and poverty. For the past twenty-seven years she has been involved in the antiviolence movement through research and teaching, and as an advocate and worker. She has served as an expert witness on battering in the federal and state courts in over fifty cases, and assisted with several clemency hearings for battered women. She is chair of the Arizona Coalition Against Domestic Violence and a founding board member of Women Living Free, a non-profit organization assisting incarcerated women and women leaving prison. She is currently writing a book, *Intimate Terrorism and Women's Criminality*.

Lori B. Girshick is a community activist and sociologist. She has worked with battered women for over ten years, and has recently published *Woman-to-Woman Sexual Violence: Does She Call It Rape?* She has been involved with prison issues for over fifteen years. Her books in that area include *No Safe Haven: Stories of Women in Prison* and *Soledad Women: Wives of Prisoners Speak Out*. Her current work focuses on transgender issues.

Esther Heffernan is professor of sociology at Edgewood College in Madison, Wisconsin. She is author of the classic *Making It in Prison*. Two recent publications include "Banners, Brothels, and a 'Ladies' Seminary': A History of Women in Federal Corrections" in *Escaping Prison Myths;* and a "Commentary" on Robyn Saviano's study of "Wisconsin's Female Offender" in *ICCA Journal* (September 2000). She consulted on issues of women in corrections with the Federal Bureau of Prisons, the Alaska Department of Corrections, and the General Accounting Office, and served as co-director of the LEAA National Study of Co-Corrections. She has been a member of the Wisconsin Legislative Council's Task Forces on the Revision of the Criminal Code and on Community Corrections, and is presently involved in the Task Force on Money, Education, and Prisons, the Task Force on Women in the Criminal Justice System of the Wisconsin Women's Network, and on the board of Dane County (Wis.) Family Connections, which monthly brings children to visit with their mothers at Taycheedah Correctional Facility.

Richard S. Jones is associate professor of sociology at Marquette University. He has conducted numerous ethnographic projects on constructed social worlds, with a particular emphasis on the relationship between social world membership and identity in prisons. His publications include "Coping With Separation: Adaptive Responses of Women Prisoners" in *Women and Criminal Justice* and *Doing Time: Prison Experience and Identity Among First-Time Inmates*.

Faith E. Lutze is associate professor and director of the criminal justice program at Washington State University. She teaches criminal justice courses related to corrections and to gender and justice. Her current research includes the rehabilitative nature of prison environments, the impact of ultramasculine environments on inmate adjustment, offender adjustment to community corrections supervision, and violence toward women. She has published in *Justice Quarterly, Crime and*

Delinquency, Journal of Contemporary Criminal Justice, Journal of Criminal Justice, and *Corrections Management Quarterly.*

Angela M. Moe is assistant professor of sociology at Western Michigan University. Her research, teaching, and activism center on women as victims and offenders in the law and justice system. Her published work focuses on societal and institutional responses to woman battering. She is currently examining the links between women's nonlethal offending and intimate partner abuse.

Thomas J. Schmid is professor of sociology at Minnesota State University, Mankato. His research has focused primarily on the relationship between identity, community, and social world membership. He is coauthor of *Doing Time: Prison Experience and Identity Among First-Time Inmates.*

Susan F. Sharp is assistant professor of sociology at the University of Oklahoma. Her interests encompass gender and the criminal justice system, gender and deviance, and the effects of criminal justice policies on families. She has worked as a substance abuse counselor, primarily with offender populations. Her recent research includes the edited book *The Incarcerated Woman,* and work published in *Women and Criminal Justice, Prison Journal, Deviant Behavior, Journal of the Oklahoma Criminal Justice Research Consortium, Journal of Youth & Adolescence,* and *Journal of Contemporary Ethnography.* She is active in the Division on Women and Crime of the American Society of Criminology.

Jim Thomas is professor of sociology and criminal justice at Northern Illinois University. He has been researching both men's and women's prisons since 1980. In addition to over two dozen articles on prisons and prison culture, he is author of *The Paradox of the Jailhouse Lawyer* and *Doing Critical Ethnography.* He is currently completing a monograph entitled *Communicating Prison Culture* and is beginning a study of spirituality and coping with prison life. He has been active in prison reform for over twenty years and is a member of the John Howard Association, Illinois' prison monitoring organization.

Barbara H. Zaitzow is associate professor of criminal justice at Appalachian State University. Both her master's and doctorate research projects involved surveys of incarcerated women in Virginia and Illinois. She has continued her research in men's and women's prisons in North Carolina and was co-investigator on a national grant–sponsored study of gangs in prisons. She has been involved in state and national advocacy work for prisoners and organizations seeking alternatives to imprisonment. She continues to work with and provide services to local and state officials as an executive board member and program evaluator of a local community corrections program, and is an instructor for members of the North Carolina Department of Corrections' unit management training. She has served as an editorial board member for the *Journal of Contemporary Criminal Justice*. She has published on a variety of prison-related topics including HIV/AIDS and other treatment needs of women prisoners, and the impact of prison culture on the "doing time" experiences of the imprisoned, which appear in the *International Journal of Offender Therapy and Comparative Criminology, Journal of the Association of Nurses in AIDS Care, Journal of Crime and Justice, Criminal Justice Policy Review, Journal of Gang Research,* and *Names*.

Index

Abbott, Jack, 186, 203n
Abolitionists, 45
Absurdity, existential, 2–3, 16, 20, 205, 208
Abuse: child, 98–99, 125; in domestic relationships, 95, 186, 189, 192–193; mental, 193–194; physical, 70; by prison staff, 109; rates, 96–98; sexual, 70, 95, 96, 125; substance, 76–78, 110–111
Acoca, Leslie, 33, 112, 126
Adaptive work, 170–172
Agozino, Biko, 146
Alarid, Leanne Fiftal, 88
Albor, Teresa, 112
Alderson Correctional Center, 39, 41–43, 57, 59–63
Alexander, Ruth M., 42, 57
Amnesty International, 32, 34
Andrews, Matthew Page, 49
Arata, Catalina M., 100
Arizona Health Care Cost Containment System, 74
Arnold, Regina, 66
Artificial prison work, 180
Auburn system, 52
Auherhahn, Kathleen, 142
Austin, James, 188
Authentic prisoner work, 180

Ball, D. W., 168

Barak, Gregg, 121, 131
Barnett, Ola, 186, 196
Barry, Ellen, 112
Bates, Sanford, 40, 41, 44, 47, 50, 62, 63
Battered women, 100
Baunach, Phyllis J., 35
Beattie, L. Elisabeth, 96, 100
Beck, Allen J., 22, 43, 111, 120, 130
Beckett, Katherine, 212
Bedford Hills Correctional Facility (New York), 28, 97, 127–128
Belknap, Joan, 71, 75, 79, 85, 91, 121, 124–127, 132, 183, 184, 189–191, 193, 195, 197
Bem, Sandra Lipsitz, 15, 208, 210, 211
Benhabib, Seyla, 139
Bennett, James, 40, 44, 47, 50, 62, 63
Berger, Peter L., 7
Bill, Louise, 111
Bill of Rights, 47
Black Codes, 54
Blackstone, William, 48, 50, 53
Bledsoe, Albert Taylor, 45
Bloom, Barbara, 96, 123, 124, 129, 130, 132, 189, 197, 200
Bloomfield, Maxwell, 49
Blume, E. Sue, 96
Bordt, Rebecca L., 82

Bosworth, Mary, 8, 11, 16, 19, 66, 138, 142, 144, 147, 153n, 155, 162, 173, 175, 177, 210
Boudin, Kathy, 128
Boudouris, James, 134
Bourdieu, Pierre, 10, 16, 17, 39, 43, 44, 47, 61, 64
Bowker, Lee, 31, 183
Bradley, Joseph, 46
Bradwell, Maria, 46
Braidotti, Rosi, 139
Brent, Margaret, 49
Brenzel, Barbara M., 58
Brockway, Zebulon, 58
Brown, J. D., 189
Browne, Angela, 75, 97, 168, 192
Burkhart, Katheryn, 28
Butler, Anne, 184, 195
Butler, Judith, 139, 141, 149

Caiazza, Amy B., 74, 78, 91
California Mother-Infant Care program, 135
Cambanis, Thanassis, 24
Camp, Christy Marie, 25, 29, 38
Career development training, 79
Carlen, Pat, 25, 26, 28, 142
Central California Women's Facility, 61, 161
Chandler, Edna W., 23
Chesler, Phyllis, 88
Chesney-Lind, 26, 66, 79, 81, 86, 98, 120, 135, 183–185, 188, 197, 200
Child abuse, 98–99
Child protective services, 85
Children: African American, 121; minors, 120–122; mother-child contact, 129–134; of prisoners, 32, 122–125, 174–178; visits by, 86–87
Christianity, 85
Christianson, Scott, 195
Chu, James A., 101
Cincinnati Workhouse, 59
Clark, Judy, 28
Clear, Todd, 123, 132, 188
Clemmer, Donald, 7, 156

Coerced conformity, 201–202
Collins, Patricia Hill, 10
Conly, Catherine, 134–135, 209–210
Connell, Robert W., 42
Connelly, Mark Thomas, 42
Convention Against Torture and Other Cruel, Inhuman, or Degrading Treatment, 105
Convict lease system, 54
Coping: strategies of, 101, 110–114; stress of, 70
Correctional misogyny, 191–195
Correctional Service of Canada, 116, 127
Cott, Nancy F., 43
Covington, Stephanie, 197–200
Cruttschnitt, Candace, 121
"Cultural sojourners," 19, 24–25, 157, 170, 172, 179–180
Culverson, Donald R., 121

Daane, Diane, 126
Dalley, Lanete P., 5
Daly, Kathleen, 35
Dangerous women, 51–53
Danner, Mona, 188
Davis, Angela Y., 66, 78, 79, 91, 95
Dearing, Susan, 36
de Beaumont, Gustave, 51, 52
de Beauvoir, Simone, 141
Degradation ceremonies, 68–71
Dependency: female, 28, 49–50; of mothers, 123; of prisoners, 102
Depersonalization, 102
Deprivation model, 7–8, 156
Destabilizing women, 139–141
Determinate sentencing, 119, 120
Deveaux, Monique, 65
Diaz-Cotto, Juanita, 33, 35, 58
Dix, Dorothea, 50
Dobash, Russell R., 82
"Doing gender," 9
Domestic violence, 95, 186, 189. *See also* Abuse
Dougherty, Joyce, 184
Doulas, 126

Drugs, 110; abuse, 110–111; offenses, 22–23; treatment, 76–78; war on, 120, 136
Drummond, Tamerlin, 128, 133
Durham, Alexis M., 26
Dutton, Mary Ann, 100, 110, 111, 114

Educational training, 78–79
Eighth Amendment, 104
Ekstrand, Laurie, 119, 125, 128, 130–131, 133, 135
English Common Law, 48, 50
Enos, Sandra, 124, 125
Entry to prison, 24–25. *See also* "Cultural sojourners"; Orientation
Equality for women, 189
Erez, Edna, 121
Esslin, Martin, 2

Faith, Karlene, 33, 102
Fallen women, 57–59
Families, impact of incarceration on, 123
Family-like relationships, 31, 88–89, 113, 130–131, 150, 167–168
Federal Correctional Institute for Women (Dublin, Calif.), 97
Feinman, Clarice, 122
Female inmates, special needs of, 31–32
Female offenders, 183; characteristics of, 22–24
Feme sole, 48, 49, 51–52, 62
Feminine subjectification, 91
Femininity: as resistance, 140–145; as entrapment, 141–145
Feminism, liberal, 139
Ferraro, Kathleen J., 18, 65, 71
Finkelhor, David, 96, 100
Flavin, Jeanne, 120
Flexner, Eleanor, 49
Flynn, Elizabeth Gurley, 61
Fogel, Catherine I., 102
Fonow, Margaret M., 138
Foster, T. W., 168
Foucault, Michel, 1, 65, 119, 121, 206, 208

Fourteenth Amendment, 46
Fourth Amendment, 104
Fraser, Nancy, 65
Freedman, Estelle, 23, 25, 42, 50, 52, 60, 150
Fuss, Diana, 139, 149

Gabel, Katherine, 131
Gallagher, Lizzie, 56
Galtung, J., 161
Gaudin, James M., 124
Gelsthorpe, Lorraine, 138
Gender: biological differences, 4; domination, 43; equality in prison, 5, 35, 61–63; hegemony, 141–142; heterogendering, 207–208; identity, 143; images, 15; "lens of gender," 211; neutrality, 135; resistance, 149–152; socialization, 184–185
Gender-specific tasks, 142
Giallambardo, Rose, 25, 61, 150, 159, 173
Gibson, M. A., 157
Giddens, Anthony, 139, 140
Gilfus, Mary E., 66, 98
Gilliard, Darrell K., 34
Gilroy, Paul, 146, 149
Girl Scouts Behind Bars program, 133
Girshick, Lori B., 16, 18, 28, 97, 104, 113, 125, 132, 133, 136, 188, 191, 197, 198
Goffman, Erving, 2, 7, 102, 138, 141, 142, 171, 207
Goodenough, Ward H., 7
Goodstein, Lynne, 3
Gordon, Robert, 186, 203n
Gorz, Andre, 213
Gray, Tara, G., 27, 91
Greenfeld, Lawrence A., 22, 75, 78, 85, 119, 121, 125
Greer, Kimberly, 5, 162, 173
Grievance processes, 82–83, 109
Guadin, James M., 125
Gunther v. Iowa State Men's Reformatory (1980), 103

Hagan, John, 123, 132

Hairston, Creasie Finney, 85, 86, 128, 131, 132
Halfway houses, 49–50
Hanna-Moffit, Kate, 103, 142, 198, 200
Harlow, Caroline Wolf, 70, 74, 75, 81
Harris, Jean Wahl, 132
Harris, Mary Belle, 39, 41, 44, 57, 63
Hart, Cynthia B., 30
Hassine, Victor, 186, 203n
Hawk-Sawyer, Kathleen M., 62
Hayner, Norman S., 7
Haywood, Thomas W., 75, 79
Health care, 32, 71–74
Heffernan, Esther, 3, 16, 17, 42, 58, 59, 61, 63, 159, 165, 167, 173
Helplessness, learned, 196–198
Heney, Jan, 101, 106, 107, 110, 111, 117
Henriques, Zelma, 131, 132, 190, 192, 194–197
Heterogendering, 207–208
Heterosexuality, 150, 186; expectations, 207
Holstein, James A., 176
Holt, K. E., 112
Homosexuality: homophobia, 150; relationships, 30–31, 60–61, 150–151
hooks, bell, 49, 139
Hopefulness, learned, 196–198
Huggins, Denise, 113
Human Rights Watch, 34, 81, 103–109, 112, 115
Humphries, Drew, 121

Identity: 16, 65, 139–141, 171; of female prisoners as mothers, 175; gender, 143; of inmates, 157; outside, 180; politics, 139–141; preservation, 171–173; social, 18–19; work, 170–172, 178, 180
Ideology, 15
Illinois prisons, 4–6
Image construction, 179
Importation model, 7–8, 156
Imprisonment, responses to, 164–165

Incest, 96
Indeterminate sentencing, 58–59
Indianapolis House of Shelter, 59
Infantilization of women prisoners, 25, 192–193, 195
Ingraham, Chrys, 50, 166–167, 207
Inmate code, 166–167
Inmate distrust, 162
Insider/outsider research, 12–13
Institutionalized oppression, 91
Institutional racism, 149
International Covenant on Civil and Political Rights, 105
Intimate dyads, 88–89, 150. *See also* Family-like relationships
Irish women prisoners, 51
Irwin, John, 8

Jacobs, James B., 11
Jails: prisoner perceptions of, 88–90; totalizing character, 81
Jones, Richard S., 8, 11, 16, 19, 159, 160, 166
JusticeWorks Community, 135

Kelly, Liz, 99, 185
Kendall, Kathleen, 101, 102, 112, 116, 200
Kent, James, 48–50, 53
Kilmartin, Christopher, 183–185, 202n, 203n
Kilpatrick, D. G., 99
Kirk, Gwyn, 183, 184
Kitzinger, Sheila, 126
Klein, Sue, 66
Klungness, Elizabeth J., 56
Koban, Linda A., 132
Kondo, Dorinne K., 16
Koons, Barbara A., 66, 75
Koss, Mary, 101, 183, 185, 186, 189, 192
Krais, Beate, 43
Kruttschnitt, Candace, 66, 89

Lake, Elise S., 99
Landes, A. B., 97
Language degradation, 107, 208

LaViolette, Alyce, 185, 189, 192
Lawrence, Steven, 32, 148–149
Leger, R. G., 167
Lekkerkerker, Eugenia C., 42
"Lens of gender," 211
Leonard, Elizabeth Dermody, 75, 97
Lerner, Gerda, 49
Lesbian relationships, 60–61, 150–151
LeShanna, L., 167
Levanthall, Rachel, 102, 111, 117
Liberal feminism, 139
Lichtenstein, Alex, 54
Lieber, Francis, 51–53
Liebling, Alison, 142
Lockwood, Daniel, 187
Long-term inmates, 26–27
Lord, Elaine, 26, 32
Lowell, Josephine Shaw, 59
Lundberg, D. A., 175
Lutze, Faith E., 19, 185, 186, 189, 199, 200, 202, 208
Lynch, Michael, 122, 127

MacKanzie, Doris L., 26, 167
MacPherson, Sir William, 149
Male guards, 105, 106
Male prisoners, 32, 15
Male privilege, 15, 187–189
Mann, Coramae Richey, 25
Mannheim, Karl, 13
Marcus-Mendoza, Susan, 81, 189, 197, 200
Markovic, Vesna, 126, 132
Martineau, Harriet, 53, 54
Maryland Correctional Institute for Women, 133
Masculine sex role stereotypes, 201
Masculinity, 184, 186–187; and violence, 184–186. *See also* Ultramasculinity
Massachusetts Reformatory for Women, 60
Mauer, Marc, 23
Mawby, R. I., 165, 167
McCarthy, Belinda, 124
McClellan, Dorothy S., 29, 97, 98, 110, 190, 192–194

McCorkel, Jill, A., 9, 173
McGinn, Elinor Myers, 56
McGowan, B. G., 165
Meisenhelder, Thomas, 165
Melish, Joanne Pope, 53
Meltzer, B. J., 159, 172
Mental health, 75–76, 112
Messerschmidt, James, 185
Metzger, Diane, 190, 194, 196
Milan Federal Detention Farm, 40
Miller, Jody, 17, 103, 113
Miller, Theresa A., 103
Mills, R., 112
Milovanovic, Dragan, 3
Moore, Joan, 123
Morash, Merry, 75, 89, 97, 128, 132, 198
Morawska, E., 157
Moses, Marilyn, 132
Mother-child contact, 129–134
Mothering, 85–88, 176–178
Mother-Offspring Life Development program (MOLD), 134
Mothers and Their Children program (MATCH), 133–134
Moyer, Imogene L., 167
Mumola, Christopher, 120, 123, 124, 129
Muraskin, Roslyn, 59, 183, 198

Newark Custodial Asylum for Feebleminded Women, 59

O'Brien, Patricia, 135
O'Keefe, Maura, 100
O'Neal, John, 205
Offenses, drugs, 22–23
Oklahoma Criminal Justice Research Center, 123
Orientation: of insiders, 165, 180–181; post-prison, 158; pre-prison, 158
Oshinsky, David M., 54–56
Outside identity, 180
Owen, Barbara, 7, 25, 27, 32, 81, 85, 88, 91, 104, 113, 126, 128, 132, 155, 159, 161, 162, 165, 166, 173, 175, 192, 193

Parchman Penitentiary (Miss.), 54–56
Parens patriae, 50
Parents and Children Together program (PACT), 135
Parkinson, Diana, 126
Participatory research, 13
Patriarchy, 46–47, 65, 211
Phenomenological model of prison experience, 156–159
Physical abuse, 70
Pima County Adult Detention Center (Ariz.), 67, 76, 82–84
"Pirandellian prison," 2, 213
Pirandello, Luigi, 1, 208
Pisciotta, Alexander W., 1
Pollack, Shoshana, 27, 29
Pollock, Joycelyn, 103–105, 110, 113, 121, 150, 192
Pollock-Byrne, Joycelyn, 66, 75, 85, 86, 91, 155, 165
Postmodernism, 139
Postrelease services, 134
Posttraumatic stress disorder (PTSD), 95–96, 99–102, 112, 116
Powerlessness, of inmates, 107
Pregnancies, 4, 31–32, 73, 112, 125–129, 190–191
Prendergast, Michael L., 36
Price, Barbara, 183
Prison: coping, 29–30, 196–198; counseling, 74–78; culture, 6–9, 30, 165; reform, 36–37; regimentation, 69–71; policies, 114–116; private, 130–131; programs, 33, 115–117; work experiences in, 79–81
Prisoners: emotions, 173; mental abuse of, 193–194; partnerships, 88–89, 167, 171–172; social control of, 187
Privacy, 68
Private prisons, 130–131
Privileged knowledge, 12, 14
Property boxes, 6, 194
Propper, Alice M., 31

Race, 62, 145–149

Racism, 148, 149
Radical Reconstruction, 54
Radwell, Maria, 46
Rafter, Nicole Hahn, 25, 32, 42, 47, 52, 53, 58, 59, 62, 79, 189, 195, 198
Rand, Michael, 96
Rape survivors, 99
Rasche, Christine, 192
Reading Family Ties Program (Fla.), 133
Reception procedures, 24–25
Reed, Diane F., 124
Reforming prisons, 35–37, 210–213
Reforms: incremental, 212–213
Reiman, Jeffrey, 127
Reinharz, Shulamit, 138
Relationism, 13
Religion, 83–85
Resick, Patricia A., 99
Resistance to conditions, 65, 82–88, 92
Retraumatization, 105
Rice, A., 70
Rich, Adrienne, 151
Richie, Beth E., 36, 66
Root, Maria P., 99, 101, 110, 114, 140
Rose, Nikolas, 45
Ross, Frederick A., 45, 66, 79–81, 83–85, 88
Ross, Luana, 32, 71
Rothman, David, 201
Rules, learning of, 69

Sabo, Don, 15, 16, 211
Sargent, Elizabeth, 81, 197
Saunders, Daniel G., 65, 100, 112
Sawicki, Jana, 65
Schaefer, Michael A., 85
Schafer, N. E., 32
Schlossman, Steven L., 50
Schmid, Thomas J., 8, 157, 158, 166, 171
Schor, Naomi, 139
Schrag, Clarence, 8
Schutz, Alfred, 170
Schwalbe, Michael, 10, 13

Schwartz, Martin, 185
Seabury, Samuel, 44–45
Security mandate, 102–103
Self-esteem, 104
Selling, L., 168
Sentencing, 135
Sexual abuse, 70, 95; of children, 125; by staff, 109
Sexual assault, 96
Sexual degradation, 34
Sexual extortion, 195
Sexuality, 149–152
Sexual misconduct of staff, 34, 108–110
Sharp, Susan F., 8, 18, 121–125, 127, 129–132
Sharswood, George, 48
Shaw, Margaret, 71, 142
Shelden, Randall G., 121
Shokeid, M., 157
Short-term inmates, 26–27
Siegal, Nina, 132, 135
Sim, Joe, 97, 111, 142, 185, 187
Singer, Mark I., 95
Sing Sing Penitentiary, 52
Slavery, 44, 46–47, 53–57
Smart, Carol, 188
Smith, Dorothy E., 12, 14, 209
Sobel, Suzanne B., 129, 175
Social capital, 16
Social identity, 18–19
Sparks, R., 156
Spivak, Gayatri, 145
Standpoint perspective, 11–14
Stanley, Amy Dru, 40–41, 44, 45, 54, 57
Stanton, Elizabeth Cady, 49
Steffensmeier, Darrell, 121
Stephens, Richard, 11, 13
Stewart, Abigail J., 117
Stigmatization, 107
Stresses of incarceration, 102
Stress response, 105
Strip searches, 106, 114, 194–195
Stunted resistance, 82–83
Substance abuse, 110–111
Subversive identities, 152–153

Suicidal thoughts, 111
Supervision, 105–108
Support networks, 189–191
Surveillance, 68
Survival, in prisons, 82–88
Swift, Carolyn, 197, 199
Sykes, Gresham M., 7, 25, 150
Symbolic violence, 9–11, 17, 43–44, 57, 61, 63–64, 210

Taub, Nadine, 46
Taycheedah Correctional Institution (Wis.), 61
Telephones, 87, 129–130
Teplin, Linda A., 75
Thirteenth Amendment, 46–47, 53, 54
Thomas, Charles W., 8
Thomas, Jim, 7, 11, 108
Timm v. Gunter, 103
Title VII of the Civil Rights Act, 103
Tjaden, Patricia, 91
Toch, Hans, 7, 185–187
Total institutions, 138, 207
Training: career development, 79; educational, 78–79; vocational, 33, 78–79
Travino, A. Javier, 119, 136
Treatment programs, 105, 198–201
Tsenin, Kay, 50
Turk, Austin, 119

Ultramasculinity, 16, 184–185, 187, 199, 205, 207–208
Universal Declaration of Human Rights, 105
Useem, Bert, 7

Vagrancy laws, 57–58
Van Maanen, John, 9, 13
Van Waters, Miriam, 60
Van Wormer, Katherine S., 183, 192, 194
Vera Justice Institute, 123
Victimization, 185
Violence, 81–82; domestic, 95, 186, 189; masculinity and, 184–186; symbolic, 9–11, 17, 43–44, 57, 61,

63–64, 210
Visits, 120–131
Vocational training, 33, 78–79

Walker, Lenore E. A., 112
Wan, Angela M., 111
Ward, David, 165, 173
War on drugs, 120, 136
Waterson, Kathryn, 28, 31, 102, 195, 209
Watts, Harold, 123
Waupin Correctional Center (Wis.), 61
Weber, Max, 12
Weigert, A. J., 171
Welch, Michael, 27, 212
Welfare assistance, 79
Wertheimer, Barbara Mayer, 48
Western House of Refuge (New York), 59
Wheeler, Patricia A., 6, 7
Widom, Cathy S., 98
Wisconsin State Prison for Women, 61
Wittig, Monique, 139
Women as slaves, 47–49
Women prisoners: as wayward children, 28; victimization of, 33–35
Women's Prison and Reformatory (Ind.), 59
Women's Prison Association (New York), 134
Women's prisoner litigation, 6
Women's reformatory movement, 61
Wonders, Nancy, 119, 121
Wright, Kevin, 187

Young, Iris M., 139, 140
Young, Vernetta, A., 122

Zaitzow, Barbara H., 3, 8, 17, 28, 33
Zamble, Edward, 203n
Zaplin, Ruth, 104, 132–134, 197, 198, 200
Zupan, Linda L., 104
Zurcher, Louis A., 173

About the Book

It is old news that the conditions and policies of women's prisons are different from those of men's prisons. Less evident, however, is how gender differences shape those policies, and how gender identity and roles shape women's adaptation and resistance to prison culture and control. *Women in Prison* explores how the gender-based attitudes that women bring to prison frame how they respond to the prison environment—and how gender stereotypes continue to affect the treatment and opportunities of incarcerated women today.

The authors focus especially on how the personal and social problems imported into the prison setting become part of the intricate web of prison culture. Their study reveals just how extensively women's prison experience reflects the control and domination they experienced in the outside world.

Barbara H. Zaitzow is associate professor of criminal justice at Appalachian State University. She has investigated prisons in Virginia, Illinois, and North Carolina and has served on the editorial board of the *Journal of Contemporary Criminal Justice*. She is active in advocacy work for prisoners and local community corrections programs and also serves as an instructor for the North Carolina Department of Corrections. **Jim Thomas** is professor of sociology and criminal justice at Northern Illinois University. He is the author of *The Paradox of the Jailhouse Lawyer* and *Doing Critical Ethnography*. He has been researching both men's and women's prisons since 1980. A member of the John Howard Association (a prison monitoring organization), he is active in prison reform.